GEORGE W. BUSH

Recent Titles in Greenwood Biographies

Halle Berry: A Biography
Melissa Ewey Johnson

Osama bin Laden: A Biography
Thomas R. Mockaitis

Tyra Banks: A Biography
Carole Jacobs

Jean-Michel Basquiat: A Biography
Eric Fretz

Howard Stern: A Biography
Rich Mintzer

Tiger Woods: A Biography, Second Edition
Lawrence J. Londino

Justin Timberlake: A Biography
Kimberly Dillon Summers

Walt Disney: A Biography
Louise Krasniewicz

Chief Joseph: A Biography
Vanessa Gunther

John Lennon: A Biography
Jacqueline Edmondson

Carrie Underwood: A Biography
Vernell Hackett

Christina Aguilera: A Biography
Mary Anne Donovan

Paul Newman: A Biography
Marian Edelman Borden

GEORGE W. BUSH

A Biography

Clarke Rountree

GREENWOOD BIOGRAPHIES

 GREENWOOD

AN IMPRINT OF ABC-CLIO, LLC
Santa Barbara, California • Denver, Colorado • Oxford, England

Library of Congress Cataloging-in-Publication Data

Rountree, Clarke, 1958–
  George W. Bush : a biography / Clarke Rountree.
    p. cm. — (Greenwood biographies)
  Includes bibliographical references and index.
    ISBN 978-0-313-38500-1 (hard copy : alk. paper) — ISBN 978-0-313-38501-8 (ebook)   1. Bush, George W. (George Walker), 1946–   2. United States—Politics and government—2001–2009.   3. Presidents—United States—Biography.   I. Title.
  E903.R68   2010
  973.931092—dc22
  [B]   2010032025

ISBN: 978-0-313-38500-1
EISBN: 978-0-313-38501-8

15   14   13   12   11   1   2   3   4   5

This book is also available on the World Wide Web as an eBook.
Visit www.abc-clio.com for details.

Greenwood
An Imprint of ABC-CLIO, LLC

ABC-CLIO, LLC
130 Cremona Drive, P.O. Box 1911
Santa Barbara, California 93116-1911

This book is printed on acid-free paper ∞

Manufactured in the United States of America

For my sons, Josh and John,
who are heirs to the Bush legacy.

CONTENTS

Series Foreword   ix

Acknowledgments   xi

Introduction   xiii

Timeline: Events in the Life of George W. Bush   xvii

Chapter 1   Great Expectations   1

Chapter 2   Growing a Bush in Texas   15

Chapter 3   The Nomadic Years   33

Chapter 4   Governor Bush   53

Chapter 5   A Historic Election Battle   67

Chapter 6   A Compassionate Conservative Becomes
            a War President   79

Chapter 7   The War against Terrorism   101

Chapter 8   The Iraq War   113

Chapter 9   Squeaking into a Troubled Second Term   131

CONTENTS

Chapter 10   The Lame Duck   147

Chapter 11   Bush's Legacy   167

Selected Annotated Bibliography   183

Index   191

SERIES FOREWORD

In response to high school and public library needs, Greenwood developed this distinguished series of full-length biographies specifically for student use. Prepared by field experts and professionals, these engaging biographies are tailored for high school students who need challenging yet accessible biographies. Ideal for secondary school assignments, the length, format and subject areas are designed to meet educators' requirements and students' interests.

Greenwood offers an extensive selection of biographies spanning all curriculum-related subject areas including social studies, the sciences, literature and the arts, history and politics, as well as popular culture, covering public figures and famous personalities from all time periods and backgrounds, both historic and contemporary, who have made an impact on American and/or world culture. Greenwood biographies were chosen based on comprehensive feedback from librarians and educators. Consideration was given to both curriculum relevance and inherent interest. The result is an intriguing mix of the well known and the unexpected, the saints and sinners from long-ago history and contemporary pop culture. Readers will find a wide array of subject choices from fascinating crime figures like Al Capone to inspiring pioneers like Margaret

Mead, from the greatest minds of our time like Stephen Hawking to the most amazing success stories of our day like J. K. Rowling.

While the emphasis is on fact, not glorification, the books are meant to be fun to read. Each volume provides in-depth information about the subject's life from birth through childhood, the teen years, and adulthood. A thorough account relates family background and education, traces personal and professional influences, and explores struggles, accomplishments, and contributions. A timeline highlights the most significant life events against a historical perspective. Bibliographies supplement the reference value of each volume.

ACKNOWLEDGMENTS

I would like to thank the University of Alabama in Huntsville for granting me a sabbatical to work on this book and related research. I would also like to thank Sandy Towers for her encouragement and invaluable help in bringing this book to fruition. The other editors and staff were very supportive and quick in their work. Family and friends were patient as I rattled on endlessly about our 43rd president, coming to terms with my own understanding of his life and presidency.

INTRODUCTION

For most of his life, George W. Bush was a person unlikely ever to hold the highest office in the United States. It's not that he didn't have the grooming for the job: he went to an exclusive preparatory school, earned a college degree from Yale, and completed a master's in business administration from Harvard. It's also not the case that he lacked family connections: his father had been president of the United States, his grandfather had been a U.S. senator, and many of his relatives were wealthy and powerful people.

No, the reason George W. Bush's rise to the presidency of the United States was such a surprise has to do with the man himself, not his opportunities. Bush was a weak student who feared flunking out of preparatory school and who graduated near the bottom of his class at Yale. For much of his life, he drank too much and didn't seem to have any direction. This self-described nomad moved from one business venture to the next, getting by largely with the help of his family and their friends. He called himself the black sheep of the Bush family, often feeling overshadowed by his father and by his talented and smarter younger brother, Jeb.

Bush's story could have ended there—a poor little rich boy (and man) who never took advantage of the opportunities afforded him. But when he was 40, he underwent a remarkable change. Although he had gone to church most of his life, it was only at this point that he had a conversion experience that made him a devoted Christian. He stopped drinking and found direction in his life. He unexpectedly won a political contest against a popular incumbent and became the first Texas governor to be elected to two consecutive terms. Then he set his sights on the White House and bested his father by winning two terms as president of the United States (while his father was limited to one).

Despite this impressive turnaround in his life, Bush's presidency was among the most turbulent and controversial in recent history. It began with an unprecedented election controversy that lasted over a month and ended when the U.S. Supreme Court ordered a halt to vote recounting in the contested presidential election in Florida.

The once-in-a-lifetime election controversy was a harbinger for the unusual events that would continue during Bush's time in office. The most devastating occurred during Bush's first year in office when terrorists hijacked planes and flew them into both World Trade Towers in New York City, as well as the Pentagon and a field in Pennsylvania. More Americans died on September 11, 2001, than died in the Japanese attack on Pearl Harbor 60 years earlier. Bush's response to the terrorist attacks involved controversial measures that included warrantless eavesdropping on both foreign enemies and Americans; the opening of an offshore detention facility for so-called enemy combatants at Guantánamo Bay, Cuba; the denial of the due process of law for detainees; and enhanced interrogation techniques to extract intelligence, which many people, including President Obama, have labeled *torture*.

While waging a war against terrorist groups in Afghanistan and the government that harbored them, Bush turned his attention to Iraq's leader, Saddam Hussein. He adopted a new policy of engaging in preventive wars against countries or groups that posed a threat to the United States. He claimed that Saddam Hussein had weapons of mass destruction—biological, chemical, or nuclear weapons—which he might deploy against the United States. In 2003, he ordered the invasion of Iraq, deposed Hussein, and occupied the country. However, no weapons of mass destruction were ever found, raising charges that

Bush had hyped the evidence against Iraq as an excuse to invade the oil-rich country.

Despite this controversy, Bush was reelected in 2004 in a close contest with Democrat John Kerry. As the occupation of Iraq dragged on, a massive hurricane devastated New Orleans in 2005. Hurricane Katrina's biggest damage came in the wake of the storm when levees protecting the low-lying city failed, leaving residents clinging to life on the tops of their flooded homes and dead bodies floating through the streets of the Big Easy. The local and state governments were overwhelmed, and the Federal Emergency Management Agency (FEMA) failed to take up the slack. Thousands of victims fleeing the storm waited for days at New Orleans's massive football stadium, the Superdome, while water and food dwindled. Bush apologized for the poor federal effort and promised to help rebuild the city.

The next year, Iraq exploded into sectarian violence after a mosque sacred to the country's majority Shia Muslims was bombed by minority Sunni Muslims. Sectarian militias began killing one another, with American armed forces caught in the cross fire. Americans turned against the war and against Bush's Republican supporters who controlled both houses of Congress. During the 2006 midterm elections, Democrats won an overwhelming victory, taking control of a House and Senate that had rubber-stamped many of Bush's policies. Nevertheless, while Americans were calling for a withdrawal from Iraq, Bush ordered a surge in troops to quell the violence. The controversial move seemed to work, as violence dropped significantly in the war-torn country.

Although Bush might have ended his presidency on this high note, it wasn't meant to be. In late 2008, the economy took a nosedive, as banks began failing because of bad investments, the stock market lost half its value, the auto industry collapsed, and unemployment passed 7 percent. By the time Barack Obama was sworn into office in January 2009, the country faced crises on multiple fronts: unemployment nearing 8 percent and rising; a failing banking system; an auto industry nearing bankruptcy; housing foreclosures at an all-time high; annual federal deficits exceeding $1 trillion; ongoing wars in Iraq and Afghanistan; and foreign crises in Pakistan, Iran, North Korea, Russia, and the Palestinian territories.

Time will tell whether Bush's presidential legacy will improve. For example, Bush insists that planting the seeds of democracy in Iraq, through elections the U.S. occupation made possible, will lead to a flowering of freedom in a turbulent and authoritarian part of the world. His administration's controversial efforts to thwart terrorist attacks may be proved wise as his successors grapple with how to keep the United States safe. And some of his policies that were overshadowed by the larger events listed here—such as his position limiting stem cell research—may look different as we move into an uncertain future.

This book will review the life of this controversial figure, particularly his time in the White House. We'll start where every biography begins: with his upbringing, before turning to his life as a businessman, a governor, a president, and an ex-president. We will consider the larger question of how the 43rd president of the United States should be remembered.

TIMELINE: EVENTS IN THE LIFE OF GEORGE W. BUSH

July 6, 1946	George Walker Bush is born in New Haven, Connecticut, the eldest child of George Herbert Walker Bush and Barbara Pierce Bush.
1948	George H. W. Bush moves with his wife and son to Odessa, Texas, to seek his fortune in the oil business.
1949	The Bush family moves briefly to California.
December 20, 1949	The Bush family's second child, Pauline Robinson (Robin), is born in Compton, California.
May 1950	The family returns to Texas, taking up residence on East Maple Street ("Easter Egg Row") in Midland. In November 1951, they move to West Ohio Avenue in Midland and then, in 1955, to Sentinel Drive.
1951–1957	George W. attends Sam Houston Elementary School.
February 11, 1953	John Ellis Bush (Jeb) is born in Midland.

October 11, 1953	Four-year-old Robin dies of leukemia at New York City's Memorial Sloan-Kettering Hospital.
January 22, 1955	Neil Mallon Bush is born in Midland.
October 22, 1956	Marvin Pierce Bush is born in Midland.
1957–1961	George W. attends San Jacinto Junior High School in Midland for seventh grade and then the private Kincaid School in Houston for eighth and ninth grades.
August 1959	The Bush family moves from Midland to Houston.
August 18, 1959	Dorothy Walker Bush is born in Houston, the youngest child of George H. W. Bush and Barbara Pierce Bush.
September 1961	George W. is sent to Phillips Academy, the venerable prep school in Andover, Massachusetts, which his father had attended.
1964	(June) George W. graduates from Phillips Academy. (Summer) He works on his father's unsuccessful campaign for the U.S. Senate. (Fall) He returns to Connecticut to attend Yale University in New Haven.
1968	(June 9) George W. graduates from Yale University with a BS degree in history. (Summer) He works on the Senate campaign of Edward Gurney in Florida; he is accepted into the Texas National Guard and assigned to the 147th Fighter Group at Ellington Air Force Base in Houston. (November–December) He is sent to Moody Air Force Base in Valdosta, Georgia, for pilot training.
1970	George W.'s National Guard service continues; he works on his father's second unsuccessful Senate campaign, this time against future vice presidential candidate Lloyd Bentsen; he graduates from Combat Crew Training School

and thereafter is required to serve one weekend a month; he moves to Houston.

1972   (May) George W. moves to Alabama to work on the unsuccessful Senate campaign of Winton ("Red") Blount; he transfers to the Alabama Air National Guard and is assigned to the187th TAC Recon Group, based in Montgomery. (July) He loses his flight status after failing to appear for a mandatory physical. (November) He returns to Houston following the election.

1973   (Summer) George W. is granted an early honorable discharge from the Texas National Guard. (September) He enters Harvard Business School.

1975   (June) George W. graduates from Harvard Business School with an MBA. (Summer) He returns to Texas and settles in Midland, where he works intermittently in the oil business before turning to politics.

1977   (July) George W. decides to run for Congress; meets Laura Welch, a school librarian, at a friend's barbeque. (Fall) He wins the Republican nomination.

November 5, 1977   George W. Bush and Laura Welch are married at the First United Methodist Church in Midland.

November 8, 1978   George W. loses the congressional election to Democrat Kent Hance; he returns to the oil business.

March 1979   George W.'s Arbusto Energy company (later called Bush Exploration Company) begins operations; the company had been incorporated in June 1977.

1980   (Summer) George H. W. Bush accepts his party's vice presidential nomination. (November)

He is elected vice president on the ticket headed by Ronald Reagan.

November 25, 1981 Twins Barbara Pierce Bush and Jenna Welch Bush are born in Midland to George W. and Laura Welch Bush.

1984 (February) Bush Exploration Company merges with Spectrum 7; George W. Bush becomes chairman and CEO of the merged company.

1985 (Summer) After conversations with an evangelical Christian preacher, George W. undergoes a religious conversion.

1986 (July) George W. resolves to stop drinking. (September) Spectrum 7 is purchased by Harken Oil and Gas; George W. becomes a member of the Harken board of directors and a company consultant.

1987 George W. moves his family to Washington, D.C., and works on his father's campaign for the Republican nomination for president, appealing particularly to evangelical Christians.

November 8, 1988 George H. W. Bush is elected 41st president of the United States. Thereafter, George W. returns to Texas.

1989 George W. joins with a group of investors to purchase the Texas Rangers baseball franchise and becomes managing partner; despite difficult political conditions, the group secures approval to build the Rangers a new stadium in Arlington, Texas, which opens in April 1994.

1992 Governor Bill Clinton of Arkansas defeats President George H. W. Bush in the November presidential election; George W. plays only a limited role in the campaign.

1993 Encouraged by political consultant Karl Rove, George W. decides to challenge popular sitting governor Ann Richards, a Democrat, in the 1994 election. Joe Allbaugh signs on as campaign manager; and Karen Hughes, as communications director.

November 8, 1994 In a decisive win, George W. is elected governor of Texas.

January 17, 1995 George W. is sworn in as governor.

1998 George W. holds exploratory talks with Republican strategists about a possible presidential run. (January) George W. and his partners sell the Texas Rangers, earning George W. $15 million.

November 3, 1998 George W. is reelected governor over Democratic challenger Garry Mauro, with 69 percent of the vote; he is the first Texas governor to be elected to two consecutive four-year terms. Jeb Bush is elected governor of Florida on the same day.

1999 (March) George W. forms an exploratory committee for his presidential run and begins fund-raising. (June) He announces his candidacy for president of the United States.

2000 (January) George W. wins the Iowa Republican caucus but a week later is bested by Senator John McCain in New Hampshire. (February) George W. wins the South Carolina primary on February 19 and goes on to take 9 out of 13 states on super Tuesday; soon afterward, Senator McCain drops out of the race, leaving George W. Bush as the presumptive Republican nominee. Bush selects Dick Cheney as his running mate.

August 3, 2000 Bush accepts the Republican nomination for president at the Republican National Convention in Philadelphia. His Democratic opponent will be Bill Clinton's two-term vice president, Al Gore.

November 7, 2000 A tumultuous election day: Despite Gore's reported lead (he indisputably won the popular vote), conflicting reports from Florida confirm that the very close election will be decided there, since Florida's electoral votes will all go to the winner of its popular vote. In a thoroughly extraordinary development, there is no clear winner on November 8, and the election hinges on a hotly contested recount in Florida that eventually rests on the decision of the U.S. Supreme Court in *Bush v. Gore*.

December 12, 2000 A bitterly divided U.S. Supreme Court hands down its decision holding that the Florida Supreme Court's recount instructions violated the Equal Protection clause of the Fourteenth Amendment and were therefore unconstitutional, in effect deciding the election in Bush's favor.

December 13, 2000 Al Gore concedes, and George W. Bush is declared the winner of the presidential election.

January 20, 2001 George W. Bush is sworn in as the 43rd president of the United States.

January 29, 2001 By executive order, Bush creates the White House Office of Faith-Based and Community Initiatives.

February 27, 2001 President Bush presents his $1.96 trillion budget for fiscal year 2002 to a joint session of Congress, arguing for a $1.6 trillion, 10-year tax-cut plan.

March The president withholds support from the Kyoto Protocol for reducing emissions of greenhouse gases because of the protocol's focus on industrialized countries.

May 1, 2001 President Bush announces plans for a national missile defense shield.

May 26, 2001 Congress approves a $1.35 trillion tax-cut plan embodying most of the president's proposals

August 9, 2001   President Bush limits federal funding for research on embryonic stem cells to a few dozen cell lines already in existence.

September 11, 2001   With hijacked planes, terrorists linked to Al Qaeda attack both towers of New York City's World Trade Center as well as the Pentagon in Washington, D.C. Another planned attack was foiled by the passengers of San Francisco–bound United Airlines Flight 93; the plane crashed 80 miles southeast of Pittsburgh, killing everyone on board. The president was flown from Florida, where he had been reading to a third-grade class, to Barksdale Air Force Base in Louisiana and then to Offutt Air Force Base in Nebraska, where he convened an emergency meeting via videoconference of the National Security Council.

September 14, 2001   President Bush and Mrs. Bush, former president George H. W. Bush and Barbara Bush, and former president Bill Clinton and Hillary Clinton are among those attending a National Day of Prayer Remembrance service at Washington's National Cathedral; the House and Senate vote to authorize the president to use "all necessary and appropriate force" against terrorists.

September 20, 2001   President Bush announces that Pennsylvania governor Tom Ridge will head a new cabinet agency, the Department of Homeland Security.

October 2001   The United States and the United Kingdom conduct air strikes against Taliban and Al Qaeda targets in Afghanistan; U.S. Special Forces launch ground assaults.

October 26, 2001   President Bush signs the USA PATRIOT Act granting broad powers to the nation's intelligence agencies and the Treasury Department to intercept private communications and otherwise investigate and pursue suspected terrorists.

November 2001   Kabul falls to U.S.-backed Northern Alliance troops; President Bush signs an order approving the use of military tribunals to try foreign nationals charged with terrorism.

December 2001   President Bush announces that the United States will withdraw from the Antiballistic Missile Treaty signed with the Soviet Union in 1972.

January 2002   The detention center for foreign nationals accused of terrorism opens at the Guantánamo Bay U.S. Naval Base in Cuba; the National Security Administration is instructed to begin warrantless wiretapping.

Bipartisan Campaign Finance Reform (McCain-Feingold) Act is signed by President Bush.

January 8, 2002   Bush signs the bipartisan No Child Left Behind Act, a package of education reform measures instituting new comprehensive math and English tests and addressing teacher standards.

January 29, 2002   In his first State of the Union address, President Bush labels Iran, Iraq, and North Korea an *axis of evil*.

February 12, 2002   Secretary of State Colin Powell testifies before Congress that the United States is considering possibilities for "regime change" in Iraq. By fall, Britain's prime minister, Tony Blair, announces that he will support U.S. military action in Iraq, whereas German Chancellor Gerhard Schroeder declares that Germany will not.

June 14, 2002   President Bush enunciates a policy of preemptive military strikes against presumed enemies; the policy becomes known as the Bush Doctrine.

September 12, 2002 In an address before the UN General Assembly, President Bush warns of "unavoidable" military action against Iraq if its leader, Saddam Hussein, does not relinquish the weapons of mass destruction he is alleged to possess.

October 10–11, 2002 The House of Representatives and the Senate, respectively, approve a war resolution against Iraq.

October 16, 2002 President Bush signs the war resolution.

November 22, 2002 President Bush relaxes clean air rules for utilities and industry.

November 25, 2002 President Bush signs the Homeland Security Act, formally creating a cabinet-level department that will oversee a variety of domestic security agencies.

January 2003 In his State of the Union address, President Bush claims that Saddam Hussein had attempted to purchase large quantities of uranium yellowcake for nuclear weapons; this claim is subsequently discredited.

March 19, 2003 Operation Iraqi Freedom commences after President Bush deems Iraqi cooperation with UN weapons inspectors to be inadequate.

April 9, 2003 U.S. military forces take control of Baghdad.

May 1, 2003 Speaking from the deck of the U.S. aircraft carrier *Abraham Lincoln*, the president declares that major U.S. military operations in Iraq have ceased. The speech is promptly dubbed the Mission Accomplished speech, after the banner hung prominently behind the president.

June 2003 The Coalition Provisional Authority, headed by L. Paul Bremer III, takes over reconstruction efforts in Iraq.

July 6, 2003   In an op-ed piece in the *New York Times*, former ambassador Joseph C. Wilson IV attacked the yellowcake claim as manipulation of intelligence to justify the invasion of Iraq. During a firestorm of administration reaction, the identity of Wilson's wife, Valerie Plame, as an undercover Central Intelligence Agency (CIA) operative is leaked to the press, a violation of the Intelligence Identities Protection Act of 1982.

September 7, 2003   In a televised speech, President Bush announces that he will request $87 billion for the rebuilding of Iraq.

November 5, 2003   President Bush signs the Partial Birth Abortion Act forbidding a controversial medical procedure for terminating a pregnancy in the second or third trimester.

November 6, 2003   Congress passes, and the president signs, the $87 billion Iraq spending package.

December 8, 2003   President Bush signs a measure intended to overhaul Medicare and rein in costs even while adding a new prescription drug benefit for seniors expected to cost $400 billion over 10 years.

December 14, 2003   The United States announces that it has apprehended Saddam Hussein, who had fled Baghdad when U.S. troops entered the city in March.

February 24, 2004   Bush calls for a constitutional amendment that would define marriage as being between a man and a woman, broaching a major battle in the American culture wars.

April 28, 2004   Abu Ghraib prison torture scandal surfaces in the form of photographs of inmates being subjected to psychological abuse at the Baghdad prison.

June 28, 2004	The governance of Iraq is formally transferred from the Coalition Provisional Authority to an interim Iraqi government.
July 22, 2004	The bipartisan 9/11 Commission releases its report, recommending that the nation's intelligence agencies be integrated under a new cabinet-level administrator.
September 2, 2004	At the Republican National Convention in New York City, President Bush accepts his party's nomination for a second presidential term.
November 2, 2004	Bush is reelected by a narrow margin over Democratic candidate John Kerry.
January 2005	President Bush calls for an overhaul of Social Security that would include the option of private investment accounts; after the ensuing uproar, he quietly drops the idea.
March 31, 2005	The Silberman-Robb Commission concludes in a scathing report that the U.S. intelligence community was mistaken in almost all of its pre–Iraq War judgments.
May 5, 2005	The leak of the Downing Street Memo politically damages both President Bush and Prime Minister Tony Blair; the highly sensitive British government internal memo includes the assessment that in the Bush administration's haste to go to war in Iraq, the "intelligence and facts were being fixed around the policy."
August 6, 2005	Peace activist Cindy Sheehan, whose son Casey had been killed in Iraq, begins a monthlong protest at Camp Casey near the Bush ranch in Crawford, Texas.
August 29, 2005	Hurricane Katrina makes landfall at New Orleans in the worst natural disaster ever to afflict the United States. FEMA mismanagement

and a variety of other missteps make it a political disaster as well.

September 5, 2005   President Bush nominates Judge John G. Roberts Jr. as chief justice of the U.S. Supreme Court. Judge Roberts had been nominated for the seat of retiring Associate Justice Sandra Day O'Connor, but the president then proposed that he succeed Chief Justice William Rehnquist instead. Judge Roberts was confirmed on September 20, 2005.

October 3, 2005   President Bush nominates White House counsel and longtime political associate Harriet Miers for the seat of Justice O'Connor. Miers later withdraws her name after criticism of her qualifications and her personal ties to the president.

October 19, 2005   Under the jurisdiction of the Iraqi government, Saddam Hussein stands trial in Baghdad. He is sentenced to death on November 5, and the sentence is carried out in ignominious fashion on December 30.

October 28, 2005   I. Lewis "Scooter" Libby, Vice President Cheney's chief of staff, is indicted on charges of perjury and obstruction of justice as a result of Special Prosecutor Patrick Fitzgerald's investigation into the leak of the identity of CIA agent Valerie Plame.

October 31, 2005   President Bush nominates Samuel A. Alito Jr. for Justice O'Connor's seat on the U.S. Supreme Court. Judge Alito is confirmed on January 31, 2006.

March 9, 2006   President Bush signs a renewal of the USA PATRIOT Act.

June 29, 2006   In *Boumediene v. Bush*, the U.S. Supreme Court decides that prisoners detained at Guantánamo Bay, Cuba, have the right to habeas corpus under the Constitution.

July 19, 2006   Bush exercises the first veto of his presidency to block a law lifting federal funding restrictions on human embryonic stem cell research.

September 2006   President Bush admits that terrorism suspects have been kept in secret prisons run by the CIA in other countries, a policy that becomes known as *rendition*.

November 7, 2006   Democrats win a large number of congressional seats in midterm elections as the Iraq War grows more unpopular; they have control of both houses of congress for the first time in 12 years; Donald Rumsfeld resigns his position as secretary of defense the next day.

December 2006   Seven U.S. attorneys are asked to resign by Justice Department officials on what prove to be political grounds, eventually leading to the resignation in August 2007 of Attorney General Alberto Gonzales, a longtime Bush friend and advisor.

January 2007   General David Petraeus's military surge begins in Iraq, increasing the strength of U.S. military forces there by some 30,000.

April 3, 2007   U.S. Supreme Court rules that the Environmental Protection Agency has violated the Clean Air Act by neglecting to impose new-vehicle emissions standards.

August 2007   Amid mounting evidence that the U.S. economy is approaching a catastrophic collapse, Bush tries to reassure Americans that the fundamentals of our economy are strong. His reassurances fail to stem the crisis of confidence among investors and the public.

August 13, 2007   Karl Rove, generally acknowledged as the chief architect of President Bush's electoral and political successes, resigns.

January 18, 2008   President Bush proposes a $145 billion federal stimulus package, mostly in the form of tax breaks, to revive the floundering U.S. economy.

February 22, 2008   President Bush announces that Southern Methodist University in Dallas has been selected as the site of the George W. Bush Presidential Center, which would include the presidential library.

March 8, 2008   President Bush vetoes a law that would have banned waterboarding and other extreme interrogation methods.

July 14, 2008   President Bush lifts the ban on offshore oil drilling on the outer continental shelf; the ban had been put in place by President George H. W. Bush.

October 3, 2008   Bush signs a $700 billion financial bailout for financial institutions, the biggest government bailout in U.S. history.

November 4, 2008   Democratic Senator Barack Obama wins the 2008 presidential election, which was largely seen as a referendum on the Bush years.

January 15, 2009   President George W. Bush delivers his farewell address to the nation.

January 20, 2009   Barack Obama is inaugurated as 44th president of the United States, ending George W. Bush's tenure in the nation's highest elective office. President Bush and Mrs. Bush return to Texas.

April 27, 2010   Crown Publishers, a division of Random House, announces that it will publish former president Bush's untraditional memoir *Decision Points* on November 9, 2010.

May 4, 2010   Laura Bush's memoir *Spoken from the Heart* is published.

Chapter 1

GREAT EXPECTATIONS

George Walker Bush, who would become the 43rd president of the United States, was born into a family that expected great things from its men. His ancestors had been notable ministers, wealthy businessmen, and national politicians. They attended prestigious schools and drew upon a network of relationships that supported their success. They generally married well and were prolific, adding many branches to the family tree. Living up to such a legacy was a daunting prospect for "Georgie," the eldest son of George H. W. and Barbara Pierce Bush, especially after his father reached the highest political office in the land.

"Poppy" Bush, as George H. W. Bush was known in a family with enough Georges to require nicknames, was pushed along by his own father, Prescott Bush, who had been a successful businessman and a U.S. senator. Prescott's marriage to Dorothy Walker was a milestone in Bush family history, adding a heavily monied branch to balance out and support the public service emphasis of the Bush clan. This tree balancing would ensure that the Bush men could afford to take risks in business early in life and enjoy support and security when they pursued public office later in life.

THE WALKER FAMILY

Dorothy Walker's roots can be traced back to a Catholic family that found itself in desperate straits. Her great-grandfather, George E. Walker (1797–1864), was a farmer from a Catholic family living just below the Mason-Dixon line in Maryland. Like many modest land owners far removed from the huge Deep South plantations, the Walkers appear to have owned a couple of slaves to support their 321-acre Cecil County farm. In the 1830s, they hit hard economic times, lost their land, and moved to the state that would become known as the "Land of Lincoln."[1] Traveling in a covered wagon to the Midwest, they claimed a homestead near Bloomington, Illinois.

Dorothy Walker's grandfather, David Davis "D. D." Walker (1840–1918), fared much better than his parents and laid the foundations for the family fortune. The youngest of eight sons, D.D. moved to St. Louis and started a dry goods business that became the largest wholesale importer west of the Mississippi River. J.C. Penney was one of his biggest clients.[2] Ely, Walker and Company is still a going concern today, selling western clothing under the Ely & Walker label. By 1914, D.D. would be one of 7,300 millionaires in the United States.[3]

D. D.'s son and Dorothy Walker's father, George Herbert "Bert" Walker, would grow up with all the advantages of a rich man's son. His father had hopes he would become a priest and sent his fifth child with a personal valet to Stonyhurst, a Jesuit boarding school in England. But Bert, a brash and independent-minded young man, had his own plans. After he returned, he fell in love with a beautiful socialite, Lucretia "Loulie" Wear, and left the Catholic Church to marry her. D. D. was so upset he refused to attend the wedding in a Presbyterian church. Although they still stayed in touch, a rift remained, which reached a peak at the end of D. D.'s life when he began giving away his fortune to the Catholic Church. Bert and his brother were attempting to have their father declared mentally incompetent when he died while the dispute was still in the courts.[4]

Bert would not need his father's fortune, though. While he was in his twenties he had struck out on his own in business, passing up the dry goods business for opportunities in finance. He opened one of the first investment banks in the Midwest, G. H. Walker and Company, and made bold investments that won and lost him several fortunes.[5] During World War I, he worked with J. P. Morgan and Company to purchase war supplies for Britain and France. His investments in railroads brought him into contact with E. H. Harriman, owner of the huge Union Pacific railroad, and his son Averell. Bert partnered with Averell in 1919, leaving St. Louis for New York to form the Wall Street firm W. A. Harriman and Company. By the end of the 1920s, Bert reached his apex in business, serving on the boards of 17 corporations.[6] Because of disputes with his investment partners, Bert pulled out of the company and liquidated his stock market holdings just before the 1929 crash, leaving the Walkers untouched by the Depression.[7]

Bert would never embrace the modesty exhibited by the northeastern, patrician Bush clan into which his daughter would marry. He spent lavishly all his life. At 25, as a newly married man with one child, he kept three live-in servants (a maid, a nanny, and a cook).[8] He and his father set aside their differences long enough in 1904 to jointly purchase property in Kennebunkport, Maine, so their families would have a retreat from the midwestern heat. Bert added to the property later and bought several other properties of his own, including an opulent, marble-floored mansion on Long Island; a home in Santa Barbara; and a 10,000-acre southern plantation in South Carolina known as Duncannon, where he took hunting parties.[9] In New York City, his Wall Street office was at One Wall Street, and his home was at One Sutton Place in Manhattan.[10] He traveled in private railroad cars, and he and his wife got around in separate chauffeured Rolls Royces. He and Averell co-owned a stable of race horses for a time, as well as a 150-foot yacht.[11]

Like the Bushes, Bert established a family tradition of athletic achievement as a standout at polo, golf, and boxing. He won Missouri's amateur heavyweight boxing title in a bare-knuckled competition.[12] He combined his wealth and influence with his interest in sports by becoming the president of the U.S. Golfing Association and founding the Anglo-American golf tournament called the Walker Cup.[13] Bert's son, George Herbert Walker Jr., kept up this tradition of combining wealth and a keen interest in sports, cofounding the New York Mets baseball franchise in 1960. "Uncle Herbie" would be one of George H. W. Bush's biggest supporters, attending all of his nephew's college baseball games, as well as supporting his business ventures.[14] But, this is jumping ahead a bit. The next section turns to the other family that was merged when Prescott Bush married Dorothy Walker.

THE BUSH FAMILY

The Bush family traces its ancestry back to a 19th-century minister, James Smith Bush, the first Bush to attend Yale University (class of 1844). Bush studied law before turning to the ministry. He worked in Orange, New Jersey, and later Staten Island, New York, with a brief adventure as ship's chaplain aboard the steamship *Vanderbilt*, when it sailed to San Francisco.[15] He met dissension in his church at West Brighton, Staten Island, which led to his resignation, the *New York Times* reported, because he "opposed the employing of games of chance to raise money for the church."[16] He moved to Concord in 1883. Two years later, he published the second of two books of sermons, *Evidence of Faith*, which argued that Christianity could be placed upon a rational basis.[17] When he died in 1889, his Yale obituary noted that his late decision to leave the Episcopal Church and become a Unitarian led to an anguish that killed him.[18]

James Smith Bush's second son, Samuel Prescott Bush, studied engineering rather than theology. He attended Stevens Institute of Technology in New Jersey before heading off to the Midwest to ply his craft in the railroad industry. He worked his way up to president of a railroad equipment manufacturer, Buckeye Steel Castings, in Columbus, Ohio, holding that position for 20 years before retiring in 1927. He served as director of some of Pennsylvania Railroad's Ohio subsidiaries as well as the Huntington National Bank. He was tapped for the War Industries Board during World War I, taking charge of the Ordnance, Small Arms, and Ammunition section, which coordinated with munitions manufacturers. He was president of the National Association of Manufacturers and a director for the Federal Reserve Bank of Cleveland.[19]

Although his wealth was paltry compared to that of the Walker family, he built an impressive mansion in the Columbus suburbs; vacationed in the seaside resort of Watch Hill, Rhode Island; and sent his children to expensive boarding schools. He had been recruited to serve on the board of one of these schools, St. George's all-boys preparatory school in Newport, Rhode Island, where his oldest son, Prescott Bush, enrolled in 1908.[20]

THE BUSH-WALKER MERGER

Prescott Bush, born at the end of the 19th century, grew up as the son of a wealthy industrialist in the Bexley mansion, just outside of Columbus, Ohio. In prep school at St. George's, he was a standout student, playing varsity baseball, basketball, and football, as well as leading several organizations, such as the glee club, golf club, and civics club. He was elected head prefect—equivalent to class president—in his last year at St. George's.[21] He continued his achievements at Yale. Full grown, he reached six feet four inches, an imposing figure who earned varsity letters in baseball, hockey, and golf. He had a wonderful bass voice that earned him a coveted spot on the recently formed a capella singing group, the Yale Whiffenpoofs, as well as the Yale Glee Club and Men's Choir.[22] He also was tapped for membership in the secretive Skull and Bones society.

Following his graduation in 1917, Prescott and several of his fellow "Bonesmen" joined the National Guard after the United States declared war on Germany, entering World War I, and he was commissioned as a captain in the army. Before Prescott and his friends were shipped overseas, they were sent to Fort Sill in Oklahoma to join their equestrian artillery unit (the army's last one) for two months. While in Oklahoma, Prescott and his fellow Bonesmen are alleged to have stolen a skull from an Apache cemetery, which they claimed to be Geronimo's. Indeed, this allegation surfaced anew in 2009, on the 100th anniversary of Geronimo's death, when the Apache warrior's descendants filed a lawsuit against Skull and Bones. They sought the return of the skull, which, rumor had it, was kept in a glass case in the secretive society's clubhouse, called the Tomb. However, even the lawyer bringing the suit admitted there was little hard evidence to support the theft, and, indeed, it appears to have been an exaggeration about what the Bonesmen actually brought back to the Tomb.[23]

Whatever frivolity occupied the Bonesmen during their two-month stay in Oklahoma, it quickly faded as Prescott and his friends were deployed to the front near Verdun, France, for the last 10 weeks of the war. Yet even here he managed to make light of his situation, leading to an unintended hoax. He sent a letter home bragging about how he had been decorated by French, British, and American military officials after saving the lives of their most famous generals (Ferdinand Foch, Sir Douglas Haig, and John Pershing). When he explained how he had used a bolo knife to divert an incoming artillery shell, he had to assume that his readers would recognize his joshing. Somehow this joke ended up presented as fact in the local newspaper back home, the *Ohio State Journal*, as well as in the *New Haven Journal-Courier*. His embarrassed mother had to write a letter to the Ohio paper correcting the record, insisting it was erroneously based upon a letter "written in a spirit of fun."[24] Bush didn't have to face the humiliation of this mistake for another year, as he continued his army duties into 1919 in occupied Germany.

Although Dorothy Walker's family was much wealthier than Prescott's, she didn't have a chance to go to college. While all of her brothers went to Yale, her father did not believe that girls needed a college education. Instead, she and her sisters were sent to an elite girls school in St. Louis before being shipped off to the exclusive Miss Porter's School in Farmington, Connecticut. They capped this education with six months in Paris to polish their social skills.[25] Like her father, she was a talented athlete, winning second place in the first National Girls' Tennis Championship in 1918.[26]

Dorothy and her sister returned from Paris in spring 1919. A few months later, following a tennis lesson, the 18-year-old Dorothy, clad in a full-length tennis dress, met the 24-year-old Prescott Bush, who had stopped by her family's home to pick up opera tickets from Dorothy's sister.[27] He had landed a position that fall in St. Louis with Simmons Hardware Company, known nationally for its Keen Kutter line of products and run by Skull and Bones alumnus and the founder's son, Wallace Simmons. Simmons knew Prescott's father, having discussed war planning with him when Samuel Bush served on the War Industries Board.[28] Prescott proposed to Dorothy the following summer in the year Mr. Walker moved his family to New York City to start a Wall Street firm with Averell Harriman. They were married on August 6, 1921, at the family's summer place in Kennebunkport, Maine, where Dorothy was born. Prescott's mother never got to see her son's wedding, however. Shortly after Prescott's engagement was announced, she was struck by an automobile while walking near the family's Watch Hill, Rhode Island, summer home and was killed instantly.[29]

Although Prescott had inherited a small sum from his mother's estate, his financial situation was a bit tenuous in the early years of their marriage. For the first few years, he worked as a salesman, dragging Dorothy and his growing family to Missouri, then Tennessee, then to Ohio to work for a rubber company in which his father had an investment. When that company was purchased by a New England firm, they moved to Massachusetts. Their second child, George Herbert Walker Bush, heir to his grandfather's name and future president of the United States, would be born there. In 1925, the family bought its first home in Greenwich, Connecticut, where Prescott could commute to his new job with U.S. Rubber Company in New York City and Dorothy and the children could be near her father.

Bert Walker helped out the young couple by paying a cook, gardener, nurse, and maid to work in their house, as well as building a bungalow at Kennebunkport for Dorothy and the children to escape the summer heat.[30] Prescott was never quite comfortable with his ostentatious father-in-law. He was brought up to be, and brought up his children to be, much more modest and thrifty with personal finances. But in 1926, Bert made him one offer he couldn't refuse: a position as vice president in the investment firm Bert started with Averell Harriman, W. A. Harriman and Company. Prescott knew the Harrimans already through Roland "Bunny" Harriman, a Skull and Bones colleague in his class at Yale.

Prescott had been on the job a couple of years when Bert Walker had a serious disagreement with the Harrimans over whether to accept margin accounts shortly before the stock market crashed in 1929. Prescott stayed, but Bert left the firm, divesting himself, fortuitously, before the crash. Prescott earned his keep during this difficult period by convincing Averell to cut costs in their foreign offices and supporting a merger with the venerable Brown Brothers and Company to form Brown Brothers Harriman at the start of 1931. Prescott was made a full partner in the new company, with a generous salary to support him until the economic tide turned. He used his new wealth to buy an eight-bedroom Victorian house for his growing family (Dorothy was pregnant with their fourth child).[31]

Prescott was a domineering presence in the Bush home, enforcing discipline on his large family in matters concerning misbehavior and even breaches of etiquette.[32] But there was a great deal of fun for the children as well. Prescott and Dorothy, as competitive athletes, encouraged friendly rivalry through family games and the many sports their children played. As the oldest son, Prescott Jr. once noted: "Listen, our family's middle name was games. Oh, we used to have tiddlywinks championships. We'd play, oh, just about every kind of game you can think of from Parcheesi to tiddlywinks to Go Fish or Sir Hinkam Funny Duster."[33]

Through the support of their grandfather and the success of their father, the Bush children would grow up, as their parents had, in a well-to-do family. They would have servants, play golf and swim at the country club, summer in Maine and at several other family resorts, attend preparatory and Ivy League schools, and turn to the Walker family for financial backing in some of their business ventures. The second son, George Herbert Walker Bush, also would follow his father into politics and set a pattern for two of his own sons.

INAUGURATING THE BUSH POLITICAL DYNASTY

The public service of the Bush family finds some roots in James Smith Bush's decision to enter the ministry and in Samuel Bush's service on the War Industries Board. But it would be Prescott who moved the family squarely into politics. He became well known in business circles, serving on the boards of Prudential Insurance, Pan American Airways, CBS, Dresser Industries, and Yale University.[34] In parlaying that reputation into a political career, he began small, winning election as the moderator of Greenwich's Representative Town Meeting. He raised money for Republican presidential candidates in 1936 and 1944. But with children still going to expensive schools, he passed on running for the House of Representatives in 1946. Only in 1950 was he ready to take the plunge, narrowly losing to Democrat William Benton after a columnist claimed he was associated with the Birth Control League (actually, it was Planned Parenthood, the organization's successor). This association did not play well in majority-Catholic Connecticut.[35] In a run for the Senate in 1952, he didn't even make it through the

Republican primary, but the sudden death of sitting Connecticut Democratic senator Brien McMahon cleared the path for his nomination for the open seat, which he won, riding Dwight Eisenhower's coattails to Washington, D.C.[36]

Prescott served in the Senate for more than a decade, earning respect for his support of Eisenhower's Interstate Highway System, for Kennedy's Peace Corps, for his stance on civil rights, and for his criticism of fellow senator Joseph McCarthy's communist witch hunt (which Bill Clinton would reference in his presidential candidate debate with George H. W. Bush).[37]

He carried his sense of decorum, civic-mindedness, and seriousness over into his duties, urging a resolution to prevent his fellow senators from waving to visitors in the Senate gallery during floor debates, opposing a proposal to raise the salary of senators from $12,500 to $22,500, and ignoring threats from energy companies against his second son's oil

Senator Prescott Bush (right) snaps the brim of a straw hat he has presented to Vice President Richard M. Nixon at a May 1953 GOP lunch. AP Photo.

business when he opposed deregulation of natural gas.[38] He did not run
for reelection in 1962 because dizzy spells and stomach pains made his
run for office difficult. He would come to regret that decision.[39]

Prescott's second son and grandson would exceed the family patri-
arch in politics, earning one term and two terms, respectively, in the
White House as president. He would build political connections that
would promote his son's political success, which, in turn, would promote the grandson's political success. Both the son and grandson could
count on the Walker side of the family to help them succeed in business, which, according to the pattern laid down by Prescott, was the
proper path to public service, taking care of family and finances first,
before turning to one's civic duties. And, indeed, both son and grandson would stick to the plan, as a brief account of George H. W. Bush's
life shows, and the remainder of this book explains in relation to his
son, George W. Bush.

GEORGE H. W. BUSH

George Herbert Walker Bush would be called "Poppy" in the Bush
home and at school, a variation of "Pop," which is what his name-
sake, George Herbert Walker, was called by the family. He was born in
Milton, Massachusetts, during that restless period when his father was
following his next job around. Poppy was the second child and the second son, following Prescott Jr., known as "Pressy." Poppy admired his
big brother and started school a year early to be near him. They both
attended the Greenwich Country Day School before leaving home for
Phillips Andover preparatory school in Massachusetts.

Poppy blossomed at Andover, as his own father had done at
St. George's, particularly in athletics. He was captain of the baseball
team and captain of the soccer team (where he was one of their all-
time best players), and he played on the varsity basketball team. Like
his father who had been chosen as prefect, he served as senior class
president. He was involved in a great many social and academic groups
as well. Although he was an average student, he was well liked. And
although he inherited a strong competitive streak from his parents, he
had a keen sense of fair play, befriending a Jewish student who nearly
dropped out of Andover when he was passed over by all the Greek

societies. An illness during his senior year required Poppy to miss a lot of school, and he had to return for a fifth year to finish.[40]

Poppy's final year at Andover brought tragedy and promise. The December 7, 1941, attack on Pearl Harbor created fear and outrage, dragging the United States into World War II. Poppy was ready to leave school and enlist, but he promised his parents he would at least finish at Andover. A couple of weeks later at a Christmas dance, Poppy met Barbara Pierce, a 16-year-old who was a distant cousin of the 14th president, Franklin Pierce. Her father was a vice president at McCall Publishing, and she ran in the same social circles as the Bushes. Barbara was athletic, but not the beauty her sister Martha was (having appeared on the cover of *Vogue* the year before). The two began dating, and Poppy took her to his senior prom. But the war was calling. Poppy defied his parents' request that he go on to college and enlisted in the navy on his 18th birthday. He proposed marriage to Barbara, the only girl he had ever kissed (he assured his mother), before he was deployed the next year.[41]

Poppy was trained as a naval pilot and, at 18, was the youngest in the navy. He was assigned to an aircraft carrier in the South Pacific where he saw a lot of action, flying 58 bombing missions. He was shot down twice over the Pacific. The second of those hits occurred on September 2, 1944, on a bombing run south of Japan. Although his plane was damaged, he still managed to drop his bombs on a Japanese installation at Chichi Jima before bailing out in the ocean. His two crew members didn't make it, but he survived, as shown vividly in vintage footage of his rescue at sea played during the 1988 Republican National Convention that nominated him for president.[42] He was awarded the Distinguished Flying Cross and three air medals. At the end of 1944, he was reassigned to the naval base at Norfolk to help train torpedo pilots. He was honorably discharged in September 1945 and entered an accelerated program at Yale in November.

Shortly after his return to the United States, he and Barbara married on January 6, 1945, in her family's church in Rye, New York. She had dropped out of Smith College after little more than a year to plan the wedding and never returned. The couple settled in New Haven, Connecticut, as Poppy began his college studies. He finished his degree in two and a half years but still managed to make his mark at Yale. He lettered in both soccer and baseball. He played in two College World Series in baseball and was captain in his senior year. In that role, he was honored to accept a draft of the autobiography of Babe Ruth for the Yale library from the Bambino himself. He majored in economics and graduated Phi Beta Kappa, performing much better than he had at Andover. He was president of Delta Kappa Epsilon fraternity and the last man tapped for Skull and Bones.

Barbara had her hands full a year into Poppy's college career after she gave birth to their first child, George Walker Bush, on July 6, 1946. Barbara's mother had given her castor oil to speed the process along.[43] Barbara would have five more children over the next decade and a half, playing the traditional role that Bush wives were given, while Poppy worked to secure their financial future.

Following graduation, Poppy decided against following his father into the investment business. A family friend, Neil Mallon, provided direction to the young man. Mallon had been in Skull and Bones with Prescott and was a close friend of the Bush family. Prescott had recommended Mallon for the presidency of Dresser Company, on whose board he sat. Mallon, in turn, helped out Poppy by getting him into the oil business, an important and growing sector of the economy. Dresser had become the largest manufacturer of oil drilling equipment, and Mallon wanted Poppy to learn the business from the ground up. Poppy started with a modest salary working for Dresser subsidiary International Derrick and Equipment Company in Odessa, Texas. Poppy left Connecticut and set off for his new life in a red Studebaker his parents had bought him as a graduation present, while Barbara and baby George flew down to the family's new home in the Lone Star State.

The couple lived frugally, initially living in a duplex apartment and sharing a bathroom with another couple.[44] After a couple of years of learning the ropes and moving from Texas to California and back, the Bushes settled in Midland, Texas. This would be the place that their infant son, George W. Bush, would consider home, the place that most shaped his values and his outlook. This would be the city that launched his father's considerable success in the oil business. That success provided the financial security for Poppy to follow his father into politics and inspired two of his sons to carry on the dynasty. The next chapter considers George W. Bush's childhood against the backdrop of his father's rising financial and political fortunes in this dusty Texas town.

NOTES

1. Jacob Weisberg, *The Bush Tragedy* (New York: Random House, 2008), 8.

2. Kitty Kelley, *The Family: The Real Story of the Bush Dynasty* (New York: Doubleday, 2004), 25.

3. Kelley, *The Family*, 24.

4. Kelley, *The Family*, 26; Weisberg, *The Bush Tragedy*, 9.

5. Weisberg, *The Bush Tragedy*, 9.

6. Kevin Phillips, *American Dynasty: Aristocracy, Fortune, and the Politics of Deceit in the House of Bush* (New York: Viking, 2004), 22–24.

7. Weisberg, *The Bush Tragedy*, 11.

8. Kelley, *The Family*, 27.

9. Kelley, *The Family*, 25; Phillips, *American Dynasty*, 23–24; Weisberg, *The Bush Tragedy*, 10.

10. Bill Minutaglio, *First Son: George W. Bush and the Bush Family Dynasty*, reprint, 1999 (New York: Three Rivers Press, 2001), 20.

11. Weisberg, *The Bush Tragedy*, 10–11.

12. Ibid., 8.

13. Ibid., 9.

14. Ibid., 24.

15. "For the Pacific Coast; Departure of the Vanderbilt and the Monadnock," *New York Times (Archive)*, 25 October 1865, 5.

16. "A Pastor Chides His Flock," *New York Times (Archive)*, 28 January 1884, http://query.nytimes.com/mem/archive-free/pdf?_r=1&res=9E02E0D61538E033A2575BC2A9679C94659FD7CF.

17. Weisberg, *The Bush Tragedy*, 11.

18. Ibid.

19. Phillips, *American Dynasty*, 21.

20. Kelley, *The Family*, 8.

21. Ibid.

22. "Music: Whiffenpoof Contest," *Time (Online)*, 2 August 1937, http://www.time.com/time/magazine/article/0,9171,770754,00.html; Weisberg, *The Bush Tragedy*, 13.

23. James C. McKinley Jr., "Geronimo's Heirs Sue Secret Yale Society Over His Skull," *New York Times*, 20 February 2009, A14; Kelley, *The Family*, 16–19.

24. Kelley, *The Family*, 20–22.

25. Ibid., 29.

26. Ibid., 31.

27. Ibid., 31.

28. Phillips, *American Dynasty*, 183.

29. Kelley, *The Family*, 34–35.

30. Kelley, *The Family*, 37; Phillips, *American Dynasty*, 183.

31. Kelley, *The Family*, 38–43; Weisberg, *The Bush Tragedy*, 14, 45–46.

32. Kelley, *The Family*, 48.

33. Minutaglio, *First Son*, 21.

34. Ibid., 19–20.

35. Weisberg, *The Bush Tragedy*, 18; Kelley, *The Family*, 46.

36. Weisberg, *The Bush Tragedy*, 18.

37. Kelley, *The Family*, 116, 158–62; Department of Transportation, "Infrastructure: A Bush at Both Ends Before and After the Interstate Era," Federal Highway Administration Web site, 2009, http://www.fhwa.dot.gov/infrastructure/rw01d.htm.

38. Weisberg, *The Bush Tragedy*, 18.

39. Ibid., 19–20.

40. Kelley, *The Family*, 64–65; Weisberg, *The Bush Tragedy*, 5.

41. Kelley, *The Family*, 66–70, 78, 87; Weisberg, *The Bush Tragedy*, 35.

42. Weisberg, *The Bush Tragedy*, 32.

43. Minutaglio, *First Son*, 23–24.

44. Ibid., 25.

Chapter 2

GROWING A BUSH IN TEXAS

Midland, Texas, was a dusty little West Texas town that would have held little interest for the northeasterners who poured into it during the middle of the 20th century, save for its location in the Permian Basin and the wealth that is hidden beneath it. The small farm and ranching community had been Comanche territory before the tribe was relocated to Oklahoma. The town was originally named Midway when it was founded in the late 19th century because it served as a way station for the Texas and Pacific Railroad halfway between El Paso and Fort Worth. Unknown at that time was that not far below the surface of the arid land lay the remains of a sea 200–300 million years old whose sedimentary bed held billions of barrels of oil, huge natural gas reserves, and significant stores of potash. The first big oil strike came in 1923 when the Santa Rita No. 1 well began operations, followed closely by several other strikes. At the peak of U.S. oil production in the 1970s, the region would account for about 20 percent of the nation's crude oil production. Because Midland sat in the middle of the Permian Basin, businesses in the fledgling oil industry began gravitating there.

In 1940, Midland was still a small town of just over 9,000, a place where the U.S. military would train bombardiers for World War II, dropping 1 million bombs in practice runs over the vast, parched desert. But Midland would nearly triple in size by 1950, spurred on by a huge oil strike in Midland by Humble Oil (later Exxon) in 1945. When the Bushes arrived at midcentury, there were more than 3,000 wells in production in the Permian Basin. That ensured that Midland would continue to grow, reaching 67,000 by 1960.

Such growth threatened traditional ways in this small southern town where alcohol sales were prohibited, schools were racially segregated, and the almost-exclusively Protestant churches were filled on Sundays. But, the influx of thousands of Yankees to the oil town would force those native Midlanders to adjust, despite the fact that, as Barbara Bush complained, some of them were "Eastern-prejudiced."[1]

For the Bushes, the first task was finding a suitable house among the wide streets of Midland that were laid out in a neat grid, many named after states and western towns. Their first home was modest: an 847-square-foot house at 405 East Maple Street in a neighborhood called Easter Egg Row. Here they lived among many of their own kind: graduates of Harvard, Yale, and Princeton who carved out a place for their own culture in West Texas by forming clubs for their fellow college alumni.[2] They were the new entrepreneurial class that made Midland a vibrant and growing city. Poppy Bush later called the place "Yuppieland West."[3]

Twenty miles away was Odessa, where the workhorses of the oil industry lived: the roughnecks, roustabouts, welders, and pipe fitters who brought the oil out of the ground and kept the equipment running. It was a blue-collar town where people labored in the hot sun but could grab a cold beer before returning to their mobile homes. Poppy had worked in Odessa in his first year with Dresser, learning the business from the ground up. The contrast between the two towns could not have been greater.

GEORGIE BECOMES A TEXAN

George W. Bush did not suffer from the fish-out-of-water experience of his northeastern parents in this hot, southern town of limited cultural opportunities. He was four when the family finally settled in Midland; his first memories were of this place, and he grew up feeling at home in Texas. The small town was a safe place for a kid to grow up, riding bikes around the neighborhoods where, Bush noted later, "other people's mothers felt it was not only their right, but also their duty to lecture you when you did something wrong."[4] George found lots of friends among the many young families that populated Midland at that time. Kids and parents alike could enjoy weather that was warm and dry enough to allow backyard barbecues, baseball games, and other outdoor activities almost year-round.

By the time the Bushes settled in Midland, there was one more child to keep an eye on: George's first sibling, Pauline Robinson Bush, called "Robin," was born just before Christmas in 1949. Barbara would push Robin around the dusty town in a pram with George hanging on to the handle.

With a growing family living in a tiny house, Poppy needed to graduate from his modest-paying Dresser job and create a financial foundation, as his father had done. He didn't have to look far for others interested in the same thing. Right across the unpaved road from the Bush home lived John Overbey, a University of Texas graduate who had worked as an oil and gas lease broker in Midland since 1947. Overbey provided the expertise and Poppy provided the capital to create the Bush-Overbey Oil Development Company in 1951. Bush raised $350,000 from his Uncle Herbie and more from several other eastern investors, including his father.[5] The partnership began buying and selling oil drilling royalty rights, setting up shop in an office building across from the county courthouse.[6] When Poppy wasn't flying to the Northeast to woo additional investors, he was scouring land records in Texas courthouses looking for owners with promising oil drilling sites.[7]

Poppy did well enough to allow the Bush family to move into a house with a little more breathing space. The three-bedroom house at 1412 West Ohio had a big front yard in a neighborhood with groves of oak trees. It was close to George's new school, Sam Houston Elementary, and a new country club the Bushes would join. Poppy was active in the community, becoming a deacon and then an elder at First Presbyterian Church; working with the YMCA; registering Republicans to vote; and socializing with fellow Yale alumni, oil company executives, or neighbors in pickup football games.[8] A photograph in a Midland newspaper shows Poppy and young George in a rare moment when the father had undivided time for his son at an electric train race. The accompanying article referred to George as "Junior"—a mistake that would be made often throughout George's life.[9]

The year George turned seven was the most tumultuous year of his young life and, indeed, in the lives of his parents. Early in 1953, the Bushes had a third child, John Ellis Bush, whom they called Jeb. Jeb would grow up to be a chief rival with George for his parents' aspirations. But the joy of a new child was overshadowed by concern for Robin, who began bruising easily and was often tired. The family doctor identified the problem: the 3-year-old had leukemia, almost always a fatal disease at the time.

Poppy called John Walker, his uncle, who was president of Memorial Sloan-Kettering Hospital in New York, where Robin was extensively tested. The family stayed at the Walker family apartment on Sutton Place, nine blocks from the hospital. Dorothy Walker sent Marion Fraser, a Bush-Walker family nurse, back to Texas to care for George and Jeb. The Bushes shuttled between Midland and New York. When Robin returned home for brief stays, George wasn't allowed to play with her. After a seven-month illness, doctors tried one last surgical procedure to save Robin, but she died.

Poppy and Barbara donated her body to science, skipping a funeral but having a memorial service. They returned home to tell young George, who wasn't aware of how sick his sister had become. They drove up to George's school in the middle of the school day, as the second grader was struggling to carry a Victrola record player down a covered walkway to the principal's office. He saw his parents' car pull up the gravel drive and assumed Robin was with them, even thinking he saw her. He sprinted ahead to his teacher and said: "My mom, dad, and sister are home. Can I go see them?" When he met them, they told him the sad news. He was devastated and didn't understand why his parents didn't tell him about her condition.

This tragedy would haunt him for years. He began having nightmares. At a Friday night football game of the Midland Bulldogs, he turned to Poppy and his oil colleagues and said: "I wish I was Robin." Poppy asked why. He said: "Because I bet she can see the game better from up there than we can here." He later asked his father if "my sister was buried standing up or in a prone position . . . because the earth rotates, they said so at school, and . . . does that mean that Robin is standing on her head?"[10]

Years later, in his memoir *A Charge to Keep*, George W. Bush explained the lesson he learned from his sister's death: "I guess I learned in a harsh way, at a very early age, never to take life for granted. But rather than making me fearful, the close reach of death made me determined, determined to enjoy whatever life might bring, to live each day to its fullest."[11] Indeed, he seems to have sought joy from life in the years that followed—perhaps too much at times.

The death of Robin also had an indirect effect on him when his mother became despondent. Barbara was the constant in young George's life, and he in hers, given his father's frequent traveling for work and the many nights he spent involved in community or church work. George responded to his mother by trying to cheer her up by telling jokes and laughing with her, becoming something of a clown. But Barbara clung too closely to her 7-year-old, as George reported later that she had been trying "to envelop herself totally around me" so that "[s]he kind of smothered me."[12] Barbara recognized the problem one day when she overheard George telling a friend that "he couldn't come out because he had to stay inside and play with his mother, who was lonely."[13]

The same year that brought the Bush family the joy of a new birth and the tragedy of a premature death also brought a business triumph that would provide long-term financial security for the family. Poppy was discussing an oil venture with a lawyer who worked on the same street as the Bush-Overbey company. Hugh Liedtke was the son of the chief counsel of Gulf Oil and a navy veteran like Poppy. They developed a plan to raise $850,000 to acquire 8,000 acres in an oil field 70 miles east of Midland. Once again, Poppy called on Uncle Herbie for investors. Liedtke had investors from Oklahoma, as well as his brother who was a partner in his law firm. They took the name Zapata Petroleum from the 1952 movie starring Marlon Brando, *Viva Zapata!* about a Mexican revolutionary. The investment paid off quickly, as the field yielded one performing well after another, eventually totaling 127 wells that together produced more than a million dollars in crude each year. A year later, they added a subsidiary, Zapata Off-Shore. With additional investments, they pioneered the field of offshore drilling. The company worked with an inventor to develop huge oil derricks, costing millions of dollars each, to drill for oil in the ocean. They started in the Gulf of Mexico and then exported the derricks around the world. Within a decade, Zapata Petroleum would merge with South Penn Oil to become Pennzoil. Poppy became a millionaire before he was 30.[14]

Poppy's prosperity permitted another upsizing in the Bush home with a move to a 3,000-square-foot brick home at 2703 Sentinel, which backed up to Cowden Park where Little League games were played. The new house had a swimming pool, which was rare in Midland.[15] In these happier circumstances, George's rambunctious personality began to show. For example, he wore a swimsuit under his blue jeans at school to remind his classmates what he had waiting at home. In Miss Austine Crosby's third-grade class, he became restless when it rained and the students weren't allowed to go out for playtime, so he threw a football through the window. In the fourth grade, after Elvis had held a concert in neighboring Odessa, he took a ballpoint pen and drew a moustache, goatee, and long sideburns on his face to emulate "the King."[16] As the oldest child in the family by seven years, George sometimes took charge of his siblings at playtime. One story Jeb related involved George, Jeb, and his two youngest brothers, Marvin and Neil, being lined up for mock executions with George's air rifle. George demanded, "O.K., you little wieners, line up," and then he would shoot each of them in the back. They would fall to the ground and play dead.[17]

Young George loved baseball—an interest shared by his father and grandfather, which he would pursue for decades to come. He collected baseball cards in a shoebox and tried to memorize the starting lineups for every major league team. He played Little League for the Midland Cubs, and, although his busy father rarely saw them, Barbara never missed a game. When Poppy's youngest brother, William "Bucky" Bush, came to Midland, he helped umpire George's game. He had come to the Permian Basin to learn the oil business from his brother, bringing a friend eager for on-the-job training, Fay Vincent. Years later, Vincent would become Commissioner of Major League Baseball.[18] By the time George was a teenager, he could go see the New York Mets and sit in the owners' box with his great Uncle Herbie, who cofounded the franchise.

Other relatives made their way to Midland, but none with more fanfare than Prescott Bush. Prescott had lost his bid for the Senate in 1950 but won in 1952 when one of Connecticut's senators died unexpectedly and breathed new life into his political aspirations. Prescott came to Midland as a celebrity, his six-feet-four-inch frame hard to miss, even among Texans.[19] The stories of Prescott's new life in Washington, D.C., playing golf with President Eisenhower, meeting ambassadors, and enjoying the cultural opportunities of the nation's capital intrigued Poppy, who began thinking seriously about a political career.

Poppy found a way to kill three birds with one stone: improving the prospects for his business, his family, and his political future. The offshore business was growing, and Poppy needed to move closer to the source of his newly spun-off company's operations.[20] In 1959, he packed up his family and moved to the grandest house yet: a seven-bedroom house with a pool, sauna, and exercise room built on a 1.2-acre lot at 5525 Briar Drive in Houston.[21] The extra room was useful because just before the custom-built home was ready to occupy, Barbara gave birth to the final member of the Bush clan, Dorothy Walker "Doro" Bush. The Bushes now numbered seven: two parents, four boys, and a baby girl.

The sons of George H. W. Bush and Barbara Pierce Bush in Houston, summer 1959: Marvin, Neil, Jeb, and George. George Bush Presidential Library and Museum.

The relocation helped his family in other ways as well. The new house was located near an exclusive prep school, the Kinkaid School, where George was accepted, leapfrogging many on a long waiting list. George was called "intense" by his teachers, and he was a popular student. He participated in baseball and other sports and had a spot on the debate team.[22]

The third advantage was realized in moving Poppy to the center of a growing Republican Party in Texas.[23] When Republican Richard Nixon ran for president against John F. Kennedy, Houston went for Nixon. Although Nixon lost, Lyndon Johnson won two races: one as Kennedy's vice president and a second in a reelection bid for his Senate seat. (Johnson was hedging his bets in case Eisenhower's vice president beat the Democratic team in 1960.) Johnson's departure from the Senate resurrected the hopes of the GOP candidate he had trounced, political science professor John Tower. Tower stood for the special election to replace Johnson and won, making him the first Republican senator elected from the South since Reconstruction. That GOP success would be repeated many times over the next several decades until the South was solidly Republican.

But the hotbed of GOP activity in Houston was problematic, because the ultraconservative John Birch Society was trying to control the party there. Looking for a bigger tent to expand its base in the million-plus metropolis of Houston, the Harris County Republican Party tapped the moderate George H. W. Bush to be its chairman in 1962. He was a hardworking chairman, visiting all 270 precincts in his district to ensure an active electorate. He also began raising money for his own run at public office, setting sights on unseating the popular Democratic senator Ralph Yarborough in the 1964 elections.[24] He hoped to ride the coattails of the party's eventual presidential contender, Barry Goldwater.

Poppy's biggest challenge wasn't raising money, but rather adapting his northeastern views to those of the conservative, southern GOP. Like most northeastern Republicans, including his father, Poppy accepted the New Deal welfare state, rejected international isolation, and favored civil rights for minorities. (Poppy was a leading campaigner for the United Negro College Fund when he was at Yale.) The southern Republicans were a different breed. So, in order to reach southern conservatives, Bush campaigned against Medicare, the nuclear test ban treaty, and the 1964 Civil Rights Act, all of which Yarborough supported.[25]

But Poppy's attempts to play the southern conservative couldn't overcome the sense of decorum he learned from his father. Thus, when he was giving a speech in Tyler, Texas, on November 22, 1963, and was told that President Kennedy had been shot, he stopped the speech, telling the crowd he believed it was inappropriate to give a political speech in light of the news. He and Barbara actually flew through Dallas that afternoon, the site of the assassination, on their way back home to Houston. Poppy suspended his campaign for the rest of the year.[26] He also refused his campaign adviser's suggestion to use his daughter's death from leukemia in a response to his opponent's charges.[27]

After he won the GOP primary race in June 1964, Poppy became an easy target for the populist Yarborough, despite the fact that the Democrat's own views were out of step with his state's more conservative leanings. Yarborough depicted Bush as a Yankee carpetbagger whose father, recently retired from the Senate, was said to be "out to buy hisself a seat in the United States Senate."[28] He used Poppy's international success with Zapata Off-Shore to claim that the cheap foreign oil he helped to produce would undermine the Texas economy.[29]

Poppy counterpunched with appearances by Nixon and GOP presidential candidate Barry Goldwater. By mid-October, *Newsweek* predicted a win for the 40-year-old oilman. The Bush campaign rented a larger hall for the election-night bash, expecting lots of well wishers following the victory. But they were stunned when the radio announced that Yarborough had beaten Bush. Goldwater's coattails were nonexistent, as Johnson took 44 states and the District of Columbia, while Yarborough beat Bush by nearly a quarter-million votes.[30]

George W. Bush cried the night his father lost. He had worked hard on his father's campaign, taping a 30-second spot in Spanish to reach Hispanic voters, riding on the campaign bus, delivering signs, compiling briefing books, and running errands.[31] But that was mostly summer work, and he missed most of the campaign because he was living in Massachusetts, having been shipped off to boarding school two years after the Bushes moved to Houston.

GEORGE LEAVES FOR SCHOOL

George's work at the Kinkaid School in Houston helped pave the way for his successful application to his father's alma mater, Phillips Academy in Andover, Massachusetts. Andover was a world away from Texas, geographically and culturally. It is 20 miles north of Boston and 20 miles west of Salem. It is the oldest incorporated boarding school in the nation with an endowment larger than many colleges. It was founded in 1778, a place where George Washington sought to enroll his nephews. It had more than a hundred buildings on a 500-acre campus and was covered with large elms and maple trees, which exploded in bright colors in the fall.

George was assigned to the dormitory America House, which was built in 1825. The song "America" was written on the front porch of the dorm by Samuel Francis Smith in 1832. The school's art museum had works by James Whistler, Winslow Homer, and Edward Hopper. Oliver Wendell Holmes attended the school, as did Dr. Benjamin Spock, Humphrey Bogart (who was expelled for "incontrollably high spirits"), and Samuel Morse (of telegraph fame).[32] The school was run by headmaster John Mason Kemper, a World War II army colonel.[33] School began early with breakfast, chapel, and an assembly, and extra-curricular activities kept the students busy until six.[34] Students were required to wear coats and ties.

George's classmates included many who would become notable for their achievements, among them Richard H. Brodhead, president of Duke University; Dick Wolf, the Emmy-winning creator, producer, and writer of the television drama *Law & Order*; and Pulitzer Prize–winning cartoonist and creator of the comic strip "Shoe," Jeffrey K. MacNelly. Other classmates were connected to high achievers, including the son of architect I. M. Pei; the son of baseball great Hank Greenberg; the godson of President Kennedy; and Alexander Sanger, grandson of pioneering birth-control advocate and president of Planned Parenthood Margaret Sanger.[35]

If the history and clientele of this formidable school wasn't intimidating enough for young George, then following in the footsteps of his father certainly was. Poppy had been chosen Best All-Around Fellow at Andover, as well as serving as president of the senior class, captain of the baseball and soccer teams, and secretary and treasurer of the student council, among many other things. A picture of Poppy Bush in his baseball uniform hung in Benner House. He was still well known around campus when George arrived.[36]

George worried about living up to his father's legacy. And he found Andover to be "cold and distant and difficult." It was a formal, regimented place that didn't quite fit with George's free-spirited personality and Texas upbringing. He was only 15 years old when he started at Andover and understandably missed his family and his home. He hadn't jumped at the chance to go to Andover, but he went because his parents believed it was important for him to do so. One of his Houston friends even asked him what he had done wrong to get himself shipped off, since that was often the fate of "troubled" rich boys in those days.[37]

But George quickly made friends at Andover, especially with his fellow Texans. Fort Worth native Clay Johnson III in particular would become a confidant for decades to come. George also got involved in a number of extracurricular activities, including playing junior varsity baseball and basketball and joining the Spanish club. George didn't go far as an athlete, but he kept his hand in varsity sports at Andover by becoming head cheerleader. Barbara supported him by jumping down by his side at one game, grabbing a megaphone, and helping him lead the cheers.[38] The Andover yearbook featured George and his seven fellow cheerleaders cramming themselves into a telephone booth in a hackneyed prank.[39]

Adjusting to the academic rigors of Phillips was tough for the young George, who struggled with his studies. For example, in his first English class at Andover, he was asked to write an essay that related an emotional experience. He wrote about the death of his sister and was looking for synonyms for *tears* in the thesaurus his mother had given him. So, instead of saying that tears were running down his cheeks, he said *lacerates* were falling from his eyes. His teacher returned the essay with a zero on it.[40] By the time he graduated from Andover, his weak performance almost torpedoed his plans to follow his father and grandfather to Yale.[41]

But, in what he called this "serious place," George still managed to have fun. He loved to play an improvised game they called "pigball," where a football was thrown up and everyone jumped on the one who caught it. But his most ambitious effort to inject fun into Andover involved his creation of a stickball league. He named himself "high commissioner" and called himself "Tweeds Bush," after Boss Tweed of Tammany Hall's corrupt New York City politics. Teams from each dorm competed with one another, and enthusiastic crowds turned out to cheer and jeer. George gave the teams crude names like "Crotch Rots." He also gave nicknames to his classmates and was very good at remembering scores of names and faces, a talent that would serve him well later in life. His cutting humor earned him the nickname "the Lip."[42]

During summer vacations, the Bush family kept George busy. In the summer of 1962, Poppy arranged for his 16-year-old son to work as a messenger and runner with the Houston law firm of Baker Botts Sheppard & Coates, where Poppy had oil business contacts. The following summer, George was sent to the Quarter Circle XX Ranch in northern Arizona, about 30 miles from Flagstaff. The owner, U.S. Senator John Greenway, knew the Bushes through the Greenway's son, Jack, who attended Andover and Yale with Poppy. George would build fences and help oversee the cattle. His roommate in a small bunkhouse was Peter Neumann, a nephew of Greenway. Neumann killed a rattlesnake one day, cut off the tail, and kept it by his bed. When a mouse dragged it away in the middle of the night, George jumped out of bed in fright. He didn't sleep any more that night.[43]

In addition to ensuring that his son got work experience, Poppy encouraged George to learn something about politics and the Republican political philosophy. In 1963, he recommended that his son pick up a copy of Barry Goldwater's *The Conscience of a Conservative,* which George read that year. The Arizona senator spoke at Andover in 1963, one year before he became the 1964 Republican Party's presidential nominee.[44] The political field changed drastically before the 1964 contest with the assassination of President Kennedy on November 22, 1963. Lyndon Johnson would become the Democratic opponent and would win a landslide against the conservative who was portrayed as too right wing for the country.

In spring 1964, as the Beatles were debuting on *The Ed Sullivan Show,* George W. Bush was making plans for college. Because of his weak academic record, Andover's dean recommended that George consider other colleges besides Yale.[45] Although George mentioned the University of Texas as a possibility, his heart was set on the family alma mater. He had a reasonably good score on his SATs at 1206. And his legacy status probably helped as well, with Bushes attending Yale since the mid-19th century, including George's father and his grandfather. Prescott also had been a member of Yale's governing body for more than a decade until 1956. George was relieved when he received a fat envelope from Yale—the telltale sign that he had been accepted.

ANOTHER BUSH MAN AT YALE

George's academic work at Yale fell far short of his father's Phi Beta Kappa achievement. He finished his freshmen year in the bottom 20 percent of his class and graduated with a C average.[46] He joked about his performance at Yale in a commencement speech at his college alma mater in the first year of his presidency, saying: "To those of you who received honors, awards, and distinctions, I say, well done. And to the C students I say, you, too, can be President of the United States." He admitted that he had partied a little too much as a student, noting: "If you're like me, you won't remember everything you did here."[47] He acknowledged his friendship with Yale dean Dick Brodhead, who had been his college classmate, noting: "We both put a lot of time in at the Sterling Library, in the reading room, where they have those big leather couches. We had a mutual understanding. Dick wouldn't read aloud, and I wouldn't snore." He referenced a *New York Times* article that included an interview of one of George's Yale professors, John Morton Blum, who admitted to the interviewer: "I don't have the foggiest recollection of him."

Although George couldn't match the academic or sports achievements of either his father or grandfather, he did well in his social life. He was a legacy when he was picked for Delta Kappa Epsilon, "the hardest drinking jock house on campus."[48] During his initiation, he impressed his fraternity brothers by naming 50 pledges, when his fellow pledges could name only a handful.[49] In his junior year, the "Dekes" elected him their president. That role brought him notoriety in 1967 when he defended a hazing ritual in the *New York Times*.[50] The pledges would be shown a hot glowing branding iron to be applied to their skin, while a heated coat hanger or cigarette would be substituted at the last second to startle the pledges. Bush told the newspaper that this wasn't really torture, but "only a cigarette burn."[51]

George's Yale days included other pranks as well. After Yale defeated Princeton in a football game, he helped lead the effort to pull down their goalposts and was caught by the police sitting on top of the wobbling structure. Another time, he was picked up by the police for stealing a Christmas wreath from a New Haven, Connecticut, storefront to dress up the Deke house for a party.[52]

While George was playing the juvenile in college, his father was ready to make another run at Congress. He quit his position at Zapata to devote his full attention to campaigning. His cause was helped by a successful lawsuit he brought, as chairman of the Harris County Republican Party, against the Democratic leaders in Texas. Democrats had controlled the state for decades and used unscrupulous means to hang on to their power, namely, refusing to restructure the state's congressional districts. No significant restructuring had taken place since 1933. A minor change had been made in 1957. But by 1963, the failure to restructure had led to significant disparities in representation across the state given the explosion in the state's population, particularly in the largest cities. The worst case was Dallas, whose district had 4.4 times more people than the smallest district, meaning that voters in Dallas had less than a quarter of the representation in Congress that they were due. The Supreme Court had determined the year before in a Tennessee reapportionment case (*Baker v. Carr*) that federal courts had jurisdiction to intervene in cases where no other avenue of loosening the grip of such entrenched power existed.

Bush v. Martin was victorious in the U.S. District Court, and the favorable ruling was upheld in an appeal to the U.S. Supreme Court the following year. That led to the creation of two new congressional districts in Houston. Poppy ran in one that was dominated by Republicans. He worked tirelessly, pounding the pavement and shaking thousands of hands. His newly moderated position on civil rights made him look more attractive to Republican voters than his opponent, who appealed to the conservative John Birch Society. It also gave him an edge in the small, but important black vote. He raised a considerable campaign war chest that afforded him help from a Madison Avenue firm that produced slick television ads. In the end, he beat his Democratic opponent handily and moved the family once again, this time to the nation's capital. Jeb was the lone holdout, staying with family friends in Houston for nine months so he could finish the ninth grade with his classmates.[53]

The year his father began his congressional career, George became engaged to a Rice University woman he met through mutual friends. The betrothal of George W. Bush to Cathy Lee Wolfman was announced in the *Houston Chronicle*'s society page. They had planned to marry before their senior year in college, but they postponed the wedding. Time apart led their relationship to cool, and they called off their plans, parting as friends.[54]

That same year, George was inducted into the most secretive and exclusive club at Yale: Skull and Bones. His father and grandfather had been prominent members of the society, so Bush was a legacy. However, his presidency of Delta Kappa Epsilon almost assured he would get an invitation to join in any case. But his 1967 class was unlike anything his father or grandfather would have seen: for the first time, the group inducted an African American, a Muslim, and two Jews. The elite and powerful group, with its mysterious induction ceremonies (involving intimate confessions made by members while lying in a coffin), would leave behind its WASP heritage and join a changing world, as Yale began to open its doors to fewer legacies and elites and more applicants of merit.[55]

Despite the network of associates George developed at Yale, he felt alienated by its culture. The reunion of Yale classmates he sponsored at the White House 35 years after his graduation would be the first he would attend. He admitted years later that "[w]hat angered me was the way such people at Yale felt so intellectually superior and so righteous. . . . They thought they had all the answers. They thought they could create a government that could solve all our problems for us."[56] Small wonder that George felt alienated: as Jacob Weisberg has noted, to the preppies at Yale, Bush's West Texas twang and mannerisms made him an outsider and oddity; but to the growing number of hippies at the elite school, he was just another conservative fraternity preppie.[57] In this environment, he followed his own path. He was a Texan, not an easterner, and he let those around him know it. He wore his leather bomber jacket and smoked unfiltered Lucky Strikes. He didn't throttle back his colorful personality a bit, burnishing his Andover reputation as "the Lip" with sarcastic comments and self-deprecating humor.[58]

The one part of the cultural changes that did influence George was the drug culture. Like Bill Clinton, Al Gore, and other political leaders of his generation, he did partake in the growing drug culture, though the extent of his involvement isn't clear.[59] What is clear is that alcohol was his preferred drug, and it would continue to be for another two decades, which he would call his "nomadic years."

George W. Bush had fallen short of the high bar set by his father and grandfather as a student, as an athlete, and as a campus leader. Perhaps he was less intelligent or less motivated than they were. Perhaps his alienation from the northeastern circles they grew up in ensured that he would never feel comfortable at Andover or Yale. Perhaps the tumultuous changes caused by Vietnam, the civil rights movement, and new technologies from television to the birth-control pill made it inevitable that even a son of an elite family would feel the earth shifting under his feet. In any case, George must have graduated from Yale feeling something of a disappointment to the parents he loved and the father who was his role model. And that feeling of inadequacy no doubt contributed to the nomadic years that followed. Most surprising, however, is that those years of wandering in a desert of indecision would eventually give way to a radical change of direction that set the eldest Bush son on a course to surpass his father's greatest achievement.

NOTES

1. Bill Minutaglio, *First Son: George W. Bush and the Bush Family Dynasty*, reprint, 1999 (New York: Three Rivers Press, 2001), 28.

2. Ibid., 29.

3. Ibid.

4. George W. Bush, *A Charge to Keep* (New York: Morrow, 1999), 17.

5. Kitty Kelley, *The Family: The Real Story of the Bush Dynasty* (New York: Doubleday, 2004), 128.

6. Jacob Weisberg, *The Bush Tragedy* (New York: Random House, 2008), 33; Minutaglio, *First Son*, 35.

7. Kelley, *The Family*, 128.

8. Minutaglio, *First Son*, 17.

9. Ibid., 39–40.

10. Ibid., 43–45.

11. Bush, *A Charge to Keep*, 15.

12. Kelley, *The Family*, 142.

13. Minutaglio, *First Son*, 46.

14. Minutaglio, *First Son*, 44; Weisberg, *The Bush Tragedy*, 34.

15. Minutaglio, *First Son*, 47.

16. Ibid., 49.

17. Weisberg, *The Bush Tragedy*, 39.

18. Minutaglio, *First Son*, 47–48.

19. Ibid., 13.

20. Weisberg, *The Bush Tragedy*, 34.

21. Minutaglio, *First Son*, 52.

22. Ibid., 56–57.

23. Ibid., 55.

24. Weisberg, *The Bush Tragedy*, 43.

25. Ibid., 44.

26. Kelley, *The Family*, 212–13.

27. Ibid., 218–19.

28. Weisberg, *The Bush Tragedy*, 44–45.

29. Kelley, *The Family*, 217.

30. Ibid., 221.

31. Ibid., 219.

32. Minutaglio, *First Son*, 59.

33. Ibid., 60.

34. Ibid., 60.

35. Ibid., 62.

36. Ibid., 61.

37. Bush, *A Charge to Keep*, 19.

38. Kelley, *The Family*, 257.

39. Minutaglio, *First Son*, 67.

40. Bush, *A Charge to Keep*, 20.

41. Weisberg, *The Bush Tragedy*, 40; Bush, *A Charge to Keep*, 22.

42. Weisberg, *The Bush Tragedy*, 39.

43. Minutaglio, *First Son*, 69.

44. Ibid., 70.

45. Ibid., 72.

46. "Why Bush Doesn't Like Homework," *CNN.com*, 8 November 1999, http://www.cnn.com/ALLPOLITICS/time/1999/11/08/bush.homework.html; "Does It Matter Whether He Can Name the Leader of Pakistan?" *Time*, 15 November 1999, 46.

47. Ronald Kessler, *A Matter of Character: Inside the White House of George W. Bush* (New York: Sentinel, 2004), 208.

48. Lois Romano and George Jr. Lardner, "Bush So-So Student but a Campus Mover," *Washington Post*, 27 July 1999, A1.

49. Kessler, *A Matter of Character*, 24.

50. "Branding Rite Laid to Yale Fraternity," *New York Times*, 8 November 1967, 80.

51. Weisberg, *The Bush Tragedy*, 40–41.

52. Bush, *A Charge to Keep*, 47.

53. Kelley, *The Family*, 226–30.

54. Bush, *A Charge to Keep*, 47–48; Kelley, *The Family*, 262–63; Weisberg, *The Bush Tragedy*, 42.

55. Kelley, *The Family*, 264.

56. Kessler, *A Matter of Character*, 31.

57. Weisberg, *The Bush Tragedy*, 42.

58. Ibid., 41–42.

59. Scott McClellan, *What Happened: Inside the Bush White House and Washington's Culture of Deception* (New York: Public Affairs, 2008), 48; Kelley, *The Family*, 265–66.

Chapter 3

THE NOMADIC YEARS

Following his completion of a degree in history at Yale, George W. Bush faced the same issue as any other young man ready to start his life: deciding what to do with it. Some of those decisions would be forced by circumstances such as the Vietnam War; others by the proddings of his family (especially his father); and still others by his personality, dreams, and desires. Whatever the causes, much of the next two decades of his life would be tumultuous, unfocused, and unproductive. Yet at the end of these nomadic years, he would make a remarkable turnaround and become one of the most unlikely political success stories in American history. The story picks up at the height of the Vietnam War.

FLYING FOR THE NATIONAL GUARD

Like his grandfather and father before him, the opportunity for military service loomed around George's college years. For Prescott Bush, it had been the United States' entry into World War I at the end of his days at Yale that led him to volunteer and to enter combat in Europe. For Poppy Bush, the call for volunteers for World War II had preceded college, and his voluntary enlistment made him the youngest pilot in the navy. George W. Bush finished college in a different era. The Vietnam War had seriously escalated under President Johnson, sparking widespread protests, especially by young people who were being drafted to fight in what they felt was an unjustified intrusion into a civil war. Young men also faced the real concern that those shipped to Vietnam might not make it back. Hundreds were dying each week by this point, especially after the Tet Offensive launched by the North Vietnamese early in 1968.

Many young men got deferments from military service by going to college. But, like George W. Bush at the end of spring 1968, when they graduated, they could no longer claim a deferment. The next best option was to join the National Guard, since almost no units were deployed to Vietnam. Obviously, waiting lines to join the National Guard were exceptionally long by 1968. George took the Air Force pilot-aptitude test and scored a lowly 25 percent, making his prospects for joining the Texas Air National Guard bleak, given the year-and-a-half waiting list to get into this unit. Although the specifics of his acceptance into the guard are disputed,[1] several others who made it into Bush's unit also were from prominent Texas families, including the son of future senator, Democratic vice presidential candidate, and treasury secretary Lloyd Bentsen; the son of former Texas governor John Connally; the sons of prominent businessmen; and other young men who had known each other when they were in exclusive preparatory schools together in Houston. The unit even had members of the Dallas Cowboys football team, whose service in Texas assured the state's favorite sport wouldn't suffer too much because of the war.[2] In his autobiography, Bush claimed simply that the guard needed pilots, but 150 young men already were in line for such duty in Texas.[3] The colonel in charge of assigning young men to the Texas Air National Guard seemed impressed that young George "wanted to fly just like his daddy."[4]

Of course, George's Air National Guard experience stateside was not quite like his father's 58 combat missions or his grandfather's infantry service in France and Germany. This was another area where he would fall short of the high bar set by his family. On the other hand, in joining the National Guard, George's obligation was longer than his father's or grandfather's military service, requiring a six-year commitment that included two years of active duty and four years of reserve obligations.

George took basic training in the sweltering summer of 1968 at Lackland Air Base in San Antonio. In September 1968, amid great fanfare, Congressman Bush pinned second lieutenant bars on his son at Ellington Air Force Base in Houston.[5] The photo op was a public relations opportunity for the military at a time when few members of Congress had sons in the military and fewer still had sons in combat.[6]

Between his commissioning and his flight training, George took a short break from active duty to help out a Republican running for the Senate in Florida. Representative Edward Gurney was up against the former governor of Florida, LeRoy Collins. George was tapped to help with the press. He called himself a "pillow toter" for the campaign, since he had to carry around a pillow for Gurney, who had been wounded by a bullet in World War II.

As governor in the late 1950s, Collins had taken a courageous stand in urging Floridians to respect the U.S. Supreme Court's order to desegregate public schools and lunch counters. That earned him a spot

Air guardsman George W. Bush has his second lieutenant's bars pinned on by his father, George H. W. Bush, during a September 1968 commissioning ceremony. U.S. Department of Defense.

in the Johnson administration as Director of the Community Relations Service, created by the 1964 Civil Rights Act. In that role in 1965, he was called to Selma to help prevent further violence between the Alabama authorities and Martin Luther King Jr. and his supporters. He convinced King to limit his second march in Selma to crossing the Edmund Pettus Bridge and avoided a repeat of the police violence of two days earlier on Bloody Sunday, March 7, 1965.

Gurney had opposed President Johnson's civil rights reforms and his War on Poverty. His supporters used Collins's work for civil rights against him in the election. Notably, they handed out photos of Collins standing next to Martin Luther King Jr. when he successfully addressed the Selma situation. The message was clear enough to white southern voters, and a textbook example of Nixon's "Southern strategy," helping Gurney win a victory with 300,000 votes to spare.[7]

After the successful campaign, George was sent to Valdosta, Georgia, for pilot training at Moody Air Force Base. He was the only guardsman there for training; the other pilots were in the regular military. But his trainers gave him good marks as a pilot.[8] He gave nicknames to a lot of his fellow pilots, just as he had in his Deke fraternity house, and spent time at the only bar in the small southern town. George's friends all knew who his father was and were rightfully impressed when a special government plane landed at their base to shuttle their comrade to Washington, D.C. George was answering a request to serve as a one-time dinner date for President Nixon's daughter, Tricia.[9]

George was assigned to Ellington Air Force Base in Houston where he had further training to fly F-102 jet fighters, a plane the air force was phasing out. His flight instructor ranked him in the top 5 percent of pilots.[10] Although his unit was never called up to serve in Vietnam, their work could be dangerous. Bush reports losing two men in his unit while he was with the 147th Fighter Group.[11] By summer 1970, Bush had finished his active duty and was placed on reserve status. He made first lieutenant before the end of the year.[12]

BACHELORHOOD, ODD JOBS, AND GRADUATE SCHOOL

With his active duty and the campaign behind him, George began planning the next phase of his life. He applied to law school at the

University of Texas but was turned down because of his weak academic record.[13] He had moved out of an apartment he shared during his flight training with a fellow guardsman, Dean Roome, and began living the life of a single man at Chateaux Dijon, an apartment complex with six swimming pools where many Rice University students, secretaries, and young businessmen lived, including the woman he would marry, Laura Welch. But George wouldn't meet her yet, despite this coincidence. Instead, he cruised around that summer in his blue Triumph with Christina Cassini, daughter of fashion designer Oleg Cassini and actor Gene Tierney.[14]

George combined his new bachelor life with work on another Senate campaign: his father's 1970 bid. He traveled around the state, sometimes speaking on behalf of his father. He started picking up his father's political mannerisms as he got a feel for the campaign trail. Unfortunately, Poppy faced Texas native and successful businessman Lloyd Bentsen. Like Yarborough before him, Bentsen played on his opponent's northeastern roots, which Poppy's patrician ways helped to reinforce. Bentsen handed Poppy his second political defeat by winning 53.4 percent of the vote.[15] But Poppy would eventually get his revenge when the Texas senator was Michael Dukakis's Democratic running mate in the 1988 presidential election.

President Nixon, who had encouraged Poppy's run for the Senate, offered the 45-year-old Republican a concession prize: a position as U.S. ambassador to the United Nations. Poppy and Barbara moved to a nine-bedroom apartment in Manhattan, where they attended numerous official and unofficial social events and enjoyed a lavish entertainment budget.[16] This would be the first of a string of appointments Poppy would take before making his own run for the presidency in 1980 and ending up as Ronald Reagan's successful running mate, earning him eight years in the White House, followed by four more with himself at the big desk in the Oval Office.

Although he was busy with his new job, Poppy kept an eye on his eldest son and didn't let him settle into his carefree bachelor life for long. He arranged a job for George with an old friend, Robert H. Gow from Zapata Off-Shore, who had started an agricultural company. George worked as a fertilizer salesman, but he spent a lot of time talking to Gow about his future, which he did not see in agricultural products. He quit after less than a year and lived off of a small trust fund he had been given by the Walkers.[17] The next job his father got him was working as a roughneck on an oil rig. That lasted only a week. Poppy was growing frustrated, telling George, "You've disappointed me."[18] George later said of that rebuke: "When you love a person and he loves you, those are the harshest words someone can utter."[19]

Despite this disappointment, Poppy sent George on another political assignment, this one to Alabama to help the U.S. Senate campaign of Winton "Red" Blount Jr. That would lead to a controversy that would haunt George when he ran for governor in 1994 and for president in 2000. In spring 1972, George requested a transfer to an Alabama National Guard unit so he could keep up his required National Guard drills. He was eventually assigned to the 187th Tactical Reconnaissance Group in Montgomery, but he apparently never showed up for drills. There were no records that he was paid for drills for six months, beginning in April 1972, and a *New York Times* interview with 16 senior members of that unit yielded no one who recalled seeing Bush.[20] A Texas Air National Guard annual evaluation, covering May 1972 to April 1973, simply noted that "Lt. Bush has not been observed at this unit during the period of the report." The commander of the 187th, Lieutenant Colonel William Turnipseed, who himself had trained in Texas, reported that he had no recollection of seeing a fellow pilot from Texas on his base.[21] There are no written reports from the Alabama National Guard showing that George drilled there.[22]

George also did not fly again, partly because he missed a physical examination in July 1972 that was required for him to continue flying. Normally, a flying evaluation board would have held a hearing in such a case, but none was convened. If he could not fly, he might have been assigned alternate duties, but there is no record of that either.[23] In any case, there is no documentation that George completed drills at the 187th for over a year. George's former roommate, Dean Roome, told *USA Today* in 2004 that he believed that George's early "gung-ho" attitude was followed in later years of his service by a "digression" and "an irrational time in his life."[24]

While serving as Blount's campaign coordinator in a losing battle against the incumbent Democratic senator John Sparkman, his fellow campaign workers noted Bush dated frequently, drank a lot, and came in late for work most days.[25] That his drinking might have been getting out of hand was demonstrated when George visited his parents' house for Christmas at the end of 1972. It was a sad Christmas because George's grandfather, Prescott Bush, had died two months earlier of lung cancer. George was out with his 16-year-old brother Marvin and drove home late so drunk that he ran into the neighbor's trash can and dragged it down the street. His father came down in his robe asking what the commotion was about. George challenged his father, asking: "You want to go mano a mano right here?" Jeb tried to defuse the situation by reporting that George had been accepted to Harvard Business School. George responded, insisting, "Oh, I'm not going. I just wanted to let you know I could get into it."[26]

Perhaps the indirection and wasted time in military service that he never intended to extend beyond his commitment had frustrated the 26-year-old. It didn't help that his youngest sibling rival, Jeb, had performed well academically at Andover, was breezing through his bachelor's degree program at the University of Texas (and would finish Phi Beta Kappa in just two and a half years), and had already met the Mexican woman he would marry. George's weak performance in school, his National Guard commitment, his indirection, and his failure to find the right woman was making his younger brother a much better prospect to carry on the family tradition of business success followed by political service.

Poppy thought he needed to help get George back on track. He called a friend in Houston, John White, a former football player who ran an inner-city program called Project PULL (Professional United Leadership League), to see if he had a place for his eldest son. George worked there for seven months, joined in the summer by his brother Marvin. They worked in a tough neighborhood, Houston's Third Ward, dominated by poverty and minorities. George reported that the "job gave me a glimpse of a world I had never seen. It was tragic, heartbreaking, and uplifting, all at the same time."[27]

That fall, after catching up on his National Guard drilling hours, George got an early honorable discharge so he could enroll in Harvard Business School, where he earned a master of business administration. He again found himself in an elite, liberal environment where he felt out of place. He didn't try to adjust to those around him but walked into classes wearing cowboy boots, chewing tobacco, and dragging friends to the only country music joint in town, the Hillbilly Ranch.[28] George caught a lot of grief as the Watergate scandal shook Nixon's White House, because his father was now serving as chairman of the Republican National Committee. Poppy had the unenviable task of shoring up the party and the president just as the evidence of Nixon's complicity in the cover-up of the politically motivated break-in came to light.

Gerald Ford was handpicked by Nixon to replace Vice President Spiro Agnew after he resigned amid a bribery scandal. When Nixon resigned a year later on August 8, 1974, Ford became the first man to take over as president who had not been elected vice president. As Chairman of the RNC and a rising star in the Republican Party, Poppy was under consideration for the now-vacant vice presidency. He was passed over for Nelson Rockefeller, but given his choice of posts. He wanted to expand his foreign policy experience to enhance his political prospects and asked to head the U.S. mission to China. This was an odd request since the United States did not even have an embassy in the country. Nevertheless, Ford made the appointment, and Poppy and Barbara moved to Peking (later Beijing). George would visit his parents there in June 1975, just after he graduated from business school, along with three of his siblings. Before the end of the year, his parents would move back to the United States where Poppy would become director of the Central Intelligence Agency (CIA) at a time when the dirty tricks of the agency (such as secretly testing drugs on humans and assassinating foreign leaders) were coming to light.[29]

MAKING A LIFE IN MIDLAND

As Poppy was preparing to travel to his fourth job in five years, George decided it was time to go home. So, with an MBA in hand and his National Guard service behind him, George set out for his childhood home of Midland and the promises of the Permian Basin. It was a good time to go into the oil business. A variety of factors, including a war against Israel and, later, an embargo by Middle Eastern oil producers, tripled the price of oil during the three years before George started in the oil business.

George rented a little apartment off an alley at the back of a family friend's house, which, appropriately, was on Harvard Street. He began working as a landman for various oilmen who knew and respected his father, reviewing court records to see who owned mineral rights on lands that might have oil beneath them. He lived on very little, driving an old Oldsmobile Cutlass; taking his laundry to the home of his friends Susie and Don Evans; and wearing hand-me-down shirts from his old schoolmate, Joe O'Neill, who also had returned to Midland. He lived like a frat boy, letting dirty clothes pile up, hitting the bars, and dating frequently. His drinking caused trouble when he visited his family at Kennebunkport in early September 1976 and was arrested for driving under the influence with his 17-year-old sister Doro in the car.[30]

But George also began participating in community and civic life in Midland, attending First Presbyterian Church regularly, teaching Sunday school, volunteering to run the United Way campaign, playing touch football, and coming out for the Midland Angels AA baseball games.[31] George highlighted this work in 1977 when he surprised everyone by announcing that he would run for a congressional seat vacated by a 43-year veteran Democrat, George Mahon of Midland. Since George had never held a job for a year and had not distinguished himself in business or in military service, his chances appeared slim. But he had the help of some friends, including Joe O'Neill; Don Evans; and a young political adviser who had been hired by Poppy when he ran the RNC, Karl Rove. His brother Neil had just graduated from Tulane and came to help out as a comanager of the campaign.

George felt that the election of Jimmy Carter and the Democratic president's efforts to regulate natural gas prices gave a pro-oil, pro-business Republican a good platform to run on in the general election. For the primary, he had to get past Odessa mayor Jim Reese, who attacked him as a northeastern, liberal, Rockefeller Republican. When George emerged victorious, he faced Democrat Kent Hance who trotted out a charge familiar to the Bushes: that George was riding his father's coattails as well as the charge that he was a rich man's son who hadn't succeeded in business. Hance repeated claims made by Reese in the primary that George's father was tied to the Trilateral Commission, a group of international business and political leaders who inspired conspiracy theories about elites who pulled strings that steered the economy. George's father was a member of that group, and calling George "Junior" apparently was sufficient connection for several Lubbock farmers who pelted Bush with questions about the organization.[32]

Although George lost the race by six points, he picked up perhaps his most valuable asset during the campaign season. Jan O'Neill, Joe's wife, had invited her childhood friend Laura Welch to a cookout to meet George. Laura lived in Austin, working as a librarian in an elementary school. Although their personalities could hardly be more different, they had an immediate connection. As George noted in his autobiography, Laura is reserved, calm, and measured, while he is outgoing, constantly in motion, and in-your-face.[33] Additionally, she was an only child, while he came from a large family. Her hobby was reading, and he preferred more social activities. She was a Democrat, and he was a Republican. On the other hand, they were very close in age, as he had turned 31 only 10 days before he met Laura, who would make that milestone four months later. They both had fathers who were successful businessmen—Laura's was a real estate developer—and mothers who were housewives involved in civic organizations. They both had graduate degrees—Laura's was in library science. And both had grown up in Midland. Laura would prove to be a nice counterbalance to George, a quiet voice to rein him in when he went over the line.

George was smitten. When he vacationed with his family in Kennebunkport a few days later, he called Laura repeatedly. When he left before the vacation was over to get back to Austin and see Laura, his family knew this woman was different from others he had dated. When George took Laura to meet his family in Houston in October, his brother Jeb decided to have a little fun and dropped down on one knee as Laura walked through the door and asked: "Did you pop the question to her, George, old boy?" Laura answered: "Yes, as a matter of fact he has, and I accepted."[34] They were married on November 5, 1977, one day after Laura turned 31, in a small wedding at the First United Methodist Church. They honeymooned in Mexico and then returned to hit the campaign trail, getting to know each other better by spending hours and hours chatting while driving through the familiar political district. They moved into a house George had bought a few months earlier.

Meanwhile, Poppy had lost his job at the CIA when Jimmy Carter came into the White House and appointed his old Annapolis classmate Stansfield Turner to clean up the agency. He returned to Houston and began planning for a run for the presidency. A few weeks after George's wedding, Poppy's uncle Herbie Walker died, but not before offering one final financial support to his favorite nephew—a check in support of a political action committee Poppy had formed to plan his presidential campaign for 1980.[35] Poppy began precampaign work in 1978, putting an organization in place, before formally launching a campaign the next year. He would face two-term California governor Ronald Reagan, who had tried unsuccessfully to wrest the Republican Party nomination away from incumbent president Gerald Ford in 1976. Poppy underestimated the 68-year-old former actor, especially after winning the early Iowa caucuses through repeated visits to the midwestern state. But Reagan roared back in the New Hampshire primaries and even went on to win Texas from his Houston-based opponent. Poppy saw the writing on the wall and surrendered his delegates before the July 1980 Republican National Convention to the man who would become known as "the Great Communicator." After briefly toying with the idea of bringing back Gerald Ford as his running mate, Reagan settled on Poppy, who helped to moderate an otherwise right-wing ticket. Given a teetering economy, an oil crisis, and an interminable hostage situation that began when Iran overthrew its American-backed leader and took American embassy officials prisoner, the Reagan-Bush ticket won handily.

George had traveled to Iowa to help his dad with the caucuses, but he mostly stayed in Midland, given his need to make a living to support two people and his new home. He had formed a company a year earlier to handle the mineral rights and royalties he had begun trading, but his congressional campaign put the business on hold. Now he turned his full-time efforts to Arbusto Energy, a name playing on the Spanish word for *bush*. He raised hundreds of thousands of dollars to fund his company's ventures through his uncle Jonathan Bush, which provided him with capital and a regular salary.

After his father became vice president, making *Bush* a household word, George changed his company's name to Bush Exploration and raised more than a million dollars to continue his operations. But investors lost three-quarters of their money as oil prices dropped in 1981 and 1982. George tried a merger with Spectrum 7, an oil drilling company, but his work at the helm of the new company could not fight the tide of red ink. Fortunately, the Bush name was seen as an asset by many in the business community, and Harken Oil and Gas agreed to buy the flagging company, which was $3 million in debt. Harken made Bush a consultant and gave him more than half a million dollars in stock. George was able to avoid the bankruptcy that plagued many oil companies in the roller-coaster ride of the early 1980s. He would stay on as a highly paid consultant until the end of the 1980s. His association with Harken helped the small company land a huge oil drilling contract with the Middle Eastern country of Bahrain.[36]

The Bushes were enjoying success on the family side as well. George and Laura had tried to have children for several years and were about to give up and adopt when Laura became pregnant shortly after Poppy was sworn in as vice president. An ultrasound revealed that she was carrying twins. Although there were some last-minute complications that forced her to spend the last two weeks on bed rest, the twins were born by ce- sarean section on November 25, 1981. They were named Jenna and Bar- bara after Laura's mother and George's mother. They were large for twins, around five pounds apiece, especially since they were five weeks early.

Jenna and Barbara were baptized the next year at First United Meth- odist Church, where George had started attending, leaving the Presby- terian church after he and Laura married. He got very involved with that church and actively involved in raising his daughters. The couple encouraged the twins to pursue their own interests and not to compete with one another—a tough lesson for Bushes to learn! George helped out with childcare and took great joy in horsing around with them. They went to ballgames, wrapping up the girls in blankets on chilly autumn nights. They sent the girls to stay with their grandparents in Kennebunk- port in the summers, which the family jokingly called "basic training."

Three months after Poppy Bush began his second term as vice presi- dent under President Reagan, he decided to begin planning for another run at the White House. The whole Bush clan, including Poppy's five children and four of his siblings, met at Camp David with campaign manager Lee Atwater and several other advisers. George and Jeb asked Atwater where his loyalties would be, since partners in Atwater's firm would be working for Poppy's Republican competitors, Jack Kemp and Bob Dole. Atwater invited the skeptics to come to his office and keep an eye on him. George took him up on his offer, moving his family to Washington, D.C., in spring 1987 to work on his father's campaign.[37]

First Lady Barbara Bush and her son George W. Bush during an August 1989 stay at the family compound at Walker's Point, Kennebunkport, Maine. AP Photo/JSA.

THE TURNAROUND

A combination of events in George's life brought about the most significant change in his personal habits and in his outlook on life in his 40 years. The transition from bachelorhood to married life and from married life to fatherhood certainly played a role in making George think about his direction in life and his family's future. The good fortune he enjoyed in avoiding economic disaster, in spite of his business losses in a turbulent economic environment for the oil business, made him thankful that he could provide for his family and enjoy a level of financial security. His father's rise to prominence as vice president and now as a serious contender for the presidency made him reflect on his role as a very public first son. Finally, what he later described as "a change in my heart" through a rededication to his Christian beliefs, provided an important impetus for change.[38]

George could actually point to a specific day when he awoke and announced that he was through with drinking. He had drunk too much and too often since his days as a fraternity pledge in college. His social life had been shaped by alcohol, from beers at barbecues to drinks in bars to late-night boozing with his old drinking buddy Joe O'Neill. But one morning after a night of drinking in celebration of Don Evans's birthday in Colorado Springs, Colorado, George woke up with an awful hangover. Nevertheless, he dragged himself out of bed and went for an early morning run, as he often did. When he returned to the hotel room, he told Laura, "I'm quitting drinking."

He knew that his drinking was sapping his energy, especially for his morning runs. Laura had warned him that he became tedious and re-petitive when he drank. He also could be ugly and confrontational, such as one night in 1986 when he chewed out a journalist in the foulest of language in a Dallas restaurant in front of his wife and four-year-old just because the columnist predicted Jack Kemp would get the GOP nomination for president.[39] That kind of behavior became more worrisome as his father sought the White House and asked his eldest son to play an important role in his campaign. As George explained to Joe O'Neill several weeks after he had stopped drinking, "Someday, I might embarrass my father. It might get my dad in trouble."[40]

Also influencing his decision was his recommitment to God. A year earlier, legendary evangelist Billy Graham had visited the Bush fam-ily at Kennebunkport and answered questions for them. George re-ported later: "And what he said sparked a change in my heart." George strolled with him on Walker's Point and "felt drawn to seek something different." The next year, Bush noted, the "mustard seed" planted by the reverend began to grow, and he began to read the Bible regularly, joined by Don Evans and another friend in a bible reading group that discussed Acts and the Gospel of Luke over many years.[41]

George's new sobriety and his new passion for Christianity made him an ideal choice to reach out to the conservative religious move-ment that had supported Ronald Reagan's victory in 1980. Poppy Bush was uncomfortable talking about his personal religious views in public, but George was becoming more and more vocal about his own religious transformation. He appealed for support for his father from Reverend Jerry Falwell, who headed the evangelical political group the Moral Majority. That was especially important in the primaries since Chris-tian televangelist Pat Robertson would run against Poppy for the Re-publican nomination.

George's campaign work was supported by Doug Wead, an Assembly of God preacher with ties to televangelists Jim and Tammy Faye Bakker and many prominent conservatives. Wead connected the campaign to evangelical leaders and helped Poppy speak to the religious right by slipping biblical references into his speeches.[42] George traveled the country for the campaign, standing in for his father, looking after those important little details, and learning to deal with the Washington press corps.

The media caused Poppy problems early in the election. *Newsweek* played up the contrast between the vice president and the larger-than-life Ronald Reagan, concluding that the slim, soft-spoken Poppy suffered from "the Wimp Factor."[43] That characterization wasn't helped by Poppy's denials that he was involved in the Iran-Contra scandal at the end of Reagan's second term. That scandal arose after Congress cut off funding to the Contras, an insurgent group trying to topple the Socialist government in Nicaragua, and it was discovered that the Reagan administration had sold arms to one of our foes, Iran, and used the profits to funnel money to this Central American group that Reagan dubbed *freedom fighters*. Poppy claimed that he was out of the loop on that scandal, playing up his lack of involvement in Reagan's White House. Yet another scandal involved a story that Poppy had engaged in an extramarital affair with one of his aides. George responded to questions about that rumor with an emphatic "N-O."

Initially, it appeared that those scandals would sink Poppy's bid for the Republican nomination. Although he was the front-runner in early polls, Poppy faltered in his first test in the Iowa caucuses, not only losing to Senator Bob Dole, but coming in third after televangelist Pat Robertson. But Poppy roared back in New Hampshire and was helped when an angry Dole growled at him about distorting the Kansas senator's record on taxes. Poppy got a huge boost by a new regional primary created by southern states to ensure they had more influence over the presidential election. Super Tuesday, held on March 8, 1988, gave a resounding victory to Poppy, who won about half the delegates he needed for the nomination. George's work in appealing to evangelicals was crucial to winning the Bible Belt.

In the general election, Poppy faced Democratic governor Michael Dukakis of Massachusetts. In the face of the Democrat's lead in the polls, Lee Atwater pushed the campaign negative, calling Dukakis a

liberal who would raise taxes. But his most notorious strategy was running a television ad featuring a black man convicted of murder in Massachusetts, Willie Horton, who had gotten a furlough from prison and
committed armed robbery and rape while out. Although the release
program had been developed by Dukakis's Republican predecessor, the
ad was effective in portraying the Democrat as a bleeding-heart liberal
who cared more about criminals' rights than public safety. Poppy swept
the South and the Rocky Mountain West and won many important
midwestern contests. George's dad would become the 41st president.

Returning to Texas to consider his next step, George made his most
significant departure from his father's path and realized his greatest financial achievement. George had tracked his father's path closely, if
less successfully, in attending Andover and Yale, serving in the military,
and going to Texas to work in the oil business. Bill DeWitt Jr., George's
business partner from the Spectrum 7 merger, called George with a

*President George H. W. Bush poses with some of his children and grandchildren
for a family photo at the White House in September 1989. Jeb Bush is at the left;
to his right are Neil Bush with Pierce; daughter-in-law Margaret Bush holding
Marshall, 2; daughter-in-law Sharon Bush and Lauren, 4; granddaughter Noelle,
11; twin granddaughters Barbara and Jenna, 7; the president; George W. Bush;
and daughter Dorothy LeBlond holding Ellie, 2. AP Photo/Doug Mills.*

business proposition. He learned that the owner of the Texas Rangers was looking to sell the baseball franchise and wondered if George was interested in putting a deal together. Both men had family in the baseball business: DeWitt's father owned the Cincinnati Reds, and George's Uncle Herbert Walker Jr. had been a co-owner of the New York Mets.

George, a longtime baseball fan, was thrilled at the opportunity and quickly agreed to help put the deal together. He got a half-million-dollar loan and put up another $100,000 for his tiny stake in the $75 million franchise, cashing out two-thirds of his Harken stock to cover the loan. The investment group he put together bought 86 percent of the franchise, and, given his prominence as the son of the U.S. president, he was made a managing partner with Ed "Rusty" Rose III. His role was to be the public face of management for the team.[44]

He relished this role and earned his keep with the team. Instead of sitting up in the air-conditioned owners' box, he sat in the front row behind the dugout. He noted, "I want the folks to see me sitting in the same kind of seat they sit in, eating the same popcorn, peeing in the same urinal."[45] He knew all the hot-dog vendors and ticket takers by

In November 1993, George W. Bush, co-owner of the Texas Rangers Major League Baseball team, presents the new Rangers ballpark in Arlington, Texas. AP Photo/Ron Heflin.

name. He had baseball cards printed up with his picture on them. He signed autographs like a baseball star and frequently interviewed with the media.

But Bush's greatest contribution was in helping the team get a new ballpark to replace the small and aging Arlington Stadium. Bush helped convince the mayor of Arlington, Texas, to support a half-cent increase in sales taxes to fund a new $190 million baseball stadium. The team's lackluster record didn't improve much during Bush's years as managing partner, especially after they traded Sammy Sosa to the Chicago White Sox in his first year. The team did hire an aging but popular Nolan Ryan, who continued as a top pitcher in his league and pitched his 5,000th strikeout shortly after joining the team—a feat unmatched by any other pitcher in history. The franchise realized huge dividends from the new stadium, and George's share of the team yielded him a $15 million profit when he sold it in 1998.[46]

A NEW DIRECTION

By the beginning of the 1990s, George and his family were flying high. He had struggled through school, his early business ventures, and his nomadic bachelor days, but he ended up with a family, a fortune, and a bright future. His father had surpassed his grandfather by making it to the highest elected office in the country. Poppy's success had opened many doors for George and would open many more. Most importantly, it provided the name recognition that would be critical to George's next adventure: his serious entry into politics. Once again, the son would return to the path set down by his father and grandfather, following business success with public service.

NOTES

1. George W. Bush, *A Charge to Keep* (New York: Morrow, 1999), 51; Kitty Kelley, *The Family: The Real Story of the Bush Dynasty* (New York: Doubleday, 2004), 240; Ronald Kessler, *A Matter of Character: Inside the White House of George W. Bush* (New York: Sentinel, 2004), 32–33; Molly Ivins and Lou Dubose, *Shrub: The Short but Happy Political Life of George W. Bush* (New York: Vintage Books, 2000), 4–12.

2. Bill Minutaglio, *First Son: George W. Bush and the Bush Family Dynasty*, reprint, 1999 (New York: Three Rivers Press, 2001), 122; Ivins and Dubose, *Shrub*, 4–5.

3. Ivins and Dubose, *Shrub*, 4.

4. Kelley, *The Family*, 240.

5. Bush, *A Charge to Keep*, 52.

6. Kelley, *The Family*, 298.

7. Ibid.

8. Ibid., 299.

9. Minutaglio, *First Son*, 126–28.

10. Kelley, *The Family*, 299.

11. Bush, *A Charge to Keep*, 55.

12. Kelley, *The Family*, 300.

13. Ibid.

14. Kessler, *A Matter of Character*, 34–35.

15. Minutaglio, *First Son*, 132–34.

16. Kelley, *The Family*, 286–87.

17. Ibid., 300–301.

18. Kessler, *A Matter of Character*, 34.

19. Jacob Weisberg, *The Bush Tragedy* (New York: Random House, 2008), 47.

20. David Barstow, "Seeking Memories of Bush at an Alabama Air Base," *New York Times*, 13 February 2004, A5.

21. Spencer Ackerman, "AWOL," *New Republic*, 9 February 2004, 10.

22. Kelley, *The Family*, 306.

23. "Why Bush Stopped Flying Remains a Mystery," *USA Today*, 16 February 2004, A5.

24. Ibid.

25. Kelley, *The Family*, 304–5.

26. Todd Purdum, "Routinely Underestimated, He Struggles to Live up to His Father," *Vanity Fair*, September 2006, 376.

27. Bush, *A Charge to Keep*, 58.

28. Minutaglio, *First Son*, 160.

29. Kelley, *The Family*, 332–36.

30. Minutaglio, *First Son*, 168–70; Kessler, *A Matter of Character*, 35, 41.

31. Kessler, *A Matter of Character*, 35.

32. Ibid., 42–43.

33. Bush, *A Charge to Keep*, 81.

34. Minutaglio, *First Son*, 185.

35. Kelley, *The Family*, 359.

36. Kessler, *A Matter of Character*, 47; Weisberg, *The Bush Tragedy*, 55; Kelley, *The Family*, 428.

37. Kelley, *The Family*, 432–34.

38. Bush, *A Charge to Keep*, 136.

39. "A Curse on Both Their Houses," *The Economist*, 18 March 2000, 34; Kessler, *A Matter of Character*, 47–48.

40. Kessler, *A Matter of Character*, 49.

41. Bush, *A Charge to Keep*, 136–37.

42. Howard Fineman, "Bush and God," *Newsweek*, 10 March 2003, 22.

43. Margaret Garrard Warner, "Bush Battles the 'Wimp Factor'; A Searching Look at the Vice President's Most Persistent Political Liability," *Newsweek*, 19 October 1987, 28–34.

44. Kessler, *A Matter of Character*, 52–53.

45. Ibid., 53.

46. Ibid.

Chapter 4

GOVERNOR BUSH

Bill Clinton ensured the end of Poppy Bush's political career. The charismatic southern Democrat won more than twice the electoral votes of the Republican incumbent in 1992, helped by a strong third-party run by Ross Perot and a persistent recession that Poppy didn't seem to do enough to address.[1] With Poppy's departure from Washington, D.C., the Bush clan suffered one of those rare periods over four decades when none of its members was in a high-profile public office. But two Bush boys stood ready to remedy that by 1994.

THE RACE FOR GOVERNOR

George had considered running for governor of Texas in 1989 but was discouraged from doing so by his mother. Barbara told reporters in the White House that she feared that anything that happened in Poppy's presidency would be laid at the feet of any son who sought office. Therefore, when asked what she thought about George's possible run for governor, she said: "I'm rather hoping he won't [run]." George dismissed this advice when journalists served as intermediaries between the two on the issue, but he dropped the idea of running a few months later.[2]

His decision to run in the 1994 governor's race came after an announcement that his brother Jeb would be running for governor of Florida in the same year. Barbara had let the cat out of the bag during a golf trip to Florida to help promote a real estate venture of Jeb's. When asked about what she would do now that Poppy had received early retirement at the hands of Clinton, Barbara offered, "We're going to play golf, write books, see grandchildren," adding: "But if by chance the most qualified man ran for governor of Florida, I'm coming down to campaign." Jeb owned up to his intention to run.[3]

That was news to George, who got no such encouragement when his parents learned he was running also. Barbara warned that the Democratic incumbent governor, Ann Richards, was too popular, warning George, "You'll lose." Poppy admitted to *Time* magazine, "It surprised me a little when he decided to run for Governor. I've always felt that people in public life should have done something in the private sector before."[4] While Laura was lukewarm as well,[5] this unequal treatment by his parents must have been hard to take. Their message was clear: Jeb *had* done something in the private sector, working in international banking, real estate, and other ventures, so *he* was ready to run; George had not and was not.

Karl Rove, a brilliant political adviser who had led the College Republicans while never managing to finish college, was more encouraging. He saw weaknesses in the armor of the colorful Texas governor, who had boosted her early political career when she told the 1988 Democratic National Convention that Michael Dukakis's rival for president, Poppy Bush, was "born with a silver foot in his mouth."[6] She had refused to sign a bill legalizing the carrying of concealed weapons in the state, sparking the ire of the National Rifle Association and its many members in this Second Amendment stronghold. She was pro-choice, hurting her with those single-issue voters who were energized by the antiabortion movement. She also appointed a handful of people to state positions who were openly gay, offending the sensibilities of some evangelicals in Texas.

Rove recommended focusing the campaign on four conservative ideas: increasing school accountability, limiting civil lawsuits, toughening laws for crimes by juveniles, and reforming welfare. Right-leaning Texans liked Bush's tough approach to crime and morality, including his call to try juveniles as young as 14 as adults, to deny welfare benefits to children born to welfare recipients who already had two offspring, and to defend an archaic antisodomy statute that gay leaders wanted repealed. He appealed to their cultural pride, insisting, "I don't want Texas to become like California."[7]

George campaigned tirelessly, visiting 27 cities in five days at one point.[8] Don Evans helped him raise plenty of campaign money, which the Bush family network made easier. This helped the young Republican match Richards's substantial war chest, which boasted donations from Stephen Spielberg, Robin Williams, Willie Nelson, and Gloria Steinem.[9] Although the Bush name was widely known, George had to distinguish himself from his father. Early in his campaign, the *Houston Chronicle* ran a story about him and mistakenly included a picture not of the candidate, but of his father.[10]

Bush flew around the state in a jet he called Accountability One, which played on his oft-repeated theme of individual responsibility. Ironically, for all his talk about accountability, when he was confronted by media about rumors that he had experimented with drugs when he was younger, he dismissed it with: "I just don't think it matters. Did I behave irresponsibly as a kid at times? Sure did. You bet." He thought the same sort of interrogation of Ann Richards's early drinking problem was out of line as well.[11] Richards's team questioned George's sale of Harken stock, whose value had plummeted two months after he sold it, but the Securities and Exchange Commission (SEC) cleared him despite his missing a filing deadline to report the sale by a board member.[12]

Richards had grown up poor in a small town outside of Waco, and she tried to contrast her background with George's wealthy, northeastern roots. She played the dynasty card, but George responded by insisting: "I'm not running because I'm George Bush's son. I'm running because I'm Barbara and Jenna's dad."[13] She tried to provoke her novice rival by calling him "the Little Shrub," "Prince George," and "Junior."[14] But George's team, filled out now with Rove, spokesperson Karen Hughes, and new campaign manager Joe Allbaugh, urged their candidate to keep his cool and stay on message.[15] Richards seized on a comment George allegedly made to a Houston newspaper asserting that only Christians go to heaven, but he retorted, "I believe God decides who goes to heaven, not George W. Bush."[16]

The strategy worked. By September, Bush had pulled even with Richards and then passed her a few weeks later.[17] A late endorsement of Governor Richards by Ross Perot—a man who had become a household name in a third-party presidential run that siphoned votes from George's father in 1992—could not turn the tide. Bush had the endorsements of the two largest newspapers in the state, the *Houston Chronicle* and the *Dallas Morning News*. Nor could Richards's race be salvaged by a debate the candidates had two and a half weeks before the election. Although Richards tried to provoke Bush by questioning his business record, he wouldn't take the bait. He countered that she had spent a lifetime in politics, and his experience was better for Texas. He stuck to his core issues and wouldn't be provoked into raising his voice or interjecting some knee-jerk response.[18]

Bush's race was aided by a national conservative movement, very powerful in the South, that reacted negatively to the election of Bill Clinton, who had received a paltry third of the votes in Texas in 1992. The overwhelming election of Republican Kay Bailey Hutchison to the U.S. Senate to replace Democrat Lloyd Bentsen (who left to become Clinton's treasury secretary) in 1993 indicated how far Republicans had come and how far the Democrats had sunk in Texas. A unique campaign was being waged by House Republicans, including Newt Gingrich, Dick Armey, Tom DeLay, John Boehner, and others who helped develop a "Contract with America" to attract conservative voters to the midterm elections in the House. It worked. In 1994, President Clinton was faced with a serious setback as both houses of Congress fell to the Republicans for the first time since 1953.

George W. Bush was carried along with the tide, hurried on by his disciplined campaign. At 10 P.M. on election day, Richards called him at the Dallas Marriott, where his campaign team was gathered, to concede the election. She had lost by the biggest margin in a Texas gubernatorial election in 20 years. Shortly after that call, George's father called from Houston to congratulate him, but the message was tinged with sadness. Ironically, the son backed earliest by Poppy and Barbara as heir apparent to the Bush political dynasty came up short against Democrat Lawton Chiles. Following the telephone call, George told his aunt Nancy: "It sounds like Dad's only heard that Jeb lost, not that I've won." Poppy told the news media: "The joy is in Texas, but our hearts are in Florida."[19]

George W. Bush, with his wife, Laura, and their daughters, Barbara and Jenna, greet supporters in Austin, Texas, on election day 1994. Bush defeated Ann Richards, the Democratic incumbent. AP Photo/George Bridges.

A BUSH IN THE GOVERNOR'S MANSION

The office of governor in Texas is a constitutionally weak one. More power resides in the lieutenant governor, who presides over the state senate, and in the speaker of the house, since they generate all legislation and keep legislators in line during their 140 days of legislative work every two years. George knew that and paid a visit to the ailing lieutenant governor Bob Bullock a few weeks before the election, assuring him that he would work with the powerful Democrat. Immediately after taking office, he started having regular, private breakfast meetings with Bullock, whom he called "Bully" behind his back, and Speaker of the House Pete Laney, a cotton farmer and owner of a used-car dealership who had West Texas roots like Bush. George had already aligned himself with their work in the election, supporting bills on education and crime that already were coursing through the state legislature.

His inauguration was a country affair, featuring the Oak Ridge Boys, Larry Gatlin, and the Dixie Chicks. Billy Graham gave the invocation as George's parents and siblings looked on. His inaugural address featured the "personal responsibility" theme of his campaign. His father recognized the occasion by giving him what would become his most prized possession: a set of cuff links that Prescott Bush had given to Poppy when he earned his navy wings in 1943.[20]

George moved his family into the upstairs living area of the antebellum, neoclassical governor's mansion in Austin. He had his office enlarged and moved in a huge mahogany desk handed down by his father, as well as his collection of 250 baseballs, many autographed by famous players and kept in a glass case at one end of his office. He surrounded his office with photos of family, including one of Prescott at a political rally. He decorated one wall with an 1830s portrait of Sam Houston, the first president of the Republic of Texas, and another with a painting of a lone rider lent to him by Joe O'Neill.

George drew many of his new staff from the campaign: Joe Allbaugh became chief of staff, Karen Hughes was the governor's spokesperson, and Karl Rove remained his political adviser. Friends and supporters were given positions. For example, Don Evans was appointed to the University of Texas Board of Regents. Even Nolan Ryan, now retired from baseball, was made a state parks commissioner.[21] He also appointed some Democrats to important positions as well as several Hispanics, including a young lawyer named Alberto Gonzales as his general counsel. Bush would later appoint Gonzales to the Texas Supreme Court, along with three other justices.

Early in his administration, Bush took up his campaign promise to work for tort reform. He felt that juries in Texas were too generous in awarding multimillion-dollar punitive damages to plaintiffs, going far beyond the actual costs of injuries sustained by plaintiffs. Texas had become a hub for tort suits because it allowed anyone injured by a company to sue in Texas if the company had any presence in the state. A movement for tort reform gained momentum in 1990 after two workers laid off from a sugar mill following a seasonal downturn sued and won $2.5 million in punitive damages (an amount subsequently reduced through a settlement).[22] Two years before Bush took office, the legislature had ended the use of Texas as a venue for tort suits for those injured outside the state. During his first year in office, the Texas legislature was considering a tort reform bill to cap punitive damages, and Bush was keen to help shape the final legislation. Bullock allowed him to send a negotiator to work with a legislative committee in developing the plan. He played tough in the face of pressure on the legislature from a group of trial lawyers and won a cap on punitive damages of two times actual damages plus $750,000.

Another major legislative effort sought to give more control to local school districts over how they achieve success, allowing greater input from parents and school boards in decisions such as choosing their own textbooks, purchasing equipment from their own chosen vendors, and experimenting with charter schools. Bush backed this return to "home rule," with some exceptions. One such exception involved teaching sex education, which Bush insisted must focus on abstinence. He also pushed to prohibit schools from distributing condoms. Although Bush won agreement that students could transfer to better schools if theirs were failing, the legislature did not go along with the idea of allowing state-subsidized transfers to private schools. Given the economic recovery from the recession that undermined Poppy's reelection bid in 1992, the bill also offered substantial increases in funding with few tax increases.[23]

In another area of education, Bush sought to increase state control over school practices. In early 1995, he received some shocking new figures about literacy in the state. The Texas Education Agency reported that almost a quarter of all the state's third graders could not read, but all but 4,000 of them were promoted to the fourth grade despite their deficiencies. George had a keen interest in reading problems—his brother Neil had dyslexia and struggled to read. Bush had discussed various reading initiatives with Barnett Alexander "Sandy" Kress, whom the lieutenant governor had appointed to a task force on school accountability. Based on recommendations of the task force, a new law tying additional school funding to test score improvements passed. George endorsed this approach with his own twist. He had become convinced— and many studies supported him—that the whole-language approach to teaching reading, championed by people like Kenneth Goodman in the 1960s, was failing to teach children how to read. Bush supported a back-to-basics approach that used phonics instruction as the central approach, where students learned the basic sounds of English grammar and worked to sound out words. Whole language relied on exposure to words, books, and stories, rather than didactic teaching and analysis central to phonics instruction.

Bush faced an uphill climb since the teaching establishment had generally accepted whole language as the best approach. Teachers would need to be retrained and convinced to use the approach. Bush tied the bill's additional funding to the use of reading instruction methods that had been proved to work, namely, phonics. The new approach seemed to work: by the end of Bush's tenure as governor, the percentage of illiterate third graders had been almost cut in half.[24]

Although Bush was seeing success in his new job, his nomadic past would come back to haunt him for years. Two years into his first term as governor, Bush was called for jury duty. This was a rare circumstance for a governor, but Bush showed up to do his civic duty. The news media came to the Travis County Courthouse to capture the governor's arrival. He told them, "I'm glad to serve," adding: "I think it's important. It's one of the duties of citizenship." He soon discovered that he was a potential juror for a drunk-driving case. Bush had his attorney petition the court to have him excused from the case on the grounds that he might be asked in the future to pardon the accused. The judge agreed, and the *Houston Chronicle* noted that Bush avoided having to answer awkward questions about his own history of driving under the influence.[25]

Later that year, George ran afoul of Speaker of the House Pete Laney and Lieutenant Governor Bob Bullock when he proposed to use a $1 billion budget surplus to support property tax cuts without discussing it with them first. The following January, he consulted the legislature before expanding his proposal to include a massive and complex tax reform plan that would revamp the financing of public schools and add a half-cent increase in the already-high (6.25%) state sales tax to fund $3 billion in property tax reductions.[26] Bush pushed the proposal hard, insisting that he was "going to kick some butts to get this thing passed," but it was defeated.[27] His effort to take on a big issue led to speculation that he was creating a record for a presidential run.[28]

In 1997, Bush had the honor of speaking as governor at the dedication of his father's presidential library. Supporters had raised $83 million to build the impressive three-building complex on the campus of Texas A&M University. It houses 40 million pages of documents from Poppy's many positions in government, as well as lots of memorabilia from his life, including a reproduction of the 1947 Studebaker he drove to Texas when he set out from New England to start in the oil business.

Twenty thousand well wishers, including national and international government officials, business people, and celebrities, turned out for the sunny November ceremony. President Bill Clinton and Mrs. Clinton attended, along with all living former presidents and first ladies, including Lady Bird Johnson, Nancy Reagan, Jimmy and Rosalyn Carter, Gerald and Betty Ford, and, of course, Poppy and Barbara Bush. Also attending were Julie Nixon Eisenhower (who could represent two presidents) and Caroline Kennedy Schlossberg (representing her father and her late mother, who had died three years earlier). Jeb Bush was master of ceremonies. President Clinton spoke graciously of his former rival, calling him "a good man whose decency and devotion have served our country well." George called his father a "war hero, loving husband, world leader, wonderful father, incurable optimist." He told the crowd that the world knew his father "as a master of personal diplomacy," adding, "We know him as the world's greatest dad."

Some Democrats criticized George for what they saw as an indirect swipe at President Clinton when he called his father "a man who entered the political arena and left with his integrity intact."[29] Although the Monica Lewinsky affair would not come to light for two and a half more months, Independent Counsel Kenneth Starr had been investigating a questionable real estate deal of the Clintons, irregularities in the White House travel office, and even the suicide of Clinton's White House counsel Vince Foster. Poppy was more gracious, joking that he was "very grateful to President Clinton who, fair and square, saw to it that I have a wonderful private life."

In 1998, George faced national media scrutiny over the scheduled execution of a convicted murderer. Karla Faye Tucker had helped her boyfriend kill two people in 1983 with a pick axe when she and her accomplice were high on drugs. Her case had been through the entire appeals process, and her execution date was set for early 1998. The petite, freckle-faced brunette drew media attention not only because she would be the first woman to be executed in Texas in 135 years, but also because she had undergone a Christian conversion and had become a model prisoner. The media began interviewing her. She appeared on Pat Robertson's religious talk show *The 700 Club*. She was interviewed by Larry King. Pope John Paul II pleaded for her life. Republican Speaker of the House Newt Gingrich asked that her life be spared. Even one of George's daughters told him at the dinner table that she opposed the execution.

As governor, Bush oversaw more executions than any governor in modern history. In all, 153 executions were scheduled, and Bush commuted only one. Tucker's was not the one. Bush insisted that his decision in death-row cases turned on two issues: (1) Is there any doubt of the guilt of the person? (2) Did he or she receive due process? If he did decide to intervene, his options were seriously limited in Texas. All he could do was commute the sentence for 30 days.

When the U.S. Supreme Court refused to step in to halt Tucker's execution, Bush made his decision, telling the press he respected the opinions of those who contacted his office but that he considered her acknowledged guilt in the case and the fact that she had recourse to the legal system to be sufficient cause to continue with the execution. Bush would not take questions from the press but returned to his office where he and his advisers listened to a speaker phone as an aide attending the execution repeated the orders during each step of her execution. Following her execution, Bush's office sent out a press release with the governor saying, "May God bless Karla Faye Tucker, and may God bless her victims and their families."[30]

Bush did commute the execution of Henry Lee Lucas for a murder to which he confessed. Lucas became notorious after authorities arrested him on an unrelated charge and he began claiming that he had killed dozens of people. The murder for which he was sentenced to death involved a woman whose body was dumped near an interstate around Austin, Texas. However, he quickly recanted, and records showed he was working in Florida on the day of the murder and cashed a check the following day a thousand miles from the crime scene. He also reported seeing a car fire that day in Florida, and investigators did find a record of such a fire. Given the doubts about Lucas's guilt, Bush had the option of commuting the sentence from death to life imprisonment, with the support of a Board of Pardons and Paroles recommendation, and he did so.

Neither decision hurt Bush's reelection. He was riding high in the polls, and even Democrat Lieutenant Governor Bullock said he had done "a fine job," despite losing the tax reform effort.[31] When former Texas land commissioner Garry Mauro ran as Bush's Democratic opponent, Bullock endorsed Bush over his party colleague. That was significant, especially since Bullock was godfather to Mauro's daughter![32] Bush's campaign was carefully managed. When the intellectual and "cottony" voiced Mauro pushed Bush to debate him, the governor's campaign staff arranged for it to be held on a Friday night in the middle of high school football season and limited the questioners to one El Paso journalist, banning CNN and the *Baltimore Sun*.[33]

Bush campaigned hard, traveling all over the state shaking hands and giving speeches. Bush held 23 press conferences in the week before the election.[34] But, early on, he found himself so far ahead of his Democratic opponent that he could afford to go to Florida and help Jeb Bush in his second run for the governorship of that state. Both brothers won handily, though George won a stunning two-thirds of the vote and made history by becoming the first Texas governor elected to two back-to-back four-year terms.

SECOND-TERM GOVERNOR, FIRST-TIME PRESIDENTIAL CANDIDATE

Although opponents of Bush had raised concerns that he would run for the presidency and leave during his second term in office, that did not hurt his reelection. And, in fact, he did begin planning for a run at the White House. Former secretary of state George Schultz began introducing the governor to a cadre of advisers on economic and foreign policy, encouraging Bush to prepare himself to take advantage of a groundswell of support for his candidacy in the 2000 presidential election. His historic reelection had proved his ability to get votes and to raise large sums of money. And, with Vice President Al Gore likely to get the Democratic nomination following eight years of prosperity and peace during the Clinton administration, the Republicans were looking for a saviour.[35]

Bush kept one eye on the White House and another on the governor's mansion as he proposed several high-profile, conservative measures for Texas. He pushed to provide state-subsidized vouchers for children to attend private schools.[36] He supported a bill requiring parental notification before a minor receives an abortion. He supported a bill to make it illegal for gays or lesbians to adopt children. He quietly undermined a hate-crimes bill that sought to protect gays and lesbians.[37] All of these efforts helped endear him to a growing and active political segment, Christian evangelicals. He had made connections with this constituency during his father's presidential campaign in 1988. Now, Ralph Reed, head of the Christian Coalition, became a campaign adviser to help him reach out to this group.[38]

By this point, Bush had a fairly well-developed philosophy of the role of government and a list of national problems that he believed needed to be tackled. He invited one of his favorite authors, Myron Magnet, to come to Austin and speak to his staff about ideas Magnet had developed that would inform much of Bush's outlook.[39] In his book *The Dream and the Nightmare: The Sixties' Legacy to the Underclass*, Magnet had blamed many of the country's problems on the cultural revolution of the 1960s for persuading criminals and the economically underprivileged that they were victims of an oppressive system. He claimed that President Johnson's War on Poverty had created a permanent underclass that relied on the state. The courts had contributed to the problem by handicapping the police in their attempts to maintain order. Embracing these positions was easy for Bush, who agreed with Reagan that government was often the problem and that "pointy-headed liberals" like those he met at Yale in the 1960s were arrogant in assuming the government could solve such problems. Bush's message of personal responsibility spoke to those beliefs and fit well with his conservative Texas upbringing.

Bush's focus on the big picture—big ideas, root causes, major initiatives—would contrast with the detail-oriented, academic, policy-wonk orientation of his major opponent for president, Vice President Al Gore. While he would be required to respond to Gore on issues like the environment, Bush would rely on his personal appeal and his general vision to woo the electorate. But first he would have to get through a formidable opponent in the Republican primary.

NOTES

1. J. Clarke Rountree, III, "The President as God, the Recession as Evil: Actus, Status, and the President's Rhetorical Bind in the 1992 Elections," *Quarterly Journal of Speech* 81 (1995): 325–52.

2. Kitty Kelley, *The Family: The Real Story of the Bush Dynasty* (New York: Doubleday, 2004), 536.

3. Ibid., 535.

4. Ibid., 542.

5. Ibid.

6. Ann Richards, "Democratic National Convention Keynote Address," Atlanta, Georgia, 19 July 1988 (downloaded from http://www.americanrhetoric.com/speeches/annrichards1988dnc.htm).

7. Bill Minutaglio, *First Son: George W. Bush and the Bush Family Dynasty*, reprint, 1999 (New York: Three Rivers Press, 2001), 278–79.

8. Ibid., 275.

9. Ibid., 8.

10. Ibid., 276–77.

11. Ibid., 282.

12. Ibid., 284.

13. Ibid., 274.

14. Ibid., 8, 285.

15. Ibid., 285.

16. Ibid., 289.

17. Ibid., 285.

18. Ibid., 286–87.

19. Kelley, *The Family*, 555; Jacob Weisberg, *The Bush Tragedy* (New York: Random House, 2008), 63.

20. Kelley, *The Family*, 555–56.

21. Minutaglio, *First Son*, 301–2.

22. Scott Pendleton, "Texas Reformers Try to Put New Caps on Frivolous Lawsuits," *Christian Science Monitor*, 25 January 1994, 13.

23. "Reforms in Texas," *The Economist*, 24 June 1995, 28.

24. Ronald Kessler, *A Matter of Character: Inside the White House of George W. Bush* (New York: Sentinel, 2004), 56–69.

25. Kelley, *The Family*, 582–83.

26. Molly Ivins and Lou Dubose, *Shrub: The Short but Happy Political Life of George W. Bush* (New York: Vintage Books, 2000), 86; Sam Howe Verhovek, "Bush Tax Plan for Texas, and 2000," *New York Times*, 30 January 1997, A12.

27. Sam Howe Verhovek, "Bush Stumbles on Taxes in Texas," *New York Times*, 31 May 1997, A7.

28. Sam Howe Verhovek, "Bush Tax Plan for Texas, and 2000," A12.

29. Maureen Dowd, "Takin' Up for Daddy," *New York Times*, 8 November 1997, A15.

30. George W. Bush, *A Charge to Keep* (New York: Morrow, 1999), 154.

31. Hugh Aynesworth, "Bush Downplays Presidential Pretensions; Sees More to Do for Texans First," *Washington Times*, 19 August 1997, A4.

32. Bush, *A Charge to Keep*, 130.

33. Minutaglio, *First Son*, 10.

34. Ibid., 5.

35. Kelley, *The Family*, 569–72.

36. Ivins and Dubose, *Shrub*, 77–78.

37. Ibid., 80.

38. Ibid., 81.

39. Minutaglio, *First Son*, 313–14.

Chapter 5

A HISTORIC ELECTION BATTLE

Although Karl Rove tried to create a sense of inevitability about George Bush's nomination as the Republican candidate for president, Senator John McCain would challenge him early. McCain was a Vietnam veteran and former prisoner of war who was a genuine hero. While Bush served his time in the Texas Air National Guard, McCain suffered torture at the Hanoi Hilton for five years.

The Arizona senator was conservative but had earned a reputation as a maverick for crossing political lines when he believed in a cause. Notably, he cosponsored the McCain-Feingold Campaign Finance Reform bill with Democratic senator Russell Feingold. Though the bill was filibustered in the 1990s, it was eventually passed in 2002.

McCain began his presidential bid shortly after voting to convict President Bill Clinton of perjury and obstruction of justice charges over the Democratic president's statements about his affair with White House intern Monica Lewinsky. McCain's memoir, *Faith of My Fathers*, became a best seller in 1999. He kicked off his campaign in the early primary battleground of New Hampshire, building on his campaign reform theme of taking back the government from special interests. He called his campaign bus the Straight Talk Express and held scores of open, town-hall-style meetings, where he took questions from all comers. Because of his heroic and maverick image, McCain presented a formidable opponent to the heir apparent of the Bush dynasty.

THE REPUBLICAN PRIMARY

Before the Iowa caucuses provided the earliest test of candidate viability, Bush had raised a considerable sum to underwrite his election bid. A slew of Republicans who were considering putting their hats in the ring pulled out in the face of Bush's campaign war chest and early polling popularity, including Elizabeth Dole, American Red Cross president and wife of the 1996 Republican presidential nominee, Senator Bob Dole; Poppy Bush's vice president, Dan Quayle; former secretary of education Lamar Alexander; and frequent Republican presidential contender and well-known conservative commentator Pat Buchanan, among a few others. That left Bush and McCain, who could raise enough for the run; wealthy publishing magnate Steve Forbes, who could pay his own way; and some lesser contenders.

Initially, it seemed that Forbes, with his idea of replacing the federal income tax with a flat tax of 17 percent for everyone, was going to be Bush's leading competition. In the Iowa caucuses, Bush won 41 percent of the vote, followed by Forbes at 30 percent. McCain, who concentrated his efforts on the first primary in New Hampshire, barely registered in the race at 5 percent. But McCain's decision to focus on the Granite State paid off when he won the nation's first primary by 49 percent to Bush's 30 percent. After polling third in New Hampshire and Delaware, Forbes dropped out of the race.

Bush worked hard to win the next primary contest in South Carolina, accepting a controversial endorsement from Bob Jones University, a South Carolina institution that prohibited interracial dating. He promised across-the-board tax cuts and took an unapologetic antiabortion position that fit well with his family values theme. McCain offered more complicated targeted tax cuts and took a softer stance on abortion, supporting exceptions in cases of rape, incest, or danger to the mother's life from a pregnancy. Bush had an advantage among Republicans, and South Carolina's closed primary (where only registered

Republicans could vote) gave him an edge and helped him win by double digits.

By super Tuesday, a contest in early March that included primaries in 11 states, Bush won 7 states and McCain was forced to pull out. In another week, Bush had enough delegates to secure the nomination. To make him acceptable to general election voters, Bush pushed ideas borrowed from the Democratic playbook, endorsing education reform, Medicare reform, and housing reform, as well as his broad-based tax cuts.

Bush also began working on identifying a vice presidential running mate to bolster his campaign. He turned to a veteran of Washington politics, Dick Cheney, to run his vice presidential search committee. Cheney came to Washington in the late 1960s as an intern for Congressman William A. Steiger, a Republican from Wisconsin. He caught the eye of Donald Rumsfeld, who recruited him to work in President Nixon's Office of Economic Responsibility. When the Watergate scandal forced Nixon to resign, Cheney followed Rumsfeld into the Office of the Chief of Staff for President Ford. When Ford moved Rumsfeld to Defense, Cheney took over as the youngest chief of staff in history at the age of 34. When Jimmy Carter defeated Ford in 1976, Cheney returned to his home state of Wyoming to work in the banking business but returned to Washington as Wyoming's only member of the House of Representatives, winning five terms. Poppy Bush tapped him for secretary of defense. When George called on him, he was running Halliburton, an oil services corporation.

Cheney was initially asked if he was interested in the second spot on the ticket, but he turned it down. A few months later, as Bush was going through the records of vice presidential candidate hopefuls Governor Frank Keating and Senators Bil Frist, Lamar Alexander, and Chuck Hegel, he approached Cheney again. This time, Cheney agreed to serve as Bush's running mate. Cheney's western roots were too similar to Bush's to provide the kind of geographic political advantage candidates typically look for in running mates; indeed, he had been living in Texas since 1993 and was required to reestablish his Wyoming residency to avoid the Constitution's Twelfth Amendment prohibition against two candidates from the same state running on the same ticket.

Presumptive Republican presidential nominee George W. Bush and his running mate, Dick Cheney, respond to applause at a rally in Springdale, Arkansas, on July 28, 2000. AP Photo/Eric Draper.

But, given his extensive record of serving in the executive and legislative branches, Cheney brought a great deal of experience to the ticket; indeed, he seemed to overshadow Bush.

As Bush would demonstrate over and over again during his presidency, he was more interested in loyalty than almost anything else. He liked the fact that Cheney was reluctant to join the ticket. Cheney's lack of interest in making his own run for the presidency in the future meant that he would concentrate on serving Bush's administration. Indeed, Cheney would become one of Bush's most trusted advisers and the most powerful vice president in U.S. history. But first they would need to defeat Al Gore and his running mate, Senator Joe Lieberman.

THE GENERAL ELECTION

The general election was a bit more crowded than usual with national figures. In addition to the Democratic vice president and the Republican governor of Texas, there were third-party runs by Ralph Nader on the left and Patrick Buchanan on the right. While these minor candidates did not garner many votes nationwide, without their participation in the general election George W. Bush would not have won the 2000 presidential race.

Although Vice President Al Gore was coming off of eight years of peace and prosperity that was the Clinton administration—featuring the largest economic expansion since before World War II—the scandal that erupted late in Clinton's second term over the Democratic president's affair with a 22-year-old White House intern had led to only the second impeachment of a president in U.S. history, though the Senate refused to remove Clinton from office. Gore's running mate, Joe Lieberman, was the first prominent Democrat to publicly criticize Clinton's conduct in the Lewinsky affair; Lieberman is a Democrat so conservative that in 2006 he could not win the Democratic primary for Senate in his home state and was forced to run as an Independent to reach the general election where Republican voters and Independents assured his reelection. Gore hoped that Lieberman's image as a leader in moral values and an early critic of Clinton's indiscretions would immunize his ticket from the taint of the Clinton scandal and attract moderates and conservative Democrats to his ticket. Bill Clinton was given a low profile in the Democratic campaign, and Gore went out of his way to stress his own strong family commitments, capping it with a long, passionate kiss with his wife when he stepped onstage to accept the Democratic presidential nomination.

Bush tried to tie Gore to the Clinton scandal, promising to restore "honor and dignity" to the White House.[1] He criticized Clinton-era policies that led to high-profile killings of American servicemen in a civil conflict in Somalia and troops engaged in nation-building in the Balkans. On the other hand, Bush endorsed Clinton's policy of opening up trade with China, which Gore was wary about given the concerns of his union supporters. Endorsing such policies of Clinton's helped Bush emphasize his interest in working in a bipartisan manner, as he had done in Texas with the Democratic leadership. Following the bitterness of the Republican-led Clinton impeachment and years of partisanship from Newt Gingrich, Tom DeLay, and others, the country was desperate for a return to civility. Finally, Bush borrowed the campaign theme he helped develop for his father, softening a hard-edged Republican stance with the image of a compassionate conservative.

Gore attacked Bush for his lack of experience on national issues. Bush was able to overcome those concerns by touting his advisers, who included experienced men such as Dick Cheney and nationally respected figures such as former chairman of the Joint Chiefs of Staff General Colin Powell. Both candidates spoke of the need to reform Social Security to ensure its solvency and of plans for the federal budget surplus Clinton and the Republican Congress had created by the end of his second term.

THE POSTELECTION BATTLE

By election day, the major candidates were running neck and neck. The polls would show that Gore won half a million more popular votes than Bush out of over 100 million cast. But the real contest was in the Electoral College, where the Constitution requires the contest to be decided. The race came down to Florida's 25 electoral votes. At 6:48 P.M. (CST), NBC became the first network to call Florida and the election for Al Gore, and all major networks followed that prediction within a few minutes.[2] But the call was erroneous because one of the tallies from the Voter News Service, which all networks drew from, was wrong. Data from Jacksonville, Florida, had an added digit that gave Gore almost 40,000 more votes than he had received.[3] It took two hours for the networks to catch the error and retract their prediction, declaring the race too close to call. Then, after 1 A.M., they were ready to call the race for Bush. Within minutes of that announcement, Gore called Bush to concede the election.

Gore and his entourage loaded into their cars to drive up to Nashville's War Memorial where his supporters were gathered to hear his concession speech. But, before he reached the location, Bush's lead had dwindled from 50,000 to less than 2,000. Under Florida law, such a close margin required an automatic recount.

Gore called Bush back to retract his concession, noting: "Circumstances have changed dramatically since I first called you. The state of Florida is too close to call." Bush was flabbergasted, asking: "Are you saying what I think you're saying? Let me make sure that I understand.

You're calling back to retract that concession?" Gore retorted, "Don't get snippy about it!" He promised that if Bush prevailed in the final count he would lend him his "full support."[4] Gore sent his campaign chairman, Bill Daley, out to address the waiting crowd in Nashville. Daley insisted that until the recounts were complete, the campaign would continue.

Florida law requires that any election decided by a half percent of the total votes or less to undergo an automatic recount, whereby ballots are run through the counting machines again and the new totals assessed. The recounts whittled Bush's lead from 1,784 votes out of 6 million cast to 327. The new totals gave heart to the Gore camp, which invoked the protest provisions of Florida's election law, asking for a hand recount of ballots in four Florida counties that were Democratic strongholds.

By this time, both candidates' teams prepared for a long battle. Bush brought in Poppy's secretary of state, James Baker, to oversee the post-election effort, and Gore countered with Clinton's former secretary of state, Warren Christopher. Baker turned to the federal courts to try to stop the hand recounts but was rebuffed. But he had an ally in Tallahassee. Although George's brother Governor Jeb Bush recused himself from involvement in the recount given his obvious conflict of interest, Secretary of State Katherine Harris proved to be a reliable ally. She was in charge of the Florida elections, even though she served as cochair of Bush's presidential campaign in Florida.

Hand recounts discovered additional votes not counted by the machines in either the original count or the automatic recount. The problem was that many counties—particularly counties that were poor, filled with minorities, and Democratic—used old voting systems that employed punch cards. Voters were required to use a stylus to punch out tiny cardboard squares to indicate their selections. Sometimes those squares, called *chads,* did not dislodge completely. When they were run through the machines, the loose chads sometimes prevented the machines from recording a vote. But hand recounters could see which chads had been punched out. However, the canvassing boards had the leeway to decide what would count as a vote—a chad hanging by one corner, by two, or simply punched in but still attached. That made the Bush team worried that Democrat-leaning counties would pick a standard that would favor Gore.

This problem would not matter if the counties' new recount totals were rejected by the secretary of state. Florida election law required that vote totals be submitted within 7 days of the election. Large counties, such as Miami-Dade, had too many ballots to go through in the time remaining. They appealed to the secretary to extend the date, but she rejected their appeal, even though under federal law she was required to wait 10 days after the election to certify the election to give time for absentee ballots (which included those from overseas military personnel) to arrive.

In the meantime, Miami-Dade County canvassing officials were continuing with their slow-moving recounts when a group of protesters gathered outside their offices, banging on the windows and yelling at the officials. The incident rattled the officials, who canceled the recount shortly afterward. The protesters were not outraged Floridians, but rather Republican staffers flown in to help in the postelection battle. The incident became known as the "Brooks Brothers riot."[5]

The Gore team filed a lawsuit to force Harris to accept late returns, and the Florida Supreme Court, which was dominated by Democrats, required her to accept them and set a new deadline. Bush appealed to the U.S. Supreme Court, which vacated the decision and asked the state court to explain the basis for its decision. Harris certified the election for Bush, and Gore drew upon another provision of Florida election law and filed a contest against the result. In a widely publicized trial, state circuit court judge N. Saunders Sauls ruled that Gore did not meet the required standard for a contest. However, in an appeal, the Florida Supreme Court noted that Judge Sauls was applying an old standard, which had been changed with a 1999 revision to the Florida statutes. In a 4–3 decision, it ordered a manual recount of all *undervote* ballots (those that did not show a selection for president) across the entire state of Florida.

The Bush campaign appealed again to the U.S. Supreme Court, and in an extraordinary move, five members of the Court voted to issue a stay and stop the recount a few hours after it began and Bush's unofficial lead had shrunk to 154 votes. The case was put on a fast track for decision. The Court heard oral arguments two days later and handed down its decision permanently halting the recounts one day later, on December 12, 2000.

The Supreme Court decision in *Bush v. Gore* is one of the most controversial decisions in the history of the court. The first problem was the breakdown of the ruling, with the five most conservative members of the court (Chief Justice Rehnquist and Justices O'Connor, Scalia, Thomas, and Kennedy) voting in favor of Bush and the four most liberal members of the court (Justices Stephens, Souter, Breyer, and Ginsberg) voting in favor of Gore. Secondly, the case involved the High Court second-guessing a state court's interpretation of state law, something almost never done, certainly not by conservatives who had defended states' rights against federal encroachment. Third, and most troubling, the legal basis for overturning the decision was incredibly weak. The majority claimed that because the Florida Supreme Court allowed the county canvassing boards to develop their own criteria for assessing what was to count as a vote, they were allowing voters in different parts of the state to be treated unequally, violating the Equal Protection Clause of the Fourteenth Amendment.

Normally, equal protection had been used to protect distinct groups, such as minorities, from unequal treatment. But there were no distinct groups harmed by the use of differing standards in this case. Furthermore, the majority cited very old precedents to support this novel equal protection claim, ignoring a more recent case, *Washington v. Davis*, that required a finding of a state's *intent to discriminate* before they would support an equal protection claim. Surprisingly, the majority had no concerns over equal protection arising from the state's use of different types of voting machines, some of which were much more likely to reject voting ballots than others, treating voters differently.

The normal resolution for such a problem would have been to send the case back to the state court with orders to ensure that equal protection was met, perhaps with a uniform statewide recount standard. But the majority claimed that the deadline for submitting final election tallies to the Electoral College was up and no recounts could go forward. Oddly, they took a statement from the Florida Supreme Court that the state would want to meet the December 12th deadline because a federal statute ensured that votes received by that deadline would not be challenged when Congress met to count the votes in January. But that deadline had been ignored before, and even conservative commentators admitted that December 12 was not a firm deadline.

Finally, the *Bush v. Gore* majority sought to prevent other litigants from citing its decision in the future with the specious claim: "Our consideration is limited to the present circumstances, for the problem of equal protection in election processes generally presents many complexities."[6] Small wonder that many commentators charged the majority with engaging in a political decision to ensure George W. Bush became the 43rd president of the United States, one who would appoint justices to carry on the conservative judicial legacy the majority had developed.[7]

Defenders of the decision, such as Judge Richard Posner, admitted that the basis of the decision was weak but insisted that the Court did the nation a favor by avoiding a constitutional crisis. That crisis might have unfolded like this: A recount might have given Gore a victory.

President Bush dances with his wife, Laura, at the Ohio Inaugural Ball, one of eight balls held on January 20, 2001, to celebrate his inauguration. AP Photo/Amy Sancetta.

The Florida legislature, controlled by Republicans, was threatening to send their own slate of electors to the Electoral College. With two slates of electors from Florida, Congress would have had to decide the election. The Republicans controlled the House, so they might have supported the Bush slate. The Senate was split 50–50 between Democrats and Republicans, so the vice president might have cast the deciding vote—that is, Al Gore. With the Congress split, the decision would have gone to the governor of the state in question, namely, Jeb Bush. Posner speculates that the Florida Supreme Court might nullify that decision and leave the entire dispute unresolved.[8]

Alternatively, it is possible that not every participant would have made a decision based solely on political allegiances. Even Posner admitted that if the voting process in Florida had worked as it was supposed to, Gore would have won.[9] As the news media reported, several factors snatched victory from Gore. Perhaps the most publicized was the infamous butterfly ballot in Palm Beach County. The Democrat in charge of elections there was trying to cram all the candidates' names on a one-page ballot and split the page into a butterfly form, with names on either side of punch holes in the center. This made it harder to identify which punch holes were meant for which candidates. Thousands of elderly Jewish voters left the polls complaining that they weren't sure whether they had punched the correct hole for Gore. Indeed, it appears that a large number of them voted for Pat Buchanan (not a favorite of Jewish voters), whose punch hole was next to Gore's, by mistake. In Seminole and Martin counties, the GOP had mailed absentee ballots to their constituents and accidentally left off required voter identification numbers. When the voters failed to add this information, Republican staffers got permission from a local Republican official to correct these ballots, in plain violation of Florida state law. Secretary of State Katherine Harris waived requirements that overseas ballots—most coming from members of the armed services—include postmarks as required by law, and these votes heavily favored Bush. Finally, Ralph Nader, the liberal consumer advocate who made a third-party run as the Green Party candidate, was the third-highest vote getter in Florida. Although he won just under 100,000 votes statewide, he peeled off thousands of votes from Gore, which would have easily won him the election. Change any of these circumstances, and Gore would have won the election.

These circumstances and the Supreme Court decision in *Bush v. Gore* helped to put Bush in the White House. But they also ensured that the heir to the Bush political dynasty would start his term under a cloud of controversy, with many Americans believing that he had stolen the election.

NOTES

1. Robert Draper, *Dead Certain: The Presidency of George W. Bush* (New York: Free Press, 2007), 91.

2. Jeff Greenfield, *Oh, Waiter! One Order of Crow!* (Waterville, ME: G. K. Hall, 2001), 58.

3. David A. Kaplan, *The Accidental President: How 413 Lawyers, 9 Supreme Court Justices, and 5,963,110 (Give or Take a Few) Floridians Landed George W. Bush in the White House* (New York: Morrow, 2001), 10–11.

4. David Von Drehle, "The Night That Would not End; with Florida in Turmoil, Tempers Frayed and Eyes Stayed on the Big Prize," *Washington Post*, 9 November 2000, A1.

5. Al Kaman, "Miami 'Riot' Squad: Where Are They Now?" *Washington Post*, 24 January 2005, A13.

6. *Bush v. Gore*, 531 U.S. 98, 109 (2000).

7. Clarke Rountree, *Judging the Supreme Court: Constructions of Motives in* Bush v. Gore, Rhetoric and Public Affairs Series (East Lansing: Michigan State University Press, 2007).

8. Richard A. Posner, *Breaking the Deadlock: The 2000 Election, the Constitution, and the Courts* (Princeton, NJ: Princeton University Press, 2001).

9. Ibid., 88.

Chapter 6

A COMPASSIONATE CONSERVATIVE BECOMES A WAR PRESIDENT

The 36-day postelection battle had left the country weary and many Democrats angry. The Secret Service was so concerned about the safety of the incoming president that, for the first time in U.S. history, the presidential inauguration was declared a "National Special Security Event," requiring anyone wishing to attend the inauguration to have permission from the government.[1] The event spawned the biggest inauguration protest in Washington, D.C., since the Vietnam War, despite the wet and icy conditions. Civil rights firebrand Reverend Al Sharpton gathered a thousand protestors in the capital during Bush's inaugural, where he insisted, "George Bush was not elected by the people."[2] Even with the heightened security, a protestor was able to strike the presidential limousine with an egg as it cruised down Pennsylvania Avenue, leading the security team to keep the First Family under cover for all but the end of the ride to the Capitol building. In his brief inaugural address, Bush sought to reassure Americans that he would "work to build a single nation of justice and opportunity."

The event was a glorious occasion for the Bush clan and its return to the White House. More than 150 of George's family members attended. George would finally realize a dream of making his parents proud in matching his father's highest achievement. He reveled in the occasion, telling attendees at the first of eight inaugural balls: "Now is not the time for speaking—it's the time for dancing." Earlier in the day President Clinton had given an address to well wishers at Andrews Air Force Base before departing the capital with his wife Hillary, the newly elected U.S. senator from New York, and their daughter Chelsea.[3] Clinton's presidency had provided an interregnum between the two Bush presidencies, and, following the second-term scandal over Monica Lewinski, the younger Bush would see his election as a restoration of honor to the presidency (notably, in replacing the man who had denied his father a second term in office).

IMPLEMENTING A CONSERVATIVE VISION

Bush quickly filled out his cabinet with pro-business and social conservatives to support his agenda and reassure his constituents that he was serious about implementing it. His least controversial choice was for secretary of state—retired general Colin Powell, a nationally known figure who served as chairman of the Joint Chiefs of Staff during the first Bush administration and was so popular that Hasbro produced a G. I. Joe figure with his likeness. Another Republican veteran, Donald Rumsfeld, was tapped for secretary of defense, a position he held a quarter-century earlier under President Gerald Ford. Former CEO of aluminum giant Alcoa, Paul O'Neill, became treasury secretary. The popular Republican governor of New Jersey, Christine Todd Whitman, was tapped to head the Environmental Protection Agency (EPA). A U.S. senator from Missouri, John Ashcroft, was chosen as attorney general after he was defeated in his 2000 reelection bid by an opponent who died in a plane crash three weeks before the election. (Mel Carnahan's widow served for the late governor until a special election could be held a year later.) Another victim of the 2000 elections, Senator Spencer Abraham of Michigan, won appointment to head the Department of Energy. Gale Norton returned to the Department of the Interior as its secretary, a place she had worked as a lawyer for the first Bush administration before serving eight years as Colorado's attorney general.

Bush wasted no time in pushing his conservative social agenda. On his first day in office, he reinstituted the controversial Mexico City

Policy begun by President Reagan and suspended by President Clinton, which denied U.S. federal aid to any international groups that offered counseling or assistance to women seeking abortions, even if that counseling or assistance was paid for from non-U.S. funds. (President Obama, like Clinton, suspended the policy when he took office.) Two years later, Bush also would sign a bill, previously vetoed by President Clinton, prohibiting a certain form of late-term abortion even when necessary to protect the health of a mother. Despite concerns that opponents had over the potential conflict with the health exception provision of *Roe v. Wade* (which legalized abortion in the country), the U.S. Supreme Court upheld the law four years later.

In August 2001, Bush went on national television to explain another change in policy concerning federal support for embryonic stem cell research. Stem cell researchers had begun using human embryos to create lines of stem cells (i.e., cells that could transform into almost any kind of cell), raising hopes that doctors might one day be able to grow replacement organs for patients; repair nerve damage in the paralyzed; and cure Parkinson's disease, multiple sclerosis, cancer, and other diseases. Many abortion opponents believe that killing human embryos is wrong, even though thousands of these embryos are destroyed every year as the unneeded by-product of widely used in vitro fertilization techniques that help childless couples have children. Bush offered a Solomonic compromise, promising to fund research using existing lines but cutting off federal money for new lines. This new policy led California to pass a $3 billion funding initiative for such research, while researchers in other states began investigating alternatives, such as the creation of stem cells from umbilical cords and the use of adult stem cells.

Late in 2001, Bush supported Attorney General John Ashcroft's challenge to Oregon's Death with Dignity Act, a provision that allowed terminal patients to receive a prescription from a willing physician for drugs to painlessly end their lives. This opposition to euthanasia was consistent with Bush's and Ashcroft's opposition to abortion, holding human life as sacred. Ashcroft contended that the federal government had the authority to restrict the use of controlled substances, such as painkillers, that would be used to end a terminal patient's life. The Bush administration defended Ashcroft's position before the U.S.

Supreme Court in 2005 but lost in a ruling that denied the federal government the authority to issue such restrictions.

Of all the conservative social policies of Bush's first term, perhaps the most significant change wrought by Bush was the creation of the Office of Faith-Based and Community Initiatives, which funneled government grants to religious organizations to provide social services to those in need. Bush had developed a smaller version of this program as governor of Texas. Although supporting religious organizations with a history of work among the poor seemed like an efficient use of funds, many critics were concerned about blurring the line between church and state. Some charged that Bush was providing payback to the religious organizations that helped get him elected. Bush's first director of the office, John Dilulio, quit after less than a year, praising Bush's decency while blaming his advisers for politicizing the office, a charge that Dilulio's assistant David Kuo detailed in his book, *Tempting Faith*. But, the work of the office grew over time, and the idea of using religious organizations was appealing enough to President Obama that he kept the program alive under a new name, the Office of Faith-Based and Neighborhood Initiatives.

On economic issues in his first term, Bush turned to his biggest campaign promise: across-the-board tax reductions. President Clinton had left office with the first budget surplus in 30 years, taking in $236 billion more than he spent in 2000. Just as he had done with the Texas state budget surplus, Bush sought to give that money back (even though the federal government was $5 trillion in debt). He justified these tax breaks as a spur to an economy that had slowed significantly since overpriced stocks in fledgling Internet-based businesses began to collapse when the dot-com bubble burst in early 2000. He also relied on a supply-side argument from economics, that if you give money back to Americans, they will spend it or invest it and grow the economy faster. Moreover, Bush, like Reagan before him, was always suspicious of government and its spendthrift ways, arguing that Americans could spend their money more wisely than the government.

The new law passed the Republican-controlled Congress (where Cheney's election as vice president had given Bush a tiebreaking vote in the evenly split Senate). It lowered the lowest tax rate from 15 percent to 10 percent and the highest rate from 39.6 percent to 35 percent, with other reductions in between. It also reduced long-term capital gains taxes, assessed on the sale of stocks held for five years or more, from 10 percent to 8 percent. Another provision that critics would call a giveaway to the rich was a huge increase in the amount of money that a person could pass on in his or her estate after death without facing federal taxation, from $675,000 in 2001 by increments to $3.5 million by 2009. The tax law also allowed for greater individual contributions to retirement accounts, further reducing tax burdens. Finally, it provided immediate tax rebates on income taxes from 2000, giving most Americans a few hundred dollars of spending money. The plan cost $1.6 trillion over 10 years, though it included a *sunset* provision that would phase it out after 9 years. The latter provision was a way to get around a Senate rule that would have allowed any senator to thwart a bill that significantly increases the federal deficit beyond 10 years. Two years later, amid very different circumstances, Bush would revisit these tax cuts and accelerate them.

Bush also kept pro-business conservatives happy by eliminating or paring back regulations, which he believed were a burden on economic growth. President Clinton had issued a number of new health, safety, and environmental regulations during his last days in office. Bush put a 60-day moratorium on those regulations the day he took office, giving him time to review them before they were put into effect. One of those regulations, which required the reduction of arsenic in drinking water, was rejected by Bush as burdensome and unnecessary. EPA administrator Christine Todd Whitman defended the decision by noting that there was no accepted consensus on what constitutes a safe level of arsenic in drinking water. The same month, the Interior Department decided to ease regulations on hard rock mining and to open up 60 million acres of national forests to logging by allowing new roads to be added.[4]

Vice President Dick Cheney became heavily involved in environmental decisions in the White House. Before he was settled into his new office, he learned about a plan to divert water from farmers and ranchers in Oregon to protect endangered salmon in the Klamath River, fish that were important to California's largest Indian tribe as well as to fishermen and environmentalists. Cheney called a low-level staffer in the Interior Department and left a message. The staffer was certain the message was a prank—why would the vice president be calling someone as low on the totem pole as she was? She deleted the message and failed to call Cheney back. She was startled when she was contacted again and promised to keep him informed about the government's actions. Cheney asked for a committee to study the matter to ensure that the dire predictions of fish kills weren't overblown. An indecisive committee ruling gave the Interior Department enough wiggle room to save the farmers from a water diversion, but 33,000 fish washed up on the banks of the Klamath River in September 2002.[5]

Cheney also appears to have been involved in talking Bush out of a campaign promise on the environment. Campaigning against Al Gore, who was a strong environmental advocate, Bush agreed that the biggest cause of global warming, carbon dioxide, ought to be regulated. Coal-burning power plants were a particularly big culprit in throwing these heat-trapping gases into the environment. When Christine Todd Whitman attended an international climate change summit in Trieste, Italy, on March 4, 2001, she understood the administration's position as backing a reduction in carbon emissions and delivered that message accordingly. Before Whitman returned and met with the president, he had already sent a letter to Republican senators stating that "the current state of scientific knowledge about causes of and solutions to global warming is inconclusive" making it "premature" for the president to propose any specific policies regarding global warming. Pulitzer Prize–winning investigative journalist Barton Gellman reported that the letter was drafted by a group of staffers led by Cheney.[6]

Bush's new position amounted to an abandonment of the Kyoto Protocol, an international agreement signed by more than 100 countries, which sought to reduce greenhouse gases significantly. Bush warned that supporting the treaty, which President Clinton supported but that had yet to be ratified by the U.S. Senate, would hurt the American economy and do too little for the environment. (The treaty did not include China, Brazil, India, and other developing countries, which were likely to account for 70% of all carbon emissions over the next half century.[7])

Cheney had strong feelings about the administration's global warming policy because he was heading up an Energy Task Force that met frequently with officials from oil, gas, and utility companies during the first third of 2001. Cheney was secretive about his work (as he would be about other work in the future), refusing to make public a list of who met with the committee in the face of complaints from environmentalists that their concerns had been ignored by the task force. Cheney fought a lawsuit over a Freedom of Information Act request for the list and won in the U.S. Supreme Court in 2004. The *Washington Post* later uncovered the names of the participants, which provided a clue that Cheney's resistance might not have been simply a defense of executive prerogatives. First, there was the overwhelming reliance on input from corporations with heavy interests in a business-friendly policy, which confirmed suspicions about the leanings of Bush and Cheney, two former oil company executives. Later, Cheney's concern over the image of the task force rose after one of the energy executives that met early with the task force became a national symbol of corporate greed and avarice. That was Kenneth Lay, an old friend and campaign contributor to George W. Bush.[8] Lay was CEO of Enron, a massive Houston-based energy company that went bankrupt when it was discovered that it had used accounting fraud over several years to make it appear very profitable. Lay had encouraged Enron employees and the public to buy stock in his company even as he and his fellow executives began selling off their own holdings. The stock plummeted from a high of $90 to pennies, costing thousands of employees their investments and retirements. The scandal also brought down the venerable accounting firm Arthur Anderson, which had supported Enron's questionable accounting practices. In 2006, Lay was convicted on multiple counts and faced a 20–30 year prison sentence when he died of a sudden heart attack.

Al Gore, who lost to Bush in the 2000 election, was so concerned about the Bush administration's position on energy and the environment that he spent the years of Bush's presidency working to raise awareness of the threat of global climate change. His work culminated in a wildly successful documentary and book on the problem, *An Inconvenient Truth*, which helped earn him a share of a Nobel Peace Prize (with the Intergovernmental Panel on Climate Change), as well as an Academy Award and a Grammy (for the audiobook version).

Not all of Bush's early decisions on the environment were supported by business. The trucking industry launched a campaign to defeat a new low-sulfur diesel emission standard proposed by the Clinton administration and implemented by the Bush administration. The National Resources Defense Council called the new diesel regulation defended by Bush "the most significant public health proposal in decades."[9]

Among Bush's most lasting achievements in his first year in office was his work on education reform. Bush had succeeded in making changes to the Texas educational system when he was governor, and now he set his sights on the nation. The effort was his most bipartisan to date, eventually attracting one of the most liberal members of the Senate, Massachusetts Democrat Ted Kennedy, as a cosponsor. The bill, which would be known as No Child Left Behind, called for schools to be held accountable for the performance of their students. It required states to set standards and to be assessed each year in their progress toward having every student meet those standards.

On the campaign trail, Bush had suggested that students be given vouchers to switch from bad schools to better ones, including private schools. Bush compromised on that point since the narrow Republican advantage in both houses of Congress required some Democratic support. The Democrats also added more federal money to the bill to help states pay for the costs of the new testing and for measures to help failing students succeed.

Unfortunately, bipartisan measures often yield bipartisan criticism, and so it would be with No Child Left Behind. Conservatives complained about Washington's heavy hand in what historically had been a local matter. Liberals complained that the frequent testing was leading teachers to "teach to the test," narrowing their pedagogical focus and providing students with a less effective education. States complained that the new federal money accompanying the law was insufficient to support the costs of the mandated testing. Even the most Republican state in the country, Utah, threatened to forego federal education funding to throw off the yoke of Washington in the program.[10]

More controversial than the program itself was the Bush administration's efforts to promote it. The Department of Education launched a public education campaign to sell the program to the American public. USA Today discovered that this campaign involved paying nationally syndicated commentator Armstrong Williams $240,000 to promote No Child Left Behind on his radio program and in his column, and to encourage other black journalists to do the same.[11] The department

President Bush signs the No Child Left Behind education reform act into law on January 8, 2002. In attendance are (left to right) Representative George Miller (D-CA), Senator Edward M. Kennedy (D-MA), Secretary of Education Rod Paige, Senator Judd Gregg (R-NH), and Representative John Boehner (R-OH). AP Photo/Ron Edmonds.

also produced "video news releases" promoting the program that were distributed to local television stations and aired without indicating that they were government produced. The Government Accountability Office determined in 2005 that these promotional methods amounted to "covert propaganda," which is illegal under U.S. law.[12] This was a harbinger of questionable, secretive actions by the Bush administration that would follow in the years to come, leading to widespread criticism and concern.

One of the biggest legislative victories of Bush's first term was the passage of a bill that vastly expanded Medicare and looked anything but conservative. The bill pushed by Bush and passed in late 2003 provides seniors with a drug benefit, a new "Part D" of Medicare, to help offset the growing costs of prescription-driven health care. Conservative *Wall Street Journal* editorialists called it a "Medicare giveaway," while others warned it would add a trillion dollars to federal expenditures

every decade.[13] Democrats complained that the bill specifically prohibited the federal government from negotiating for better drug prices, as
the Veterans Administration and other government programs allowed.
Others were worried about a "doughnut hole" in the plan, whereby
coverage would halt after the first $2,250 of coverage, only to pick up
after $3,600 was spent. Despite the obvious compromises of the bill,
it was a new benefit that addressed a growing problem for seniors and
represented a big victory for the president, who managed to thread the
political needle by getting enough conservatives and liberals to pass
the measure.

FACING FOREIGN THREATS

Foreign policy was considered Bush's weakest area, which is not unusual for a man whose only political experience was as a governor, even
if he served in a state bordering Mexico. On the campaign trail, Bush
had warned against involving troops in nation building as Clinton had
done in Bosnia, Somalia, and Haiti. Bush was suspicious of the value of
international tribunals such as the United Nations, whose work tended
to be hamstrung by the irreconcilable differences of its members and its
lack of offensive military force.

Bush's first major challenge on foreign policy came on April 1, 2001,
when a U.S. Navy surveillance plane collided with a Chinese military
jet in international waters off the coast of China, forcing it to make
an emergency landing in Linshui on Hainan Island in southern China.
Twenty-four American crew members were taken into custody, and the
Chinese initially refused to allow them to contact American officials.
The crew was released 11 days later, after the United States issued a
carefully worded letter of regret over the death of the Chinese pilot who
collided with the American plane and for the unauthorized landing the
navy plane made in China. The Bush administration refused to agree to
halt surveillance flights near China, which monitored missile deployments threatening Taiwan (which the Chinese government still considers part of China). The Chinese kept the sensitive military plane for
three months, returning it to the United States in disassembled pieces.

Bush could not have imagined what a minor afterthought this run-in
with the Chinese would represent before the end of the year. Already in

the works was a plan by Islamic radicals from the Middle East to launch a devastating attack that would forever change the United States and Bush's understanding of his role as president.

There were warning signs. During the transition, Clinton officials had briefed Bush and his staff on the threat from a Middle Eastern terrorist organization known as Al Qaeda, led by a Saudi exile named Osama bin Laden. Less than a week after Bush took office, Richard Clarke asked National Security Council director Condoleezza Rice for a high-level meeting on the threat posed by Al Qaeda. Clarke had worked in the Reagan, Bush I, and Clinton administrations. Clinton promoted him to chief adviser on terrorism for the National Security Council. In June 2001, Clarke warned Rice that six different intelligence sources were pointing to an imminent attack on the United States.

Bush was vacationing at his ranch in Crawford, Texas, on August 6, 2001, when he received a Presidential Daily Brief (PDB) headlined: "Bin Laden Determined to Strike in the U.S." Intelligence sources had been warning for months about attacks on "U.S. interests," though there were no specifics regarding when or where an attack might take place. The Bush administration issued general warnings to embassies, airlines, intelligence agencies, and foreign governments and raised the threat level at the U.S. Central Command to "Delta," its highest level. Bush later reported that the August 6 PDB was reassuring to him because it noted that 70 investigations were under way concerning the threats.[14]

On September 4, 2001, Clarke finally got his high-level meeting on Al Qaeda. He and Central Intelligence Agency (CIA) director George Tenet warned Rice, Secretary of State Colin Powell, and Secretary of Defense Donald Rumsfeld about the threat posed by Al Qaeda. Powell suggested putting pressure on Pakistan to help rein in Al Qaeda and their supporters, Afghanistan's Taliban government. Rumsfeld thought that Iraq and other terrorist threats were more significant. Rice asked Clarke to draw up a policy proposal for the president to sign.[15] That policy would not be ready in time to make any difference.

A week later, on September 11, 2001, a plane struck the North Tower of the World Trade Center in New York City at 8:46 A.M. (EST). Within 3 minutes, national television networks began broadcasting images of a gaping hole above the skyscraper's 90th floor where smoke

President George W. Bush leaves the Pentagon with Secretary of Defense Donald H. Rumsfeld (second from left), Vice President Dick Cheney (second from right), and National Security Advisor Condoleezza Rice (left), in August 2001. U.S. Department of Defense.

was billowing out. Stunned viewers tried to make sense of what they were seeing as news anchors interviewed witnesses who reported seeing a plane crash into the building.

Nine minutes after the crash, Condoleezza Rice called President Bush from the White House to tell him that either a "twin-engine aircraft" or a "commercial aircraft" had struck the World Trade Center.[16] Bush was in Sarasota, Florida, to promote his education policies with a visit to Emma E. Booker Elementary School. Unknown to either Rice or Bush was that the Federal Aviation Administration had been notified by American Airlines 35 minutes earlier that one of their planes probably had been hijacked.

Vice President Dick Cheney was in the White House when an assistant told him about the crash. He turned on the news to see the coverage of the aftermath in time to see a second plane crash into the South Tower of the World Trade Center on live television at 9:03 (EST). At that minute, Bush was entering the elementary school to begin his visit.

The president was introduced to the elementary school students and was about to begin reading a book, *My Pet Goat*, with the class when his chief of staff, Andy Card, whispered in his ear: "A second plane hit the second tower. America is under attack."[17] What happened next would be a matter of speculation for years to come. Instead of excusing himself from the classroom, Bush sat down for the reading lesson, which lasted from 5 to 7 minutes. Bush told a commission investigating the attacks that he did not leave immediately because he did not want to alarm the students and wanted to project strength and calm. One can imagine the guilt that he might have felt at possibly having missed a warning sign and failed in his chief responsibility to protect the American people. Also, he probably never conceived of himself as a war president, since his major interests were in domestic issues involving education, tax, and regulatory reform. This tragedy required Bush to think of himself in completely different terms.

Around 9:15, Bush left the classroom for a holding room where a television was replaying the attack, and he was briefed by staff. He made telephone calls to Cheney, Rice, New York governor George Pataki, and Federal Bureau of Investigation (FBI) director Robert Mueller. Strangely, despite the evidence that the country was under attack, the Secret Service did not hustle the president out of the school for his safety or the students' safety (since such a coordinated attack might include an attack on the commander in chief). At 9:29, still unaware of the hijackings that supported the attack, Bush stepped before the television cameras. He announced to the nation, "Today we've had a national tragedy" and referred to the airplane collisions into the World Trade Center as "an apparent terrorist attack on our country." Echoing his father's words following Iraq's invasion of Kuwait ("This will not stand"), the younger Bush pledged: "Terrorism against our Nation will not stand."

Although Bush announced that he would be returning to Washington, D.C., the Secret Service had other ideas. They rushed to the Sarasota-Bradenton International Airport where *Air Force One* was waiting. In the meantime, the White House got news that American Airlines Flight 77 had apparently been hijacked and was headed toward Washington, D.C., at a high rate of speed. Bush called to ensure that Laura and his daughters were safe. Vice President Cheney was moved to a bunker in the White House, and the Capitol building was evacuated.

Three minutes later, the plane plowed into the western side of the Pentagon, killing 125 employees and causing part of five stories of the massive building to collapse.

Air Force One made an emergency ascent, slamming the president back against his seat as it rocketed quickly to a high altitude to evade any ground-to-air threats against the plane. By the time Bush's plane was in the air, the rest of the planes in the country were grounded (though it would take several hours to land them all). They would stay grounded for three days as a precaution. Bush's plane circled Sarasota for 40 minutes while a decision was made as to where to take the president. In the meantime, a fourth hijacked plane, United Airlines Flight 93, crashed in a field 80 miles southeast of Pittsburgh after passengers stormed the cockpit. Through cell phone conversations, they had learned the hijackers' intentions to crash the plane.

Bush called Cheney again, telling him, "We're at war." He instructed Cheney to give congressional leaders a briefing. After he hung up the phone, the significance of the word *war* obviously had sunk in with his staff. Bush rallied them: "That's what we're paid for boys. We're going to take care of this. And when we find out who did this, they're not going to like me as president. Somebody is going to pay." In talking to Cheney a half hour later, he pledged, "We're going to find out who did this and we're going to kick their asses."[18] Bush's blood was boiling. He was already over the shock of the attack and ready to deliver some Texas justice to the terrorists.

As the towers continued to burn, some people trapped on the upper floors above the flames who could find no means of escaping began leaping to their deaths in a horrific scene captured on live television. Just before 10 A.M., the South Tower collapsed, killing everyone remaining inside and sending up a huge plume of dust and smoke. Less than a half hour later, the second tower would follow. Deaths from the passengers aboard the four planes and the collapse of the two buildings would reach almost 3,000.

Unaware that the final hijacked plane had crashed in Pennsylvania, White House officials were told that another aircraft was headed for Washington, D.C. Around a quarter after 10, Vice President Cheney informed defense officials that they had permission to shoot down any commercial aircraft that posed a threat to the capital. A later report by the 9/11 Commission was unable to establish that Cheney had received prior authorization from the president when he related that shoot-down order, though Bush insisted he had given such permission (perhaps after the fact?).[19] Cheney was a take-charge man who obviously had the complete confidence of the president.

But Cheney's order did not reach the pilots who first arrived in Washington, D.C., airspace. They were unaware of the attacks and were more focused on the kind of attack they had trained for: a threat from Russia. They were operating under stricter orders that would have required confirmation before shooting down an aircraft. The 9/11 Commission concluded that if passengers had not taken on the hijackers on Flight 93, causing the crash in Pennsylvania, the hijackers might have succeeded in a fourth attack on either the White House or the Capitol building.[20]

Security officials finally decided to fly the president to Barksdale Air Force Base in Shreveport, Louisiana. He landed and was quickly surrounded by a wall of soldiers armed with M-16s who warily escorted the president to a building with a media center where the president made a second address to the nation, exclaiming:

> Freedom, itself, was attacked this morning by a faceless coward, and freedom will be defended. I want to reassure the American people that the full resources of the Federal Government are working to assist local authorities to save lives and to help the victims of these attacks. Make no mistake: The United States will hunt down and punish those responsible for these cowardly acts.[21]

As crews prepared Air Force One for departure, Bush questioned his CIA briefer on the attacks. Bush asked who could have carried out the attacks, and his intelligence officer said, "I would bet everything on bin Laden," reassuring Bush that they would likely confirm the attackers' identities within days. Bush flew to Offutt Air Force Base in Nebraska where he teleconferenced with this national security advisers. CIA director Tenet seconded the idea that bin Laden was behind the attacks. Although the Secret Service wanted to keep Bush away from Washington, D.C., he was adamant about returning to the White House, insisting, "The American people want to know where their president is."[22]

Bush's chief speechwriter, Michael Gerson, begin drafting an address Bush would deliver to the nation that night. In the span of just a few hours, this speech would set out a new policy toward terrorism. At 8:30 P.M., the president addressed a confused and fearful nation. After acknowledging that "our way of life, our very freedom came under attack" from the terrorists, Bush reassured Americans that while "[t]hese acts shattered steel . . . they cannot dent the steel of American resolve." He reassured the country that life, business, and their government would go on. Then he added his new approach, insisting: "We will make no distinction between the terrorists who committed these acts and those who harbor them."[23] That position put a bull's-eye on the back of the government of Afghanistan, which was run by a group of Islamic fundamentalists—the Taliban—whom the United States had supported in an insurgency against the Soviet Union after they invaded the poor and barren country in late 1979. Now the Taliban were hosting several terrorist training camps, including some run by those who attacked the United States on 9/11.

Bush held an expanded national security meeting after the speech. But his day was not over. At 11:08 P.M., the Secret Service hustled Bush, in his running shorts and T-shirt; Laura in her robe and without contacts; and several senior advisors still in the White House down to a bunker. There were reports of an unidentified plane flying toward the White House. The plane was soon identified, and Bush chose to return to the residence rather than sleep in the uncomfortable bunker. He wrote a brief entry in his diary that night: "The Pearl Harbor of the 21st century took place today."[24]

The next day, Cheney approached Bush about taking responsibility for chairing a war cabinet of the principals, but Bush dismissed the idea, insisting that this was a commander-in-chief function. He wanted to ensure that no one misunderstood who was in charge.[25] A meeting with CIA director Tenet confirmed that three of the hijackers had links to bin Laden and his Afghan training camps. The attacks also were consistent with the earlier intelligence indicating that bin Laden was seeking to attack the United States soon. He directed Tenet to investigate the possibility of using a coalition of Taliban foes in Afghanistan—the Northern Alliance—to challenge the Taliban.

Bush ramped up his public discourse against the terrorists, telling reporters in the White House that the attacks of the previous day were not merely terrorist acts, but acts of war. He warned of the difficulty of fighting this new, elusive enemy. He proclaimed: "This will be a monumental struggle between good and evil. But good will prevail."[26] He continued that theme on September 14th when he spoke at a memorial service for the victims of the attacks at the National Cathedral. Drawing upon his own deep-seated faith, he sounded more like a minister than a political leader, stating: "We are here in the middle hour of our grief. So many have suffered so great a loss, and today we express our nation's sorrow. We come before God to pray for the missing and the dead, and for those who loved them." He bolstered faith in God that had been shaken by the tragedy, insisting: "This world [God] created is of moral design. Grief and tragedy and hatred are only for a time. Goodness, remembrance and love have no end, and the Lord of life holds all who die and all who mourn." Quoting Romans, he added: "As we've been assured, 'neither death nor life nor angels nor principalities, nor powers nor things present nor things to come nor height nor depth can separate us from God's love.' " He drew a sweeping lesson from the attacks, asserting: "our responsibility to history is already clear: to answer these attacks and rid the world of evil."[27] A photographer captured Bush sitting during the memorial service with Laura and his parents, when Poppy reached across and squeezed George's hand. His family would be a source of support in the trying days to come.

Later that day, Bush rallied rescue workers trying to find survivors amid the collapsed towers of the World Trade Center. As he spoke, one of the workers said he couldn't hear the president. Bush grabbed a bullhorn and provided a response that helped cement his image as a leader who would take charge, saying: "I can hear you. I can hear you. The rest of the world hears you. And the people who knocked these buildings down will hear all of us soon."[28]

Bush's most important address on the terrorist attacks came on September 20, 2001, in a speech to a joint session of Congress and heard by 80 million Americans. Bush called the United States "a country awakened to danger and called to defend freedom." Following the shock of the attacks, he insisted: "Our grief has turned to anger, and anger to resolution. Whether we bring our enemies to justice, or bring justice to our enemies, justice will be done."[29] Bush identified the attackers as members of Al Qaeda, a group responsible for previous deadly attacks on U.S. embassies in Kenya and Tanzania, as well as for the

October 12, 2000, attack on the USS *Cole* (which killed 17 sailors and injured 39). He noted that they practice an intolerant, "fringe form of Islamic extremism" and were linked to the Taliban government in Afghanistan. He insisted that the main reason they attacked us is because "[t]hey hate our freedoms—our freedom of religion, our freedom of speech, our freedom to vote and assemble and disagree with each other." He insisted they were bent on spreading their ideology throughout Asia and Africa.

Bush then addressed the government of Afghanistan directly, demanding they turn over the terrorists or "share in their fate." He also warned the rest of the world: "Every nation, in every region, now has a decision to make. Either you are with us, or you are with the terrorists. From this day forward, any nation that continues to harbor or support terrorism will be regarded by the United States as a hostile regime."

He prepared Americans for the long fight ahead, warning:

> Americans should not expect one battle, but a lengthy campaign, unlike any other we have ever seen. It may include dramatic strikes, visible on TV, and covert operations, secret even in success. We will starve terrorists of funding, turn them one against another, drive them from place to place, until there is no refuge or no rest. And we will pursue nations that provide aid or safe haven to terrorism.[30]

Bush delivered on his promise to wage an unconventional war, directing officials to "take the gloves off" in this fight. He had the State Department lining up allies and pressuring reluctant countries (especially Pakistan), the Defense Department gearing up to deliver bombs and boots to Afghanistan, the CIA undertaking covert operations to destabilize Al Qaeda's network and to capture or kill its members, and the FBI to begin looking for the next threat with domestic connections.

A YEAR OF TRANSFORMATION

Bush began the year planning to implement his conservative agenda and succeeded quite well. As a former businessman skeptical, like

Ronald Reagan had been, of the government's ability to wisely spend taxpayer money and efficiently regulate business, he passed one of the largest tax cuts in history and eased some regulations (especially those left over from Clinton). He made progress toward passing a major education reform bill with bipartisan support (which he would sign in early 2002), passed a law limiting certain kinds of abortions, and used executive orders to limit support for abortion counseling by international organizations and to limit federal money for stem cell research.

These policies put a palpable conservative stamp on the country in Bush's first year. But they would not define his presidency. The events of 9/11 would radically change his focus to foreign affairs and the threat posed by terrorism. It would lead him to take drastic measures to ensure that the homeland was not taken by surprise again. Bush's religious convictions would reinforce the black-and-white view of the world he promoted in this new war on terrorism. The formula was simple: America is good, the terrorists are evil, and any means used to defeat evil could be justified. The implications of this view would be far-reaching and would make Bush's role as a war president the most controversial since Nixon's in the Vietnam war.

NOTES

1. Jeff Greenfield, *Oh, Waiter! One Order of Crow!* (Waterville, ME: G. K. Hall, 2001), 298.

2. David E. Rosenbaum, "The Inauguration: The Demonstrations," *New York Times*, 21 January 2001, A17.

3. "Bush Gets Keys to White House, Flexes First Presidential Muscles," *CNN.com*, 20 January 2001.

4. Eric Pianin and Cindy Skrzycki, "EPA to Kill New Arsenic Standards," *Washington Post*, 21 March 2001, A1.

5. Barton Gellman, *Angler: The Cheney Vice Presidency* (New York: Penguin, 2008), 211–13; Don Thompson, "California, Tribe, Fishermen Mark Anniversary of Klamath Fish Kill," Associated Press, 26 September 2003.

6. Gellman, *Angler*, 81–85.

7. "Bush's Legacy on Global Warming," *Christian Science Monitor*, 18 April 2008, 8.

8. Michael Abramowitz and Steven Mufson, "Papers Detail Industry's Role in Cheney's Energy Report," *Washington Post,* 18 July 2007, A1.

9. David Brooks, "Clearing the Air," *New York Times,* 20 April 2004, A19.

10. Amanda Ripley, Sonja Steptoe, Melissa August, Nadia Mustafa, and Maggie Sieger, "Inside the Revolt Over Bush's School Rules," *Time,* 9 May 2005, 30–33.

11. Greg Toppo, "Education Dept. Paid Commentator to Promote Law," *USA Today,* 17 January 2005.

12. Robert Pear, "Buying of News by Bush's Aides Is Ruled Illegal," *New York Times,* 1 October 2005, A1.

13. Dana Milbank, "Conservatives Criticize Bush on Spending; Medicare Bill Angers Some Allies," *Washington Post,* 6 December 2003, A1.

14. *The 9/11 Commission Report: Final Report of the National Commission on Terrorist Attacks Upon the United States* (New York: W. W. Norton, 2004), 260.

15. Richard Clarke, *Against All Enemies: Inside America's War on Terror* (New York: Free Press, 2004), 237–38.

16. *The 9/11 Commission Report,* 35.

17. Scott McClellan, *What Happened: Inside the Bush White House and Washington's Culture of Deception* (New York: Public Affairs, 2008), 102.

18. Bob Woodward, *Bush at War* (New York: Simon & Schuster, 2002), 17–18.

19. *The 9/11 Commission Report,* 40–41.

20. Ibid., 45.

21. George W. Bush, "9/11 Remarks at Barksdale Air Force Base," Barksdale, Louisiana, 11 September 2001, http://americanrhetoric.com/speeches/gwbush911barksdale.htm.

22. Ronald Kessler, *A Matter of Character: Inside the White House of George W. Bush* (New York: Sentinel, 2004), 143, 147.

23. Bush, "9/11 Remarks at Barksdale Air Force Base."

24. Woodward, *Bush at War,* 37.

25. Ibid., 38.

26. Ibid., 35.

27. George W. Bush, "Remarks at the National Day of Prayer and Remembrance," Washington, D.C., Episcopal National Cathedral, 14 September 2001, http://americanrhetoric.com/speeches/gwbush911prayer&memorialaddress.htm.

28. George W. Bush, "Bullhorn Address to Ground Zero Rescue Workers," 14 September 2001, New York, http://americanrhetoric.com/speeches/gwbush911groundzerobullhorn.htm.

29. George W. Bush, "Address to a Joint Session of Congress Following 9/11 Attacks," 20 September 2001, http://americanrhetoric.com/speeches/gwbush911jointsessionspeech.htm.

30. Ibid.

Chapter 7

THE WAR AGAINST TERRORISM

Bush's September 20, 2001, address to a joint session of Congress had announced a "war on terror," which was a breathtakingly broad new foreign policy. It pledged to find, stop, and defeat not just Al Qaeda, but "every terrorist group of global reach."[1] A confluence of personal and practical factors would shape Bush's approach to fighting this war in a way that would make him one of the most controversial presidents in recent history. Specifically, Bush stretched the limits of executive power to the breaking point—some would say beyond the breaking point—in an effort to combat this new threat to the United States.

He would take these actions in the midst of the pervasive fear that existed in the United States during the days and weeks after 9/11. In a single day the attackers had killed more people than had died at Pearl Harbor—more people indeed than any other single foreign attack in this country's history. They had demolished the symbol of American economic power, the World Trade Center's Twin Towers, as well as damaging the symbol of our military power, the Pentagon. Had the fourth plane not been stopped by its heroic passengers, the White House or the Capitol building also might have been destroyed.

*President Bush stands atop a burned-out fire truck with
firefighter Bob Beckwith while rescue efforts continued at
the site of New York City's World Trade Center, three days
after the tragedy of 9/11. AP Photo/Doug Mills.*

The American people had witnessed much of the mayhem on live
television, from the smoking of the North Tower and the crash of the
second airplane into the South Tower to the collapse of both towers,
from people leaping to their deaths from 100 stories to billowing smoke
coming from the Pentagon. They had seen their president whisked away
to hide out for a day in various military bases around the country while
the terrorist's leader, Osama bin Laden, remained at large (which he
remained throughout Bush's entire presidency). Their assumptions—
that we were the mightiest power on earth; a beloved and respected
beacon of freedom for the world; and an oasis far-removed from the
seemingly endless history of violence between Israelis and Palestinians,
Chechens and Russians, and the Irish and the British, among others—
were shattered in an instant. They were fearful, confused, and looking
for a leader to protect them.

Personally, George W. Bush was fully prepared to take whatever action was necessary to protect the country. He was a pragmatic politician who had no time for abstract debates about presidential power, legal constraints, or warnings about what he couldn't do. He was a man of action who wanted to get things done—in this case, heading off the most serious threat to the American homeland since the cold war threatened nuclear annihilation or, before that, the Japanese followed Pearl Harbor with minor attacks on the West Coast. Bush had a black-and-white view of the world, a deep patriotism, and a keen sense of justice. He didn't like to play defense but wanted to be proactive. He also never liked policies that merely looked good on paper, however well meaning, and he certainly didn't want to take actions that would simply appear to address the threat rather than actually doing something meaningful.

His most influential adviser, Vice President Dick Cheney, had been in the executive branch when Richard Nixon's misuse of the presidential office led to a series of new laws intended to check the power of the executive and limit the abuses of law enforcement and intelligence agencies. Cheney disagreed vehemently with what he viewed as legislative encroachment on executive power, believing they unconstitutionally limited the power of the president, particularly in times of war. As a congressman, Cheney had taken a stand for a strong executive by dissenting from a congressional finding that President Reagan had overstepped his authority in supporting an insurgency against the Socialist government in Nicaragua by selling arms to Iran and using the proceeds to fund the Contras after Congress cut off funds for that purpose. He and seven colleagues claimed that it was Congress that was abusing its authority in trying to limit Reagan's actions in foreign policy. In 2001, Cheney and his legal counsel, David Addington, would be instrumental in challenging legislative and other constraints on executive action in helping to wage the war on terrorism.[2]

Pushing agents in the Central Intelligence Agency (CIA), Federal Bureau of Investigation (FBI), military, and other government agencies was going to be a challenge though. The legislative efforts to rein in executive abuses included the criminalization of operations like wiretapping without a warrant. International tribunals were trying cases against those who committed crimes against humanity, and Amnesty International and other watchdog groups were keeping an eye on governments and their operatives. Those who would have to carry out operations in the war on terrorism were understandably gun-shy about overstepping legal boundaries, even though they were strongly motivated after 9/11 to stop the next attack.[3] Unfortunately, within a week, Americans would fall victim to another attack.

THE ANTHRAX ATTACKS

On September 18, 2001, five letters were mailed from a Trenton, New Jersey, post office box to national media companies. The letters contained deadly anthrax spores. Three weeks later, two more letters containing deadlier forms of anthrax were mailed to the offices of Democratic senators Tom Daschle and Patrick Leahy. More than 20 people were infected by the spores, and 5 of them died. The congressional mail service had to be shut down for a time while equipment was decontaminated.

The letters had messages that seemed to link them to Islamic extremists, and initially, the Bush administration pointed fingers at Al Qaeda and Iraq. However, several months after the attacks, scientists identified the DNA of the anthrax as originating in U.S. military facilities. It would be seven years before the FBI was ready to bring charges against anyone. They identified Dr. Bruce Ivins, who worked in a U.S. biodefense laboratory at Fort Detrick in Frederick, Maryland, as the sole culprit. On August 1, 2008, before he could be arrested, Ivins apparently committed suicide. Critics of the FBI's case claimed that the evidence was only circumstantial and that the FBI had hounded Ivins to his death with two raids on his home.

Whatever domestic source was behind the anthrax attacks, they exacerbated the fears of the American public. Americans were ready to give the president carte blanche to do whatever was necessary to protect the country. And Bush was ready to take unprecedented steps to prevent additional attacks. He saw his ultimate role as protector of the country, a role at which he had failed on 9/11 and with the anthrax attacks. "Don't ever let this happen again," Bush reportedly told Attorney General John Ashcroft the day after the 9/11 attacks.[4] Then Bush set out to clear the road of any legal obstacles that might impede his ability to stop terrorists determined to kill more innocent Americans.

TAKING THE GLOVES OFF

Bush prepared to take the gloves off, roll up his sleeves, and take on the threat to Americans. He parlayed the fear of additional attacks into legislation that would give him new tools to counter terrorism. With the help of the president's staff, Congress quickly developed a bill that became known as the USA PATRIOT Act, which gave law enforcement officials new powers to track down and stop terrorists. The law expanded the authority of federal agencies to search a variety of records: telephone, e-mail, financial, medical, and even library records. It gave immigration officials greater discretion in detaining (even permanently) and deporting immigrants suspected of terrorism. Because of concerns over the potential weakening of civil rights protections through the bill, a sunset clause would end some of the more controversial expansions of authority on the last day of 2005. The act was passed by wide margins in both houses and signed by President Bush on October 26, 2001.

One of the most controversial provisions of the act allowed the FBI to avoid having their searches approved by a judge simply by issuing a National Security Letter (NSL) if a local FBI official believes e-mail, telephone, financial, or other records are relevant to an investigation. It put a gag order on telephone companies, Internet service providers, libraries, and others who were issued these letters, making it difficult to challenge them. The FBI issued thousands of NSLs under this provision, working hard to track down even long-shot leads in an effort to stop the next terrorist attack.

Although the PATRIOT Act provided considerable new authority to track down terrorists, the Bush administration was establishing a different legal basis to do even more. Vice President Dick Cheney and David Addington weren't convinced that the president needed the PATRIOT Act in any case to take new, robust actions to track down and stop terrorists. Cheney urged Bush to sign a presidential authorization on October 4, 2001, as the PATRIOT Act was being debated, secretly extending federal authority to conduct more extensive surveillance than the PATRIOT Act authorized. The program was such a closely held secret that not even National Security Adviser Condoleezza Rice's legal counsel was aware of it, though leaders of congressional intelligence committees were eventually briefed on the program.

This Terrorist Surveillance Program addressed a key problem in hunting down the next terrorist threat: finding enemies and plots the government didn't already know about. Wiretapping the telephone of a
known terrorist was easy enough to do, but what if unknown terrorists—
possibly already living in the United States—were hatching a plot? How
could you find them? Intelligence agencies wanted a means for collect-
ing huge masses of data—billions of e-mails, faxes, telephone calls, and
other records—so they could sift through them and perhaps detect patterns that might reveal terrorist plots.[5] The existing Foreign Intelligence
Surveillance Court did not issue warrants for such drift-net approaches
to intelligence gathering, so they were left out of the loop.

When the program was unearthed by the *New York Times* in late 2005,
Bush administration officials criticized the media for writing stories on
a classified program and helping the enemy, insisting that the president
had the authority to run the warrantless wiretapping program under his
authority as commander in chief and under Congress's authorization
for the president to use military force in the war on terrorism. They insisted that the surveillance always involved an international call with
someone in the United States where one of the parties was a terrorist suspect. Critics challenged these claims and accused the president
of running a much more expansive and illegal clandestine operation.
Several lawsuits were filed against telecommunications companies that
had given records to federal authorities without requiring a court order.
But even the Democrats were willing to help the administration at this
point, passing the Protect America Act in 2007, which blocked such
lawsuits and authorized the president to conduct warrantless wiretaps
aimed at stopping terrorists, with some provisions for modest checks on
those activities. Near the end of Bush's second term, ABC News aired a
stunning report from two former National Security Agency (NSA) employees claiming that they had monitored and even transcribed calls to
the United States by American journalists, aid workers, and American
military personnel working in the Middle East.[6]

ROOTING OUT TERRORISTS IN AFGHANISTAN

At the same time Bush was intensifying his efforts to protect the
homeland, he was overseeing a war against those who attacked the

United States and the Afghanistan government that harbored them. He began the effort, called Operation Enduring Freedom, with a low American profile. CIA operatives and Army Special Forces supported an insurgency by the Northern Alliance, a group of Afghans who opposed the ruling Taliban government, beginning on October 7, 2001. This was followed by a U.S. bombing campaign of Al Qaeda training camps and major cities held by the Taliban, as well as a force of 1,000 American soldiers who helped hold Mazar-i-Sharif, previously taken by Alliance troops, to give the American-led coalition an air base to launch operations against Kandahar and the capital Kabul. By mid-November, the Taliban was in full retreat and the capital had fallen to coalition forces. The next month, the coalition took Kandahar and many Taliban fighters retreated into Pakistan. A group of Al Qaeda fighters holed up in the mountainous region known as Tora Bora. British and American forces pounded the area, and the terrorist group stalled while they discussed a surrender. That appears to have given them enough breathing space to sneak their leader, Osama bin Laden, out of Afghanistan.

An American-educated Afghan exile named Hamid Karzai was put in charge of an interim government while American forces established a military command north of Kabul at Bagram Air Base. The speedy defeat of the Taliban government proved a hollow victory given the years of continuing conflict and commitment of American troops and treasure to come in the war-torn country. Afghanistan also would be relegated to a secondary front in Bush's war on terrorism, which would soon shift its primary focus west.

The war in Afghanistan led to the capture of a number of Al Qaeda and Taliban fighters who presented a unique challenge in this unusual conflict. The Bush administration quickly opened a detention facility at the U.S. naval base in Guantánamo Bay, Cuba. Gitmo, as it was called, began receiving scores of suspected terrorists in early 2002. Bush already had decided that these detainees, and others who would be captured around the world in this global war on terrorism, would not be treated as prisoners of war. They were irregular fighters to be sure, and Al Qaeda members weren't tied to any particular nation.

In consultation with Cheney, Bush made one of the most controversial decisions of his presidency: He would treat those captured in the war on terrorism as "enemy combatants," denying them access to the courts, trying them (if at all) in military commissions, and holding them indefinitely without charge if necessary. He also decided that these suspects were not covered by the Geneva conventions, which opened the door to the use of "enhanced interrogation techniques" on these prisoners. Years later, the public would learn, and former vice president Dick Cheney would admit, that even waterboarding—a form of simulated drowning used in the Spanish Inquisition and prosecuted as a form of torture in the United States as early as 1947—was one of the techniques approved for use against some terrorist suspects.[7] Bush's Office of Legal Counsel (OLC) had tried to give the administration legal cover for such controversial interrogation techniques. Although that office is supposed to produce objective analyses, the OLC concluded that torture might be argued to include only "serious physical injury, such as organ failure, impairment of bodily function, or even death."[8] The CIA set up black sites overseas to hold and interrogate suspects, whom they sometimes kidnapped from foreign countries and secretly whisked away in a process called *extraordinary rendition*. The public would not learn of the lengths to which the Bush administration was going in its interrogations until 2004 in the context of another war that Bush was planning.

A RADICAL NEW WAR DOCTRINE

Bush had pledged in his September 20, 2001, address to Congress and the nation on the terrorist attacks to make no distinction between the terrorists and those who harbor them. That provided a justification for taking down the Taliban regime in Afghanistan, which hosted Al Qaeda training camps. It also provided the basis for what would become known as the Bush Doctrine, which provided an offensive twist to existing American foreign policy. The theme was elaborated in a graduation speech that Bush gave at West Point on June 1, 2002, in which he warned: "We cannot defend America and our friends by hoping for the best. We cannot put our faith in the word of tyrants, who solemnly sign nonproliferation treaties, and then systemically break them. If we wait for threats to fully materialize, we will have waited too long." He vowed to "take the battle to the enemy, disrupt his plans, and confront the worst threats before they emerge." He insisted "our security will require all Americans to be forward-looking and resolute, to be ready for preemptive action when necessary to defend our liberty and to defend our lives."[9]

Although Bush didn't mention Iraq in this speech, he had dubbed the Islamic country part of an "axis of evil" in his State of the Union address six months earlier, along with North Korea and Iran. He insisted that these three countries were seeking weapons of mass destruction (WMDs), had terrorist allies, and "could attack our allies or attempt to blackmail the United States." The two speeches together provided Bush's justification for preemptive war, something the United States had never undertaken.

Vice President Cheney jumped the gun in calling for a preemptive attack on Iraq in August 2002, insisting there was "no doubt" that it had WMDs it could use against U.S. interests. A Bush spokesman dismissed the call, but behind the scenes, officials were already at work preparing for that very contingency.[10] On September 8, 2002, Cheney told NBC's *Meet the Press*, "We do know, with absolute certainty, that [Iraq's president Saddam] Hussein is using his procurement system to acquire the equipment he needs in order to enrich uranium to build a nuclear weapon." The same day, in what appeared to be a Bush administration news blitz, National Security Adviser Condoleezza Rice told CNN: "The problem here is that there will always be some uncertainty about how quickly [Hussein] can acquire nuclear materials. But we don't want the smoking gun to be a mushroom cloud." Bush jumped on the media bandwagon four days later when he stated in a United Nations address that Iraq's "Saddam Hussein continues to develop weapons of mass destruction. The first time we may be completely certain that he has nuclear weapons is when, God forbid, he uses one." He called Iraq "a grave and gathering danger."[11]

Bush administration officials began urging Congress to pass a resolution authorizing the use of force against this "gathering danger," which was overwhelmingly approved on October 11, 2002. Bush prepared the American public for this unprecedented preemptive attack by devoting much of his 2003 State of the Union address to the threat posed by Iraq. He included a claim that four months later would have to be retracted, that "[t]he British government has learned that Saddam

Hussein recently sought significant quantities of uranium from Africa." With the implication that a nuclear weapon might be nearing completion, Bush also claimed that "Saddam Hussein aids and protects terrorists, including members of al-Qaida." He warned: "Secretly, and without fingerprints, he could provide one of his hidden weapons to terrorists, or help them develop their own."[12]

The next month, the Bush official with the greatest international standing, Secretary of State Colin Powell, made the case against Iraq before the Security Council at the United Nations. He showed satellite images of trucks, which he reported had been identified as mobile labs to develop biological weapons. He claimed that Iraq had chemical weapons and was seeking to acquire nuclear weapons. He insisted that timely action was required, because "[t]he gravity of this moment is matched by the gravity of the threat that Iraq's weapons of mass destruction pose to the world."[13]

The Security Council did not pass a resolution supporting the use of force against Iraq. They had weapons inspectors inside Iraq who insisted that they could assess the threat posed by Saddam Hussein within a few months. But Bush was in no mood for delays. He was able to persuade Prime Minister Tony Blair of Britain to support an invasion, along with several other countries that contributed very minor forces to a Coalition of the Willing that would invade Iraq on March 20, 2003.

This invasion would mark a turning point in Bush's presidency, leading to a quagmire that would harm the country and threaten his legacy as president. He saw it as a turning point in the war on terrorism, changing the focus from a defensive to an offensive posture that would provide a serious warning to any country considering developing WMDs and harboring terrorists.

NOTES

1. George W. Bush, "Address to a Joint Session of Congress Following 9/11 Attacks," 20 September 2001, http://americanrhetoric.com/speeches/gwbush911jointsessionspeech.htm.

2. Jack Goldsmith, *The Terror Presidency: Law and Judgment Inside the Bush Administration* (New York: W. W. Norton, 2007).

3. Ibid.

4. Ibid., 74.

5. Barton Gellman, *Angler: The Cheney Vice Presidency* (New York: Penguin, 2008), 141–45; Dan Eggen, "Negroponte Had Denied Domestic Call Monitoring; Administration Won't Comment on NSA Logs," *Washington Post*, 15 May 2006, A3.

6. Brian Walter Ross and Vic Schecter, "Exclusive: Inside Account of U.S. Eavesdropping on Americans," *ABC News*, 9 October 2008.

7. Walter Pincus, "Waterboarding Historically Controversial," *Washington Post (Online)*, 5 October 2006; Alexi Mostrous, "Cheney: Interrogations Problem Is a 'Political Act,'" *Washington Post (Online)*, 31 August 2009.

8. Mike Allen and Dana Priest, "Memo on Torture Draws Focus to Bush: Aide Says President Set Guidelines for Interrogations, Not Specific Techniques," *Washington Post*, 9 June 2004, A03.

9. George W. Bush, "Graduation Speech at West Point," United States Military Academy, West Point, New York, 1 June 2002, http://georgewbush-whitehouse.archives.gov/news/releases/2002/06/2002 0601-3.html.

10. Dana Millbank, "Cheney Says Iraqi Strike Is Justified," *Washington Post*, 27 August 2002, A1.

11. Qtd. in Scott McClellan, *What Happened: Inside the Bush White House and Washington's Culture of Deception* (New York: Public Affairs, 2008), 138.

12. George W. Bush, "State of the Union Address," Washington, D.C., 20 January 2003, http://georgewbush-whitehouse.archives.gov/news/releases/2003/01/20030128-19.html.

13. Colin Powell, "Speech to the Security Council of the United Nations on the Iraqi Threat," 5 February 2003, http://americanrheto ric.com/speeches/wariniraq/colinpowellunsecuritycouncil.htm.

Chapter 8
THE IRAQ WAR

The United States has had a convoluted relationship with Iraq. In 1979, a U.S. ally and leader of Iraq's neighbor Iran, Shah Mohammad Reza Pahlavi, was overthrown in the Iranian Revolution. Fifty-two Americans working in the U.S. embassy were taken hostage by student revolutionaries for 444 days, causing a crisis that contributed to President Jimmy Carter's reelection loss to Ronald Reagan. In response to Iran's belligerence, the United States turned to Iraq, a competitor with Iran for dominance in the Middle East. When Iraq's leader, Saddam Hussein, wanted to wage war on Iran, the United States supported the effort, which involved a bloody eight-year conflict that ended in a stalemate. During that conflict, Hussein used chemical weapons against his own people, who were rising up against him, killing thousands of men, women, and children.

In 1990, Saddam Hussein took on a smaller challenge when Iraq invaded its tiny, oil-rich neighbor Kuwait. The first President Bush was in office and rallied a broad coalition of nations and quickly expelled Iraqi forces from Kuwait. The coalition stopped short of marching on Baghdad, but it created no-fly zones in the north and south, which kept full control of over half of Iraq out of Saddam's hands. Following Saddam's defeat, the Bush administration urged those living in these protected zones—the majority Shiites in the south and the persecuted Kurds in the north—to rise against the hobbled minority Sunni leader. Unfortunately, General Norman Schwartzkopf made a critical error when he agreed to let Saddam fly helicopters (but not fixed-wing aircraft) in the no-fly zones. The dictator employed helicopter gunships to crush the rebellion, killing thousands.[1]

Now, as the younger President Bush began beating the drums of war against Iraq, these persecuted groups were wary. But this post-9/11 president would prove to be much more willing to throw American blood and treasure at the problem of Saddam Hussein over an extended period in the hope of planting the seeds for democracy to grow in the Middle East to provide a buffer against future terrorism.

PREPARING FOR A SECOND WAR

The Bush administration had been concerned about Iraq from the time he entered the presidency. American pilots were still patrolling the no-fly zones, engaging in minor skirmishes with Iraqi defenses. Bush didn't like this game of "swatting at flies" and wanted to do something more permanent. The attacks of 9/11 and the new Bush Doctrine provided a rationale for taking major action against the Butcher of Baghdad. George Tenet, the director of the Central Intelligence Agency (CIA), assured Bush that the evidence that Saddam had weapons of mass destruction (WMDs) was a "slam dunk." Bush had his justification for war in protecting Americans against WMDs, and he believed that he could transform Iraq and, thereby, transform the Middle East.

Just as he was overseeing the start of the war in Afghanistan in late 2001, General Tommy Franks, the head of Central Command (which oversaw a large region that included the Middle East), was asked to begin formal planning for a possible war against Iraq.[2] These war plans went through multiple drafts as Secretary of Defense Donald Rumsfeld peppered military planners with questions, alternative timelines and scenarios, and requests for out-of-the-box thinking. The military ground forces, which one army general told Congress would need to number in the hundreds of thousands, was pared down by Rumsfeld to 150,000 troops for the invasion, in the belief that a quicker, lighter force could do the job.

The senior administration official with the greatest military experience, Secretary of State Colin Powell, was wary of war with Iraq. He warned Bush privately: "You are going to be the proud owner of 25 million people. . . . You will own all their hopes, aspirations and problems. You'll own it all." He worried about the image of an American general running a Muslim country, of the uncertainties of victory or how it might even be defined, and of the overwhelming amount of time and energy that would be devoted to this war rather than to other pressing matters.[3] Despite his concerns, when the president made the decision to go to war, Powell did his duty like a loyal soldier and backed the war publicly. As noted in the previous chapter, he made the case to the United Nations that Iraq still had WMDs, bringing his credibility to support the case for war. Powell would discover later that much of the intelligence he relied upon rested upon assumptions that proved to be false and, in the case of alleged biological weapons, upon a single unreliable source.[4]

While the Defense Department made plans for waging war in Iraq and dealing with the consequences afterward, the CIA was working Iraq from the inside. The United States had almost no human intelligence sources inside Iraq. In July 2002, a small contingent of CIA operatives set up a base of operations in northern Iraq, in the no-fly zone protected by the United States and controlled largely by the Kurds. With huge bundles of US$100 bills and the aid of Kurdish dissidents, this group quickly enlisted informants inside the Iraqi military, issuing many of them satellite telephones to give live updates of troop movements, weapons caches, Iraqi defensive strategy, and the like. At one point, just before the commencement of the primary American invasion, intelligence identified the location of the elusive Iraqi leader, Saddam Hussein, and his family. Two F-117 stealth bombers were deployed with "bunker-buster" bombs to hit the fortified compound.[5]

This potential decapitation of the Iraqi leadership almost didn't come off. The United Nations was considering a resolution authorizing the use of force against Iraq for failing to fully comply with UN weapons inspectors. France was likely to veto the resolution in the UN Security Council (where a single veto can stop any resolution), so Bush decided not to wait for that process to play out. With a congressional authorization to use force in hand, in mid-January 2003 he began warning publicly that Saddam's time was running out. His State of the Union address two weeks later suggested that Saddam had chemical, biological, and possibly nuclear weapons and might be working with terrorists. On March 17, 2003, he addressed the country on national television, reporting that "events in Iraq have now reached the final days of decision." He accused Saddam of using diplomacy as a ploy and of failing to fully disarm as required by an earlier UN resolution. He asked the Iraqi army to lay down its arms and avoid sabotaging oil wells, whose revenue Bush hoped to use to rebuild Iraq. And he gave the Iraqi leader a time frame for leaving, warning: "Saddam Hussein and his sons must leave Iraq within 48 hours. Their refusal to do so will result in military conflict commenced at a time of our choosing."[6] When the CIA first received the intelligence on Saddam's alleged whereabouts, they were still inside Bush's 48-hour grace period for the dictator to leave. Franks was worried about violating that promise. But, reports suggested that Hussein would be at the compound overnight, enlarging the strike window.[7]

Surprisingly, Bush was cautious about approving the strike—after all, he had just ordered the invasion of Iraq. He questioned whether the intelligence was reliable, and Tenet assured him it was "as good as it gets."[8] He was worried about the women and children accompanying Saddam and how it would look if these were the first casualties of the war on parade before the media. He asked for opinions from Tenet, Rumsfeld, and Cheney. He even turned to the CIA agent reporting the information and asked what he would do. Unused to making policy decisions, the agent told the president he was sorry that the commander in chief had to make this decision. By then, Bush appears to have decided.[9]

Bush moved up his announcement to the American people in light of the strike, speaking on March 19 at 10:15 P.M. (EST). Special Forces units had begun their stealth invasion of Iraq from the west and the north nine hours earlier. The president reported that 35 countries were providing support for Operation Iraqi Freedom, though only the British were supplying troops in significant numbers (at a 10th of the American contingent). The invasion force was small, with about 145,000 troops (counting the British), 247 tanks, and about the same number of Bradley fighting vehicles. There were less than three army divisions, a marine division, and a British division. The force was much lighter than some generals had suggested, which would lead to problems later.[10]

Bush assured Americans: "Our forces will be coming home as soon as their work is done."[11] But that return would stretch beyond Bush's second term in office, leaving his successor to plan for an ever-elusive withdrawal date. One hour after the speech, the F-117s had cleared Iraqi airspace, slipping back out without incident. Although reports from CIA informants said that Saddam had been carried away on a stretcher, those reports were later determined to be false.[12] Indeed, Richard Perle, Chairman of Bush's Defense Policy Board Advisory Committee, told Congress two years later that the information on Hussein's whereabouts probably was provided by a double agent working for the Iraqi regime to throw off the Americans.[13] The risky assault and the move-up of the invasion had been unnecessary and may have played into the hands of the Iraqi dictator.

A NATIONAL DISASTER INTERRUPTS PLANNING FOR WAR

As Bush and his military leaders were engaged in this intense period of war preparation, Bush was required to address the second national tragedy to unfold on American televisions in less than a year and a half. On February 1, 2003, the Space Shuttle *Columbia* was ripped apart during its reentry from orbit. Burning pieces of the spacecraft could be seen shooting across the skies of east Texas and Louisiana, leaving eerie trails. Seven astronauts perished, never making their landing in Florida.

Columbia was the first shuttle to fly a space mission, landing after a three-day mission on April 14, 1981. Newly elected president Ronald Reagan, recently released from the hospital after an assassination attempt, told the astronauts: "Through you we all feel like giants once again."[14] *Columbia* would fly 27 missions, taking into orbit the first sitting member of Congress, Bill Nelson, and the first female commander of any American spacecraft, Lieutenant Colonel Eileen Collins. It had serviced the Hubble Telescope and was scheduled to be retrofitted with an airlock so it could service the International Space Station.

A subsequent investigation determined that a large chunk of insulating foam had broken off during launch and collided with the left wing of the spacecraft, creating a hole that allowed superheated air to penetrate the wing during reentry and melt its aluminum frame. NASA officials were criticized for becoming lax about safety, and the shuttle program was given a termination date. Less than a year later, undaunted by this tragedy, Bush would propose sending Americans back to the moon and then on to Mars.

THE FALL OF BAGHDAD AND ITS AFTERMATH

The invasion of Iraq initially appeared to be going incredibly well. The army had advanced 150 miles into Iraq in only three days, meeting little resistance. But many in the Iraqi army had disappeared into the civilian population only to return later in civilian clothes and wage attacks on armored columns, sometimes firing from civilian homes and even mosques. Troops in the north received resistance from one of Saddam's son's military units, the Fedayeen Saddam, but they were quickly overwhelmed. To the surprise of some commanders, some resistance came from Shiite militias, which hated Saddam but were not happy about an American occupation. By April 9, American troops took Baghdad and the Iraqi government fell. A group of Iraqis—some of them returning exiles flown in by the military—created an iconic image when they used a crane to topple a 20-foot statue of Saddam.

Concerns about a humanitarian crisis, about Saddam using WMDs against Coalition troops, and about oil fields being set ablaze never materialized. Franks arranged a meeting of Iraqi representatives outside of Baghdad to begin discussions of putting Iraq into the hands of Iraqis. One of Rumsfeld's envoys speculated that they could probably reduce the American force to 30,000 troops by August. That would prove not merely optimistic, but naïve.[15]

The first sign that things weren't going according to plan was the rampant and widespread looting following the fall of the government— looting of government buildings, hospitals, museums, and even private homes. Images of ordinary Iraqis carrying away everything from office chairs to priceless antiquities were beamed across the world. American soldiers were shown standing by, watching but doing nothing. The light footprint that allowed Rumsfeld's troops to move so quickly did not provide enough boots on the ground to protect much more than the oil fields that were to be the cash cow for reconstruction. When asked about the chaos, Rumsfeld referred to it as "untidiness."[16]

Lieutenant General Jay Garner was supposed to help avoid or alleviate this "untidiness." He had been pulled out of military retirement and work at his defense contractor company by Rumsfeld to oversee postwar operations, which the secretary of defense managed to put under his department's control. Despite significant work done by the State Department on handling the postwar situation reflected in a planning document entitled *The Future of Iraq*, Garner learned very little about their work. He was brought in just two months before the invasion and worked hard to get up to speed. When he recruited expertise from the State Department and elsewhere, Rumsfeld stymied him, insisting that Garner use Department of Defense people. Vice President Cheney's office put in its two cents' worth as well, apparently making Garner fire a State Department official he recruited who had worked in the Clinton administration.[17]

This dispute reflected an interagency conflict between Rumsfeld and Powell, as well as unresolved disagreements about how the postwar governance issue would be handled. Some Defense officials were pushing for Ahmed Chalabi, an Iraqi exile who headed a group called the Iraqi National Congress, to help form a new political regime in Iraq. But President Bush himself had insisted publicly that the Iraqis would choose their own leaders, otherwise the Americans might be seen as setting up their own puppet leader in the volatile Middle Eastern country. Additionally, Bush wanted to create a democracy in the Middle East, to help transform a region that was a breeding ground for anti-American terrorists. Some in his administration were not convinced that this was feasible. The competing visions of the transition were never resolved, and Bush never took steps to stop the conflicts between State and Defense that were undermining an efficient postwar process. Bush's tendency to delegate, to avoid asking probing questions and digging into details, and to stop the destructive infighting among his departments contributed to a lack of coherency and effectiveness in the postwar operation.

President Bush prematurely declares the end of major combat operations in Operation Iraqi Freedom in a May 1, 2003, speech delivered from the deck of USS Abraham Lincoln. *The United States remained mired in Iraq for years afterward. AP Photo/J. Scott Applewhite.*

Despite the well-publicized chaos in the streets of Baghdad, Bush felt good enough about the success of the war to take a victory lap. On May 1, 2003, he donned a flight jacket, sat in the copilot's seat of an S-3B Viking jet, and flew to meet the USS *Abraham Lincoln*, an aircraft carrier steaming its way to San Diego after a lengthy mission. He bounded out of the plane with his flight helmet tucked under one arm to the cheers of the assembled sailors, disappeared inside and changed into a suit and tie, and returned to give a nationally televised speech on the Iraq War. With a banner announcing "Mission Accomplished" framed behind him, Bush insisted that the invasion had "removed an ally of Al Qaeda and cut off a source of terrorist funding . . . [and that] [n]o terrorist network will gain weapons of mass destruction from the Iraqi regime, because the regime is no more."[18] Although there was work left to do in Iraq, Bush announced the end of major combat operations. This speech would later come back to haunt Bush, as the Iraq War dragged on through his two-term presidency and his claims about Saddam's threat to the United States proved unfounded.

While Bush appeared on national television smiling and soaking in the adoration of the crew of the *Abraham Lincoln*, Jay Garner was working hard to stabilize a country coming apart at the seams. Unfortunately, Garner never had adequate support from the man who sent him there. Weeks after he arrived in Baghdad, Rumsfeld informed him that he was being replaced. L. Paul "Jerry" Bremer III would have only two weeks to get up to speed before he assumed the position of an American viceroy in Iraq, President Bush's special envoy, who reported to Bush through Rumsfeld.

Bremer's first acts as head of the Coalition Provision Authority (CPA) shocked Garner, who was staying over for a brief transition.[19] A RAND study had estimated that more than three times the number of troops Rumsfeld sent to Iraq was required to oversee the postwar situation.[20] Because he was so shorthanded, Garner had planned to use existing Iraqi institutions, including the Iraqi military, police, and civilian force, to create a secure environment and help rebuild Iraq. They had the expertise, knowledge of the country, and experience to keep basic services going and maintain order in the streets. Furthermore, keeping them employed would ensure they didn't join the ranks of the disaffected in Iraq, including half the workforce that was already unemployed in this country that had long suffered economic sanctions. Although Iraqi military, police, teachers, and others in this force had been members of Saddam's Baathist Party—that was the only way to get such jobs—Garner figured he could fire a small number of people at the top who were among the elite of the fascist party and keep the people below who simply joined to get a job.

Yet Bremer's first order as head of the CPA, issued May 16, 2003, was to fire the top three layers of civilian employees—including junior managers—in a de-Baathification effort that precluded them from ever working for the government again. That action gutted the government of management expertise in education, utilities, agriculture, and more than a dozen other areas crucial to sustaining Iraq and rebuilding its institutions. Next, Bremer dissolved the Iraqi military and police, putting hundreds of thousands of armed Iraqis out of work, on the streets, and angry at their American occupiers. In a third act, Bremer rejected a council of Iraqi leaders that Garner had supported to begin discussions on the governance of Iraq by its citizens. This stymied early efforts to create political legitimacy for the occupation, exacerbated by Bremer's repeated reminders to Iraqis that "you're not the government. We are. And we're in charge."[21] Those decisions would quickly come back to haunt Bremer. Because of such decisions, former House Speaker Newt Gingrich, a Republican, called Bremer "the largest single disaster in American foreign policy in modern times."[22]

Oddly, despite the magnitude of these decisions, there has been some controversy over where this de-Baathification decision originated. Garner had briefed the president and Rumsfeld on limiting cuts to top managers, which they appeared to endorse. Yet Bremer told Garner he would implement the new policy because, he insisted, "I have my instructions."[23] He further claimed that "[t]he president told me that de-Baathification is more important [than the efficiency of the rebuilding effort]."[24] Much later, Bremer seemed to take more personal responsibility, noting:

> I did that because I thought it was absolutely essential to make it clear that the Baathist ideology, which had been responsible for so many of the human-rights abuses and mistreatment of the people in the country over the last forty years, had to be extirpated finally and completely from society, much as the American government decided to completely extirpate Nazism from Germany at the end of the Second World War.[25]

Bob Woodward, whose four books on Bush as a war president drew upon hundreds of interviews with principal participants, discovered that the de-Baathification effort did not go through an interagency process, where principals in the planning process provide input for major decisions. Indeed, the chairman of the Joint Chiefs of Staff, General Myers, did not provide input on the policy. Rumsfeld insisted that it originated outside his department, though Bremer claims he ran drafts of the policy by the secretary of defense.[26] National Security Adviser Condoleezza Rice reported that she was not involved in discussions of the policy. Stephen Hadley, Rice's assistant, insisted that the policy had not been endorsed by the White House. Yet, Bremer told his staff that "[t]he White House, DOD and State all signed off on this."[27] In his 2006 book, *My Year in Iraq*, Bremer insisted that the policy had been approved in Washington, but no one seems to want to take responsibility for this fateful decision.

In 2007, Bush was interviewed by Robert Draper for a book he was writing. Draper asked him about Bremer's order to disband the Iraqi army and fire most of the managers working in Iraq civil service sectors. Bush reported that this was a policy reversal, because "[t]he policy had been to keep the army intact." Bush's reaction to the change was, "[t]his is the policy, what happened?" But, Bush didn't do anything to change that policy. Indeed, just after the de-Baathification policies were announced, Bush wrote a letter to Bremer assuring him: "You have my full support and confidence."[28]

Bush's philosophy of picking the right people and then delegating authority to them perhaps accounts for his acceptance of this change in policy. His surprise at such reversals, though, is partly the responsibility of those under him who refused to make clear their concerns. For example, when Jay Garner left Iraq disgusted with the policies Bremer had implemented and with his unwillingness to consider the dire consequences likely to follow, he had a meeting with the president. Instead of conveying his grave concerns, Garner said Bremer was hardworking, very bright, articulate, and "a good choice." Garner said nothing of his concerns over the fateful de-Baathification decisions. He left Bush with a rosy story of meetings with Iraqis that ended with their statement: "God bless Mr. George Bush and Mr. Tony Blair. Thank you for taking away Saddam Hussein."[29] Bush's penchant for backing his people, delegating, and not asking probing questions kept him in what *Newsweek* would later refer to as the "Bush Bubble."[30]

THE INSURGENCY GAINS GROUND

Predictably, the lack of security, frequent electricity outages, little progress on handing over authority to Iraqis, and widespread unemployment exacerbated by Bremer's policies led to growing discontent in the Iraqi population. On June 2, 2003, about 1,000 former Iraqi soldiers gathered outside Bremer's headquarters to protest the army's disbanding. They warned that if their grievances weren't addressed, they would resort to suicide attacks on American forces. Bremer dismissed them as blackmailers and terrorists.[31]

Steadily over the ensuing months, an insurgency gained ground in Iraq. The disaffected and unemployed Iraqi security forces undoubtedly took part in the daily attacks on coalition forces. Indeed, evidence was unearthed of a plot by Saddam to distribute weapons around the country for just such a postinvasion insurgency. Saddam's sons Uday and Qusay appear to have led a resistance movement until they were killed in a Special Forces raid in Mosul in July. The Bush administration frequently blamed Al Qaeda, which eventually did set up a franchise in Iraq. There also may have been participation in the attacks by radical Islamists who opposed the presence of foreign infidels in the Middle East and believed the West was waging a war against Islam.

Frustrated by the violence and the erosion of confidence in the war, Bush responded to a question at a news conference on July 2, 2003, about the threat represented by the insurgency in Iraq. Bush provided a Texas tough-guy response, saying: "There are some who feel that the conditions are such that they can attack us there. My answer is, 'bring 'em on.'" The next day, 20 soldiers were wounded in attacks.[32] Bush would later voice his regrets over this casual bravado.

Whatever group or combination of groups was to blame for the attacks, it made the task of rebuilding in Iraq nearly impossible. And when the UN mission headquarters in Baghdad was attacked on August 19, 2003, international partners began to get squeamish. The truck bomb killed 22 people, including Sérgio Vieira de Mello, the UN high commissioner for human rights, and injured 150 others. Bush and Condoleezza Rice were particularly disturbed by Vieira de Mello's death because they helped convince the veteran diplomat to head up the UN mission. In his weekly national radio address on August 23, 2003, Bush called Vieira de Mello "a good man serving an important cause." He described the attack and then yoked it to a suicide attack in Jerusalem on the same day, saying they both were the work of terrorists. In the face of this carnage, he assured Americans: "Whatever the hardships, we will persevere. We will continue this war on terror until all the killers are brought to justice. And we will prevail." He pressed his national security team to figure out how to better protect their people in Iraq, how to "harden the soft targets" that might attract the next attacks.[33]

The prospect of an early withdrawal of American troops became dimmer each day. Leaving in such circumstances would look like defeat, and the power vacuum in the shaky country would likely lead to a civil war. But the hopes for success were hindered by what became a chicken-and-egg problem: On the one hand, the United States could not win the support of the Iraqi people so long as unemployment remained high, basic services such as electricity and water were spotty, and the security situation remained dangerous. On the other hand, with mounting attacks, it was difficult to bring in civilian workers to fix sewers, electrical grids, and the like, or to free up already-strapped American forces to undertake some of those tasks.

Bremer realized that he needed to involve Iraqis in the governing process he had previously stressed belonged to him alone. He returned to Garner's group and expanded it into an interim Governing Council. But Bremer's insistence that he would be the ultimate decision maker left some Iraqis believing he was looking for "lackeys" rather than a group of governors.[34] Gradually, the council began to exercise some authority, sending a representative to international organizations and passing some legislation. One of their most controversial decisions would have put family law in Iraq under the strictures of Islamic law, called Shari'a law, which threatened to limit the rights of women in marriage, divorce, alimony, and the like. Iraq had been among the most secular of Middle Eastern countries, and women had long enjoyed many freedoms of the Western world. Ironically, the invasion of Iraq pushed this secular country toward a more theocratic form. Bremer was put in the awkward position of threatening to veto the new law.

THE SEARCH FOR WMDS

All of the challenges facing Iraq had drawn attention away from the reason Bush touted for the preemptive attack: the WMDs that Saddam was allegedly harboring. The small group sent into Iraq with the initial invasion force had not unearthed anything. The group's leader, General James "Spider" Marks, quickly realized that the data on almost 1,000 suspected sites for WMDs was outdated and unreliable.

In late May, Bush heard a report that the group was homing in on two suspected biological weapons labs, and he told European leaders he was visiting: "We found the weapons of mass destruction." But Bush's jubilation was premature. A report already on its way to him found that the labs were probably used to produce hydrogen for weather balloons. Frustrated, a few days later Bush talked to Bremer and Rumsfeld together and asked who had primary responsibility for hunting down WMDs in Iraq—obviously, he had not inquired about these important responsibilities earlier. Bremer pointed to Rumsfeld, and Rumsfeld pointed to Bremer. Bush went ballistic.[35]

Bush reassigned the WMDs search to the CIA, who recruited David Kay to head the new Iraqi Survey Group. Kay had been the chief nuclear weapons inspector in Iraq for the United Nations in the 1990s. He decided to ignore the old list that Marks had been using and look for the people in Iraq who had worked on Saddam's weapons programs. In late July, Kay reported back to Bush that no stockpiles had been found. Bush told him to "keep at it" and assured him that he would be patient while Kay did his work.[36]

A DISSENT LEADS TO A SCANDAL

Bush would need all the patience he could muster on the WMDs search, because the failure to find them was beginning to raise concerns that the president and his administration had hyped the case against Saddam Hussein to justify an unprecedented preemptive strike. The most controversial claim Bush made prior to the war was in his 2003 State of the Union address, in which he warned that Saddam might be close to developing a nuclear bomb, reporting that "the British Government has learned that Saddam Hussein recently sought significant quantities of uranium from Africa."[37] Although that claim had been discredited by the CIA and removed from a draft of an October 7, 2002, speech by the president, somehow it found its way back into this most important of speeches right as Bush was marching toward war.

One reason the CIA knew that the claim was false was because it had sent former ambassador Joseph Wilson on a trip to Africa to check out the claim. The document was obviously a forgery, because the signature on it was by a Nigerian official who was not in power on the date the document was signed. That very ambassador, whose work had been ignored, held his tongue through the invasion but spoke up afterward when no WMDs had been found. On July 6, 2003, he published an op-ed piece for the *New York Times* in which he speculated about why his report was ignored, wondering:

> If my information was deemed inaccurate, I understand (though I would be very interested to know why). If, however, the information was ignored because it did not fit certain preconceptions about Iraq, then a legitimate argument can be made that we went to war under false pretenses. (It's worth remembering that in his March "Meet the Press" appearance, Mr. Cheney said that Saddam Hussein was "trying once again to produce nuclear weapons.") At a minimum, Congress, which authorized the use of military force at the president's behest, should want to know if the assertions about Iraq were warranted.[38]

White House Press Secretary Scott McClellan reported the Bush administration's response to this challenge in his book *What Happened*, noting that "[t]o defend itself against the accusations of deliberate dishonesty leveled by Joe Wilson, Vice President Cheney and his staff were leading a White House effort to discredit Joe Wilson himself."[39] Less than a week after Wilson's op-ed was published, conservative columnist Robert Novak revealed: "Wilson never worked for the CIA, but his wife, Valerie Plame, is an agency operative on WMDs. Two senior administration officials told me that Wilson's wife suggested sending him to Niger to investigate the Italian report."[40] The story line implied that this was a sort of nepotistic junket (though Wilson said he did the work pro bono). But, devastatingly, in revealing Plame's CIA status, Novak outed her as a covert agent, ending her career.

The revelation created a firestorm. Bush initially claimed that he would fire anyone involved in the leak of Plame's identity but two years later waffled and said he would fire anyone who "committed a crime" in leaking that information.[41] McClellan lost credibility with the press after he told them that Vice President Cheney's chief of staff, I. Lewis "Scooter" Libby, and political adviser Karl Rove were not involved in the leak, following assurances from Bush and Cheney.[42] In fact, when Rove assured McClellan he had no role in the outing, McClellan notes bitterly,

[t]here was no mention of a phone conversation Karl had on July 11, 2003, with *Time* magazine's newest White House correspondent, Matt Cooper, which would remain under "double super secret" anonymity (Cooper's wit, not mine) for nearly two more years. That is when it would be revealed publicly and to me that Rove had disclosed Plame's identity to Cooper during that call.[43]

The assurances on Libby proved false as well. Libby revealed Plame's identity to a number of reporters, most notably the *New York Times'* Judith Miller, who spent 85 days in jail for refusing to reveal to Special Prosecutor Patrick Fitzgerald that Libby had spoken to her.[44] Libby would become the only official to be prosecuted by Fitzgerald, on four counts of perjury and obstruction of justice stemming from the investigation. Before his court case, Libby resigned, but he wasn't completely left on his own. President Bush commuted Libby's sentence of 30 months in jail, though he didn't pardon Libby or forgive his $250,000 fine. At a presidential press conference on July 12, 2007, Bush assured the public that it was "a fair and balanced decision." He took no action against Karl Rove or Deputy Secretary of State Richard Armitage, both of whom were also involved in the leak. Indeed, McClellan claims that

[f]rom the outset of the investigation, the president made a decision not to pursue the matter internally. He said he wanted to get to the bottom of the questionable activity surrounding the leak episode, but he did not order any White House staff members to mount an investigation, nor to take any other proactive steps to uncover the truth or inform the public.[45]

This episode became a national scandal and embroiled the Bush administration in years of controversy. However, and surprisingly, none of the problems of 2003—this scandal, the failure to find WMDs in Iraq, the increasing toll in Iraq and Afghanistan, the failure to hunt down Osama bin Laden—was sufficient to undermine Bush's bid for reelection in 2004. Not even a new scandal that threatened the very foundations of American values in 2004 would prevent George W. Bush from outdoing his father by winning a second term as president.

NOTES

1. Thomas E. Ricks, *Fiasco: The American Military Adventure in Iraq* (New York: Penguin, 2006), 6.

2. Ibid., 32–33.

3. Bob Woodward, *Plan of Attack* (New York: Simon & Schuster, 2004), 150.

4. Ricks, *Fiasco*, 90–91.

5. Woodward, *Plan of Attack*, 383–92.

6. "Bush: 'Leave Iraq within 48 Hours,'" *CNN.com*, 17 March 2003, http://www.cnn.com/2003/WORLD/meast/03/17/sprj.irq.bush.transcript/.

7. Woodward, *Plan of Attack*, 279, 294, 371–72, 379.

8. Ibid., 387.

9. Ibid., 387–91.

10. Ricks, *Fiasco*, 117.

11. "Bush Declares War," *CNN.com*, 19 March 2003, http://www.cnn.com/2003/US/03/19/sprj.irq.int.bush.transcript/.

12. Woodward, *State of Denial: Bush at War, Part III* (New York: Simon & Schuster, 2006), 152.

13. Ricks, *Fiasco*, 117.

14. Bill Prochnau, "Shuttle Sent into Orbit," *Washington Post*, 13 April 1981, A1.

15. Woodward, *State of Denial*, 160–63.

16. Daniel Williams, "Rampant Looting Sweeps Iraq," *Washington Post*, 12 April 2003, A1.

17. Woodward, *State of Denial*, 128.

18. George W. Bush, "President Bush Announces Major Combat Operations in Iraq Have Ended: Remarks by the President from the USS *Abraham Lincoln*, At Sea Off the Coast of San Diego, California, 1 May 2003, http://georgewbush-whitehouse.archives.gov/news/releases/2003/05/20030501-15.html#.

19. Ricks, *Fiasco*, 158–59.

20. Woodward, *State of Denial*, 190.

21. Ibid., 197.

22. Qtd. in Mortimer Zuckerman, "A Mountain of Mistakes," *New York Daily News*, 15 October 2006, 39.

23. Ricks, *Fiasco*, 159.

24. Michael Hirsh, Rod Nordland, and Mark Hosenball, "About-Face in Iraq," *Newsweek*, 24 November 2003, 30.

25. Qtd. in Ricks, *Fiasco*, 160.

26. Edmund L. Andrews, "Envoy's Letter Counters Bush on Dismantling of Iraq Army," *New York Times*, 4 September 2007.

27. Woodward, *State of Denial*, 193–98.

28. Ibid., 196.

29. Woodward, *State of Denial*, 219–26.

30. Evan Thomas and Richard Wolfe, "Bush in the Bubble," *Newsweek*, 19 December 2005.

31. Woodward, *State of Denial*, 211.

32. Romesh Ratnesar and Simon Robinson, "Life Under Fire," *Time*, July 14, 2003, http://www.time.com/time/magazine/article/0,9171,1005196,00.html.

33. Woodward, *State of Denial*, 246.

34. Patrick E. Tyler, "Overseer Adjusts Strategy as Turmoil Grows in Iraq," *New York Times*, 13 July 2003, A1.

35. Woodward, *State of Denial*, 209–13.

36. Ibid., 237.

37. George W. Bush, "State of the Union Address," Washington, D.C., 20 January 2003, http://georgewbush-whitehouse.archives.gov/news/releases/2003/01/20030128-19.html.

38. Joseph C. Wilson, IV, "What I Didn't Find in Africa (Editorial)," *New York Times*, July 6, 2003, http://www.nytimes.com/2003/07/06/opinion/06WILS.html.

39. Scott McClellan, *What Happened: Inside the Bush White House and Washington's Culture of Deception* (New York: Public Affairs, 2008), 171.

40. Robert D. Novak, "Mission to Niger," *Washington Post*, July 14, 2003, A21.

41. David Stout, "Bush Says He'll Fire Any Aide Who 'Committed a Crime,'" *New York Times*, July 18, 2005, http://www.nytimes.com/2005/07/18/politics/18cnd-rove.html.

42. McClellan, *What Happened*, 183, 217.

43. Ibid., 181.

44. "Reporter at Center of CIA Leak Retires," *CNN.com*, November 10, 2005.

45. McClellan, *What Happened*, 228.

Chapter 9

SQUEAKING INTO A TROUBLED SECOND TERM

As 2003 neared its end, the president's approval ratings were slipping with the rise in casualties in Iraq, the failure to find weapons of mass destruction (WMDs), and the lingering wars in Iraq and Afghanistan. In December, Patrick Fitzgerald was named special prosecutor assigned to investigate the outing of Central Intelligence Agency (CIA) agent Valerie Plame. Reporters became more confrontational with the president, given these controversies and the fact that he would have to face them more in this election season.

A FIELD DAY FOR THE PRESS

Despite his image as an easygoing, sociable Texan, Bush and his team carefully managed his interactions with the press. During his first three years in office, he held only 12 press conferences, which is about the same as President Nixon during his scandal-plagued second term. Only two of those press conferences were held in prime time. Partly he got a "pass" because of the unprecedented attack on 9/11, which bolstered his standing as commander in chief, suggesting that he had a lot on his plate and didn't need the distraction of meeting frequently with the press. When he did meet with the press, he called on carefully selected reporters and was well rehearsed with answers to the most likely questions from them.[1]

But starting at the end of 2003, reporters began to challenge him. Diane Sawyer of *Good Morning America* interviewed Bush in December 2003, citing a poll that showed that half of Americans believed that his administration had hyped the evidence against Saddam Hussein in the buildup to war. Bush denied that he had exaggerated the threat and offered a response that would be the administration's go-to answer to such criticisms in the future, insisting: "Saddam was a danger and the world is better off because we got rid of him."[2]

In January 2004, David Kay resigned as head of the Iraqi Survey Group, testifying before Congress that no stockpiles of WMDs could be found in Iraq. In light of this revelation, Tim Russert of *Meet the Press* asked the president in February whether he thought the Iraq War had been a war of choice or a war of necessity. Bush didn't seem to understand the question, and asked for elaboration, but then insisted that "we had no choice, when we look at the intelligence I looked at, that says the man [Saddam Hussein] was a threat."[3] Of course, Bush's radical, preemptive strike against Iraq had been predicated on the assertion that Saddam was an urgent threat, a ticking time bomb close to going off, not merely a threat.

But Bush's biggest gaffe with the press came in his April 13, 2004, press conference. John Dickerson of *Time* magazine threw the president a curve by asking him what he considered to be his biggest mistake as president. Bush fumbled:

> I wish you would have given me this written question ahead of time, so I could plan for it. John, I'm sure historians will look back and say, "Gosh, he could have done it better this way or that way." You know, I just—I'm sure something will pop into my head here in the midst of this press conference, with all the pressure of trying to come up with an answer, but it hasn't yet.[4]

Bush could not come up with a single example, despite several examples he could have drawn from questions that preceded Dickerson's. For example, Terry Moran of ABC News had just asked Bush:

Mr. President, before the war, you and members of your administration made several claims about Iraq, that U.S. troops would be greeted as liberators with sweets and flowers, that Iraqi oil revenue would pay for most of the reconstruction, and that Iraq not only had weapons of mass destruction, but as Secretary of Defense Rumsfeld said, "We know where they are." How do you explain to Americans how you got that so wrong? And how do you answer your opponents who say that you took this Nation to war on the basis of what have turned out to be a series [of] false premises?[5]

Elisabeth Bumiller of the *New York Times,* had just referenced a report from the 9/11 Commission, a bipartisan group which studied the failures that led to the attack and the response to it:

[Y]ou, yourself, have acknowledged that Osama bin Laden was not a central focus of the administration in the months before September 11th. "I was not on point," you told the journalist Bob Woodward. "I didn't feel that sense of urgency." Two-and-a-half years later, do you feel any sense of personal responsibility for September 11th?[6]

David Gregory of NBC News had even noted a perceived problem with Bush's leadership: that "you never admit a mistake." Even reporters in the press room were stirring uncomfortably as Bush fumbled for an answer to the question about his biggest mistake.[7]

Of course Bush could have pointed to mistakes, but he was too stubborn to admit them. He told Dan Bartlett, White House communications director: "I kept thinking about what they wanted me to say—that it was a mistake to go into Iraq. And I'm not going to. It was the right decision."[8] This attitude made Bush came across as out of touch and obstinate. He went so far as to tell the assembled press that even if he had known they wouldn't find actual WMDs, he would have ordered the invasion of Iraq.

THE ABU GHRAIB SCANDAL

Nine days after Bush's troubled press conference, *60 Minutes II* broke a story about the abuse of prisoners by American personnel at Abu

Ghraib, a prison that Saddam Hussein had used to torture dissenters. The CBS producers of the weekly television news program had agreed to delay the story for two weeks at the request of the Department of Defense and the chairman of the Joint Chiefs of Staff, General Richard Myers, because of the tension in Iraq. The story included graphic pictures showing naked Iraqi prisoners stacked up in a human pyramid, a female soldier holding one end of a leash attached to a naked Iraqi man, and soldiers posing with the cowed prisoners and smiling sadistically. One photo showed a hooded prisoner standing on a box and covered with a shroud with wires dangling down. Dan Rather reported that the prisoner was told that if he fell off the box, he would be electrocuted.

An army investigation of the abuse was already under way, which eventually led to the convictions of about a dozen soldiers. But several investigative journalists tied the abuses to the Bush administration's new approach to the war on terror, to which the Iraq War was repeatedly tied by Bush. As noted in Chapter 7, the Bush administration began developing new policies on the treatment of prisoner in the gloves-off war on terror. Some forms of enhanced interrogation techniques looked a lot like torture. And this attitude seems to have spilled over into Iraq, where untrained national reservists were told to "soften up" prisoners for CIA interrogators. The *Washington Post* reported that Lt. General Ricardo Sanchez, a senior military officer in Iraq, authorized interrogation tactics that used "military dogs, temperature extremes, reversed sleep patterns, sensory deprivation, and diets of bread and water on detainees whenever they wished," as well as stress positions, isolation, and other means to coerce prisoners to cooperate.[9]

In light of these media revelations, Donald Rumsfeld drafted a letter of resignation and gave it to Bush. But Bush was not ready to let his secretary of defense step down. He thought Rumsfeld's work on transforming the military to address new threats was vital.

The reaction to the images of abuse from those in the Middle East was outrage. Violence in Iraq exploded, punctuated by a massive truck bomb near the American military's protected Green Zone in Baghdad. Bush went on Arab television to assure viewers that the Abu Ghraib abuses were the fault of a few bad apples, stating:

I want to tell the people of the Middle East that the practices that took place in that prison are abhorrent and they don't represent

America. They represent the actions of a few people. Secondly, it's important for people to understand that in a democracy that there will be a full investigation. We want to know the truth.[10]

Despite these assurances, images from Abu Ghraib would haunt Bush for the rest of his time in office, leading people to question his approach to the war on terrorism.

THE PRESIDENTIAL RACE OF 2004

All this negative media coverage couldn't have come at a worse time. Bush was gearing up for the 2004 presidential election where he would try to best his father's one-term record. He was gambling that the country wanted a leader who was able to make tough decisions and stand behind them.[11] But a few days after his Democratic opponent, Senator John Kerry of Massachusetts, won the March 2nd super-Tuesday primary, Bush found himself behind by six points in a Gallup poll. Speculation in the media predicted that Kerry might create a "unity" ticket featuring Republican senator John McCain as his running mate—the man Bush had defeated in the 2000 presidential primaries.[12] Although McCain never joined his Democratic colleague on the ticket, Bush's campaign team realized it had an uphill battle to stay in the White House.

The architect of Bush's first presidential victory, Karl Rove, developed a campaign to portray Kerry in a negative light, putting him on the defensive. They would warn that Kerry was weak on national defense, likely to roll back Bush's tax cuts, and supportive of gays at a time when Bush was arguing for a constitutional amendment to declare marriage a union between a man and a woman.[13] This last charge would fire up social conservatives that made up Bush's base. The issue of gay marriage was put front and center in 2004 after San Francisco mayor Gavin Newsom began issuing marriage licenses to gay couples, despite his state's ban on the practice. Massachusetts began allowing gay marriages after its state supreme court ruled on May 17, 2004. While Kerry didn't support gay marriage, he also did not support a constitutional amendment to ban it.

On security matters, Kerry looked like a good choice to challenge Bush. With wars in Iraq and Afghanistan, in addition to the war against terrorism, the decorated Vietnam veteran looked like a strong candidate for commander in chief, especially compared with Bush, whose modest National Guard service record was even in doubt. But the Bush campaign got support from a third party that questioned Kerry's record. Calling themselves "Swift Boat Veterans for Truth," this group of veterans who operated on gunboats as Kerry had in the jungle rivers of Vietnam claimed that Kerry's three Purple Heart medals were undeserved. They were funded largely by a wealthy Texas Republican and included claims by individuals who, the *Washington Post* noted, either were not on Kerry's boat or whose new claims contradicted what they had stated years earlier about Kerry's record. Kerry's shipmates came to his defense, but the barrage of ads raised questions that tarnished Kerry's image as a war hero.[14]

When the Democrats began their convention in Boston in late July, Bush headed for his ranch in Texas to get away from the campaign. He had substituted mountain biking for running after his knees began to go. He told reporters that bike riding made him feel like a kid again. But on this trip, Bush would feel his age after he tumbled over the handlebars during a steep descent, landing on his back with the bike crashing down on top of him. Nevertheless, the health-conscious president managed to complete a rugged 18-mile ride in 80 minutes, suffering only a minor cut on his leg.

When the Republicans held their convention, they featured an unusual keynote speaker: Democratic senator Zell Miller, a firebrand from Georgia. Three years earlier, Miller had introduced Kerry as "one of this nation's authentic heroes." But before the Republicans in Madison Square Garden, Miller launched an attack on Kerry's record, claiming he had repeatedly voted against defense projects, concluding: "This is the man who wants to be commander in chief of our U.S. armed forces? U.S. forces armed with what? Spitballs?"[15]

Kerry criticized Bush for cutting taxes during war time, overselling the danger of Saddam Hussein, failing to capture Osama bin Laden, and not preventing the abuses at Abu Ghraib. But his efforts at attack were not sufficient to carry him to a victory. The race ended on an eerily familiar note, with victory turning on a single state, Ohio, whose 20 electoral votes would decide the winner. A 2 percent final margin in the Buckeye State favored Bush, though nationwide he received more than 50 percent of the vote and beat Kerry by almost 3 million popular votes. (He had lost to Gore by a half million votes four years earlier, while eking out a victory in the Electoral College.)

Although the election yielded Bush a modest victory, he took it as a mandate that gave him political capital to spend. But it wouldn't take him very far, particularly in light of a controversial bill he tried to push to change Social Security, an entitlement program crucial to so many politically active seniors that it is called "the third rail" of politics— which on subway lines is the rail that is electrified and will kill you if you touch it. That capital also would be dissipated by quagmires in Iraq and Afghanistan, and yet another televised national disaster that exposed weaknesses in the Bush administration.

BUSH IN THE BUBBLE

In April 2005, Bush went to Texas to give a major speech on his proposal to reform Social Security. He noted that he had campaigned on the issue the year before in an effort to "mak[e] sure the safety net of Social Security is available for younger generations of Americans."[16] He reminded his Galveston audience of a serious demographic problem: baby boomers, those members of the post–World War II population spike, were nearing retirement age. That spike would lead to record numbers of Social Security recipients, straining the system. Although the issue had been discussed and studied for decades, few presidents had pushed for changes to ensure the financial stability of the retirement program.

Bush's solution involved the creation of a new form of Social Security investment directed by individuals. Specifically, he suggested that "younger Americans ought to be allowed to take some of their own payroll taxes, some of their own money, and invest it in a savings account, a personal savings account, an account they call their own."[17] Bush insisted that such an investment would yield greater returns for Social Security recipients.

Critics noted that this represented a radical change to the system. A safety net overseen as a public trust by the government would now become a private investment. What if those investments went bad? Wouldn't that undermine the whole idea that we're looking after one another? But this was the very thing that attracted Bush, who called for a new "Ownership Society" that displaced the need for public entitlements with new forms of private property. Bush also didn't explain where the trillion dollars or more would come from to divert these payroll taxes—currently used to pay today's Social Security recipients—to this program.

Republicans and Democrats alike were nervous about the proposal. When Bush met with a congressional delegation to discuss the idea, he enthusiastically talked up the plan. But everyone knew the plan was dead on arrival—even Republicans weren't ready to touch the third rail. *Newsweek* used the story to suggest that Bush was out of touch, quoting one House Republican's complaint: "I got the sense that his staff was not telling him the bad news. This was not a case of him thinking positive. He just didn't have any idea of the political realities there. It was like he wasn't briefed at all."[18]

One reason Bush was out of touch is that he did not use his second term as an opportunity to shake up his cabinet and bring in new people with new ideas, as many presidents do. Instead, he replaced Secretary of State Colin Powell—one of the few vocal dissenters in his administration—with Condoleezza Rice, his national security adviser. When his attorney general, John Ashcroft, resigned, he turned to his White House counsel, Alberto Gonzalez, to take over the Justice Department. Bush's press secretary at the time, Scott McClellan, characterized Bush's personnel changes as "elevat[ing] people who were known Bush loyalists," ensuring that Bush remained in a "bubble" (as *Newsweek* called it), where his views would be reinforced.[19]

Loyalty was a primary characteristic that Bush sought in selecting his staff. And, in fact, he showed great loyalty to them, such as when he refused to accept Donald Rumsfeld's resignation after the Abu Ghraib scandal surfaced. Loyalty might have clouded his judgment at the end of 2004, however, when he awarded CIA director George Tenet and the director of Iraq's Coalition Provisional Authority, Jerry Bremer, the Presidential Medal of Freedom, the nation's highest civilian honor. As noted previously, Tenet is credited with two of the worst intelligence failures in history: first, the failure to foresee and warn the president about the attacks on 9/11, and then, the assurance that it was a "slam dunk" that Saddam Hussein had WMDs. Bremer's de-Baathification policies had put tens of thousands of armed Iraqi security forces out of work, giving them time and motivation to attack American troops, which they did regularly. Furthermore, Bremer was unable to account for some $9 billion in reconstruction money.[20]

Perhaps the most disconcerting display of loyalty by Bush would be his support of Michael Brown, Bush's selection to run the Federal Emergency Management Agency (FEMA). Brown didn't have a great background for the job—he had been commissioner of the International Arabian Horse Association before the appointment. Brown had found his way into Bush's cabinet through loyalty to a third party. Joe M. Allbaugh, who managed Bush's 2000 presidential campaign, had been friends with Brown for 30 years.[21] Unfortunately, Brown took the job just before the most destructive natural disaster in American history.

HURRICANE KATRINA

Hurricane Katrina, which developed over the last week of August 2005, affected the Gulf Coast from Florida to Texas, hitting Louisiana, Mississippi, and Alabama particularly hard. Its storm surge breached New Orleans's protective levee system, and left 80 percent of the city under water.[22] Hurricane Katrina caused almost $100 billion in property damage. Four hurricanes in the previous year (Charley, Frances, Ivan, and Jeanne) managed to wreak only $46 billion in damages. Three hundred thousand homes were damaged enough to require evacuation.[23]

Millions of people lost power from the raging winds, which spread across an area the size of Great Britain. In the largest dislocation since the Dust Bowl of the 1930s, three-quarters of a million people were displaced.[24] Eighteen hundred people died, making Katrina the most lethal hurricane since 1928.[25]

Steps taken by local, state, and federal authorities before the storm hit largely failed. New Orleans mayor Ray Nagin ordered an evacuation of the city 48 hours before the storm hit but didn't make it mandatory for another 24 hours. And the large number of poor people in the city undermined the evacuation effort, since 100,000 residents had no automobiles.[26] Hundreds of buses that might have been used to evacuate residents were under water. The city had gotten a $7 million federal grant for communications equipment to use in just such an emergency, but the batteries were quickly drained, leaving the city without a means to centrally direct efforts.

Governor Kathleen Blanco made a general request to the White House the day after the hurricane hit, asking Bush for "everything you've got," following that request later with a list: "40,000 troops; urban search-and-rescue teams; buses; amphibious personnel carriers; mobile morgues; trailers of water, ice and food; base camps; staging areas; housing; and communications systems."[27] But, federal deliveries were hampered by the storm damage and the lack of adequate preposi-tioned supplies and equipment.

Despite mistakes at the state and local levels, the most conspicuous failure came from FEMA director Michael Brown. He waited almost 5 hours after the storm hit before he proposed sending 1,000 federal workers to help. That proposal was hard to send up the chain of com-mand. After 9/11, Bush and Congress had created the Department of Homeland Security (DHS) to coordinate efforts to fight terrorism. FEMA had been relocated under the new department, and many of its funds had been redirected to preparation for terrorist attacks. Brown had to go through DHS secretary Michael Chertoff for support. DHS assumed that state and local authorities would take charge of disasters for the first 72 hours, but Katrina had already wiped out their capacity to deal with the catastrophe.

In an effort to evacuate poor residents to higher ground, 10,000–12,000 people were moved into New Orleans's Superdome. But high winds prevented deliveries of food and water to the stadium for days. Television cameras covered the unfolding disaster at the football sta-dium as toilets backed up, the August sun began to bake those under the uncooled dome, and the hungry and injured evacuees became rest-less. DHS secretary Chertoff seemed oblivious to what many Ameri-cans saw unfolding, dismissing concerns over chaos at the stadium as mere rumors.[28]

More dramatic footage emerged of people standing on the tops of their houses begging to be rescued. Bodies floated down the middle of the streets of the Big Easy. Reports came in of the government's bum-bling. Bush's communication team made a poor decision in releas-ing a photo of him looking down at the disaster from *Air Force One*, making him appear out of touch. The same idea was conveyed when he went to Mississippi and stood before the devastated vacation home of Senate Republican Majority Leader Trent Lott, assuring everyone that it would be rebuilt and that he would come back and sit on Lott's porch. One can only imagine how poor homeless residents of New Orleans felt.

In an exchange with reporters, Bush tried to explain the inadequacy of the federal response when he insisted that the failure of the levees following the hurricane had not been anticipated. But reporters quickly discovered that government studies had warned of that very possibility for decades. With the public losing confidence in the government, Bush found himself in front of cameras standing beside Michael Brown. He praised the inexperienced FEMA director, insisting: "Brownie, you're doing a heck of a job. The FEMA Director is working 24—they're working 24 hours a day."[29] Scott McClellan, whose job had been to present the administration in its best light, reported years later:

> Even Brown looked embarrassed, and no wonder; most Americans had already concluded that the FEMA director was in over his head. They were simply beginning to wonder how and when he would get the ax and who would replace him. (Brown ultimately resigned ten days later, on September 12.) For Bush to commend him publicly suggested either that the president's well-known belief in personal loyalty was overwhelming his judgment or that he still didn't realize how bad things were on the Gulf Coast. Either way, the incident said something bad about the Bush administration.[30]

In the end, the federal government's effort was significant, but late. All told, the Coast Guard rescued and evacuated more than 33,000 people from New Orleans, FEMA Urban Search and Rescue teams saved another 6,500, and the Department of Transportation assembled 1,100 buses to evacuate New Orleans residents to several states and the District of Columbia. The Department of Defense mounted the largest civilian airlift on American soil in U.S. history.[31] But, the U.S. government appeared overwhelmed, as even poor countries like Cuba offered help.

Federal Emergency Management Agency (FEMA) director Michael Brown points out map locations to President Bush and Department of Homeland Security director Michael Chertoff (front, second from right) at an equipment shed in Mobile, Alabama. President Bush toured the region on September 2, 2005, five days after Hurricane Katrina made landfall in the New Orleans area. AP Photo/APTN.

Two weeks after Hurricane Katrina, President Bush accepted responsibility for the federal government's poor response to the disaster, offering: "To the extent that the federal government didn't fully do its job right, I take responsibility."[32] He addressed the nation on September 15, 2005, from Jackson Square in the French Quarter of New Orleans, assuring the battered residents "that our whole nation cares about you, and in the journey ahead you're not alone," adding: "tonight I also offer this pledge of the American people: Throughout the area hit by the hurricane, we will do what it takes, we will stay as long as it takes, to help citizens rebuild their communities and their lives." For the rest of his presidency, he would be criticized for not doing enough. Restoring New Orleans to its former glory was certainly an impossible task, but after the federal fumbling over the disaster, Louisiana residents had lost faith in Bush. Four years after the disaster, when Bush left office, New Orleans had reclaimed only about 70 percent of its pre-Katrina population.[33]

The Hurricane Katrina debacle left Bush hobbled for the rest of his presidency. With three years left to go, he began resembling a lame duck, incapable of mustering the kind of support he had enjoyed in his first term. Yet, despite this drag from his sagging popularity and from the seemingly unending wars in Iraq and Afghanistan, Bush's lame-duck status seemed to embolden him to act fearlessly in an attempt to shape his legacy.

NOTES

1. Scott McClellan, *What Happened: Inside the Bush White House and Washington's Culture of Deception* (New York: Public Affairs, 2008), 204.

2. Ibid., 200.

3. Ibid., 202–203.

4. George W. Bush, "The President's News Conference," *Weekly Compilation of Presidential Documents* 40, no. 16 (2004): 590.

5. Ibid., 584.

6. Ibid., 585.

7. McClellan, *What Happened*, 205.

8. Ibid., 207.

9. R. Jeffrey Smith and Josh White, "General Granted Latitude at Prison," *Washington Post*, 12 June 2004, A1.

10. George W. Bush, "President Bush Meets with Al Arabiya Television on Wednesday: Interview of the President by Al Arabiya Television," The Map Room, 5 May 2004, http://georgewbush-whitehouse.archives.gov/news/releases/2004/05/20040505-2.html.

11. Bill Sammon, *Strategery: How George W. Bush Is Defeating Terrorists, Outwitting Democrats, and Confounding the Mainstream Media* (Washington, DC: Regnery Publishing, 2006), 11.

12. Ibid., 16.

13. Ibid., 17.

14. "Swift Boat Smears," Editorial, *Washington Post*, 12 August 2004, A22.

15. John F. Harris, "Cheney Calls Kerry Unfit; Democrat Joins Vice President in Barrage Against Challenger," *Washington Post*, 2 September 2004, A1.

16. "President Participates in Social Security Roundtable in Texas," The University of Texas Medical Branch, Galveston, Texas, 26 April 2005, http://georgewbush-whitehouse.archives.gov/news/releases/2005/04/20050426-3.html.

17. Ibid.

18. Evan Thomas and Richard Wolffe, "Bush in the Bubble," *Newsweek*, December 19, 2005, 30–39,

19. McClellan, *What Happened*, 247.

20. "Audit: U.S. Lost Track of $9 Billion in Iraq Funds," *CNN.com*, 31 January 2005.

21. Elizabeth Bumiller, "Casualty of a Firestorm," *New York Times*, 10 September 2005, A11.

22. *The Federal Response to Hurricane Katrina: Lessons Learned*, Special White House Report, February 23, 2006, 1, http://georgewbush-whitehouse.archives.gov/reports/katrina-lessons-learned/.

23. *Federal Response to Hurricane Katrina*, 7.

24. *Federal Response to Hurricane Katrina*, 8.

25. Estimates differ widely, given the difficulty in accounting for the missing. The White House reports 1,330 deaths (*Federal Response to Hurricane Katrina*, 153). The Louisiana Department of Health and Hospitals puts the number of Louisiana deaths at 1,464 ("Reports of Missing and Deceased," *Louisiana Department of Health and Hospitals*, 6 August 2006 [http://www.dhh.louisiana.gov/offices/page.asp?ID=192&Detail=5248]). *The Times-Picayune* reports the number of Louisiana deaths at 1,577 (Michelle Hunter, "Deaths of Evacuees Push Toll to 1,577," *Times-Picayune*, 19 May 2006 [online]). Deaths in other states were in the hundreds. The *St. Petersberg Times* in 2007 put the "official death toll" at 1,836, though it did not cite the basis for that number ("Ask the Times," *St. Petersberg Times*, 19 October 2007, A2).

26. Mark Thompson, Amanda Ripley, Karen Tumulty, James Carney, Nathan Thornburgh, Cathy Booth Thomas, Tim Padgett, Brian Bennett, Hilary Hylton, Siobhan Morrissey, Michael Peltier, Eric Roston, Mike Allen, and Sally B. Donnelly, "Four Places the System Broke Down," *Time*, 19 September 2005, 34–41.

27. Ibid.

28. McClellan, *What Happened*, 285.

29. Ibid., 288.

30. Ibid., 289.

31. *Federal Response to Hurricane Katrina*, 38–40.

32. Richard Sisk, "Prez Takes Blame for 'Cane Blunders," *(New York) Daily News*, 14 September 2005, A2.

33. "Census Bureau: New Orleans Population Revised Up," Associated Press, 7 January 2010.

Chapter 10

THE LAME DUCK

The last years of Bush's presidency following the bungling of Hurricane Katrina were turbulent ones for the man from Midland. The Iraq War would take a significant turn for the worse. His party would suffer serious setbacks in two straight elections. He would turn over the keys to the White House to a Democrat in the midst of the most serious economic crisis since the Great Depression. Yet through it all, he remained upbeat, even defiant, and took bold steps to address the crises he faced.

SECTARIAN VIOLENCE IN IRAQ

Although sectarian violence had been growing in Iraq since the fall of Saddam Hussein, it threatened to become a full-scale civil war after February 22, 2006, when Sunni insurgents attacked a Shia holy site in Samarra. The attackers detonated two bombs inside the al-Askari Mosque. The mosque, which is more than 1,000 years old, is one of the most important Shia mosques in the world. The explosions shattered the mosque's distinctive golden dome, destroying a treasured landmark of Shia Muslims around the world. A second attack on the Golden Mosque a year later destroyed two minarets that remained.

Bush quickly condemned the attacks, blaming "terrorists in Iraq" whom he called "enemies of all faiths and of all humanity." He pleaded with Iraqis "to exercise restraint in the wake of this tragedy and to pursue justice in accordance with the laws and Constitution of Iraq." He warned that "[v]iolence will only contribute to what the terrorists sought to achieve by this act."[1] But Bush's entreaties could not stem the revenge attacks that would follow. Almost immediately, a round of indiscriminate attacks began against Iraqi Sunnis, who were dragged from their Baghdad homes and executed in the streets.

Although insurgents against the new Iraqi government were certainly to blame, the attack reflected frustration by Sunnis with their new role in Iraq. Iraq had been governed by Sunnis under Saddam Hussein; but with a majority Shia government in charge, the country was now in the hands of those who had suffered under the regime. Sunnis overwhelmingly opposed the new Iraqi constitution approved in large numbers by Shia and Kurdish voters in 2005. Parliamentary elections on December 15, 2005, saw voters casting ballots largely along ethnic lines.

Despite the Bush administration's efforts to help Iraq develop a centralized, ethnically diverse, and religiously neutral national security force overseen by evenhanded administrators, the army and police were viewed as the arm of a Shia administration. Furthermore, national security forces were inadequate, so local militias began filling the vacuum, and those militias were largely Shia controlled. These gangs with guns often attacked Sunnis, leading Sunnis to fight back, creating a cycle of violence.

The increasing violence ensured that American forces would be tied down in Iraq for years to come, playing referee between the warring factions. The alternative was to leave Iraq and allow the ethic groups to fight it out, creating casualties on a catastrophic scale and potentially destabilizing the entire Middle East. Furthermore, the power vacuum undoubtedly would lead Iraq's neighbors to jump into the fray, especially Iran, which shares a long border with Iraq. Because Iran has been a vocal opponent of the United States since the Iranian Revolution that unseated the American-backed Shah of Iran in 1979, abandoning Iraq might mean ceding it to an enemy.

In the face of rising violence and an Iraqi government that seemed to make little progress in taking control of its own security, Bush kept insisting that Americans needed to be patient and "stay the course." That stance included keeping Donald Rumsfeld on as Secretary of Defense, despite calls for new leadership and a new direction. The American public was losing confidence in Bush, Rumsfeld, and the Republicans on foreign policy—an area where they typically edged out Democrats who were often considered too soft on our enemies. In the midterm congressional elections at the end of 2006, the voters demonstrated their dissatisfaction with the status quo and overwhelming voted for Democrats. The Republicans lost 6 seats in the Senate and 27 seats in the House, giving the Democrats control of both houses for the first time since 1994.

The loss of Congress was a blow to Bush, who had enjoyed the support of a friendly legislative branch during his first six years in office. Republican committees had not held the president's feet to the fire over the failures of 9/11, the elusive weapons of mass destruction used to justify the invasion of Iraq, the questionable use of warrantless wiretapping, the scandal over torture at Abu Ghraib, or the weak federal response to Hurricane Katrina. With the Democrats in charge, he was now open to scrutiny as he had never been before.

Following the losses, Bush decided it was time to let Donald Rumsfeld step down. The day after the midterm losses, he announced Rumsfeld's departure and nominated Robert Gates to be secretary of defense. The former director of the CIA, president of Texas A&M, and member of the bipartisan commission on the 9/11 attacks was so well respected that President Obama kept him on in that position after he assumed the presidency. Republicans who lost in the face of Bush's obstinate "stay the course" position were resentful that Bush hadn't taken action a few weeks earlier.

Not only did Bush change the leadership at the Pentagon, he announced a radical new military plan in an address to the nation on January 10, 2007. In that speech he admitted, "[i]t is clear that we need to change our strategy in Iraq." He explained that there were too few troops to secure areas that had been cleared of terrorists—something General Eric Shinseki, the army chief of staff, had told Congress before the 2003 invasion, only to be rebuked by Bush's Iraq War planning team. The lack of troops meant that when troops cleared an area and left, the terrorists would move back in. Bush called for a "surge" in troops in Iraq by about 20,000. He insisted that getting control of the security situation would ensure that "daily life will improve, Iraqis will gain confidence in their leaders, and the government will have the breathing space it needs to make progress in other critical areas."[2] Eventually, the return to peaceful routines would allow the Iraqis to come together and rule their own country.

Bush's plan was radical. It put a strain on a military already stretched to the breaking point, with soldiers serving multiple deployments and many suffering from injuries, physical exhaustion, and post-traumatic stress disorder. It flew in the face of the recommendations of a bipartisan commission appointed by the new Democratic-controlled Congress. That commission was cochaired by Bush's father's secretary of state, James Baker, and former Democratic congressman Lee Hamilton. It recommended in a December 2006 report that the United States initiate a robust diplomatic effort to involve Iraq's neighbors in a stabilization plan (which would require an effort on the Israeli-Palestinian peace front as well) and begin a complete drawdown of American combat forces accompanied by a shift in their role to that of training Iraqi forces. Bush was doing the opposite of what the commission recommended, so Democrats and even some Republicans criticized the surge plan. Senate Democratic Majority Leader Harry Reid went so far as to call for the president to admit that "the war is lost."[3]

Bush ignored congressional calls to draw down forces. He was not ready to admit defeat and leave Iraq. But the surge, which ballooned to 30,000 additional troops, meant more confrontations with those engaged in a fledgling civil war and, initially, more American casualties. The death toll among American troops would crest with the surge in 2007, passing 900 (and 1,000 including the war in Afghanistan), up 10 percent from the previous year.

The counterinsurgency operation supported by the surge and run by General David Petraeus brought soldiers out of fortified compounds and into neighborhoods surrounding Baghdad. This new deployment allowed the soldiers to get to know the people, form networks, and patrol regularly. In the troubled Anbar province, Sunnis actually reached out to the Americans to protect them against Al Qaeda leaders who attacked those who did not fight the Americans. The Anbar Awakening, as it was known, became a model for Petraeus in turning communities against the agitators. Instead of trying to fight the militias exercising local control, the military began working with them, providing money, logistical support, and even weapons to foster their work as the eyes, ears, and security adjuncts of the military. Petraeus even got unexpected help from one of the most prominent critics of the American occupation, Shiite cleric Muqtada al-Sadr. In August 2007, he surprised everyone by ordering his Mahdi army to stop attacking American forces.[4]

Bush's bold move soon began to pay off. By 2008, the number of American casualties had dropped by two-thirds. That number halved again during the first year of Obama's presidency. On the other hand, the surge turned into more of an escalation, with the additional troops staying in Iraq until President Obama, who campaigned on pulling out of Iraq, began withdrawing troops from major cities in June 2009. The current plan calls for a complete withdrawal of combat forces by the end of 2011, but the security situation was still called "fragile" by General Petraeus in 2010.[5] Most commentators believe that tens of thousands of U.S. troops will remain in Iraq for years to come, regardless of who is president.

THE ECONOMIC CRISIS

Just over one year before Bush finished his second term in office in December 2007, the worst recession in 70 years began. The primary cause was related to a housing crisis. For many years, housing prices had been increasing in value as more and more Americans became home buyers vying for the same properties. Easy credit, relatively low mortgage rates (including low down payment, adjustable rate mortgages), and a belief that housing prices would continue to rise led more people into the market and more financial institutions to offer mortgages. At the same time, the world was awash in money seeking investments with good returns, and enterprising financial institutions began bundling together mortgages and selling securities to back them, providing a better return than was available in, for example, U.S. treasury bills. Rating agencies seemed as optimistic as consumers about the stability of the housing market and gave high ratings to these securities, encouraging more investment.

But, the inevitable happened: the housing bubble burst. Adjustable rates mortgages were starting to reset at higher rates, people purchasing *subprime* mortgages found that they had taken on more debt than they could afford, declining housing prices put many mortgage holders under water (owing more than their homes were worth), and security-backed mortgages began taking a hit. That was bad enough, but some big financial firms had insured those mortgage-backed securities against losses (through a new instrument called *credit default swaps*) and now they were going to have to pay out hundreds of billions of dollars to cover losses from those tanking securities.

The government shared some of the blame for this problem. President Reagan had begun the deregulation of the banking industry. President Clinton passed reforms that allowed traditionally conservative commercial banks to start operating more like investment banks in some areas. The Securities and Exchange Commission under George W. Bush had allowed banks to leverage their investments and take on much more debt. Federal regulators had refused to regulate credit default swaps and other such *derivatives* contracts, which had increased exponentially in recent years, creating enormous risks for some of the largest financial institutions in the United States.

The first casualty of the crisis was one of the top-five investment banks in the country, Bear Stearns. Two of the company's hedge funds had invested heavily in subprime mortgages—those were the riskiest consumer mortgages, made to customers with the weakest credit. In June 2007, the funds collapsed, threatening the venerable firm's survival. In March 2008, Bush administration officials brokered a deal for JPMorgan Chase to take over Bear Stearns. The U.S. government agreed to take on $30 billion in liabilities to sweeten the deal. In September, Fannie Mae and Freddie Mac, two government-sponsored mortgage lenders who control the lion's share of the U.S. mortgage market, began teetering on the brink of bankruptcy, and the government took control of them. When another huge investment firm, Lehman Brothers, began defaulting because of the collapse in the housing market, the Bush administration decided not to intervene and allowed the company to fold. The same month, the government injected $85 billion into the huge insurance giant AIG, which had issued billions of dollars in credit default swaps, preventing another bankruptcy. The choice to save Bear Stearns and AIG while leaving Lehman Brothers to fail left many on Wall Street unsure about when the government would intervene.

Bush himself was philosophically opposed to government bailouts. Like most Republicans, he was a believer in markets and preferred to let companies that make poor investments fail, making room for stronger, better managed companies. But when his treasury secretary, Henry Paulson, warned him that allowing the collapse of the largest players in the financial system would lead to a second Great Depression, even he jumped on board. He pushed Congress to pass a massive $700 billion rescue package to buy up toxic assets that were dragging down financial institutions and the economy. In his weekly radio address of September 20, 2008, Bush admitted that "[t]hese measures require us to put a significant amount of taxpayer dollars on the line," but he said that he was "convinced that this bold approach will cost American families far less than the alternative." He warned that "[f]urther stress on our financial markets would cause massive job losses, devastate retirement accounts, further erode housing values, and dry up new loans for homes, cars, and college tuitions."[6]

Even if Bush were successful in reaching the American people, he was stymied by members of his own party, who voted 2–1 against the measure in the House of Representatives, where it was defeated on September 29, 2008. The stock market responded negatively to this failure, suffering one of its biggest one-day losses since Black Monday on October 19, 1987. Indeed, the decline on Wall Street had begun a year earlier, following the Dow Jones Industrial Average's peak of 14,164. But the financial crisis and Washington's inability to address it accelerated that decline, with the Dow hitting 9,625 on election day, November 4, 2008; and 7,949 on January 20, 2009, the day Barack Obama was sworn in as Bush's successor. All told, the market lost almost 44 percent of its value during the last 16 months of Bush's presidency.

The collapse of the stock market led to the devaluation of the retirement portfolios of millions of seniors, causing a great deal of pain and forcing many to postpone retirement. But, for the economy as a whole, the collapse of the financial system was much worse. Cash-strapped banks stopped lending. Businesses could no longer get credit. Without that credit they couldn't sell cars or other goods requiring financing. They also couldn't cover their payrolls, leading to layoffs. The fall of consumer confidence followed the collapse of housing prices, which served as piggy banks for many Americans (who took out equity loans on their homes) and made everyone feel less confident in their own finances. Americans cut back on purchases, which hurt the economy, which led to further job losses, which again undermined consumer confidence, in a vicious spiral. At the end of 2007 when the crisis began, unemployment was 5.0 percent. But by the time Obama was inaugurated, it had jumped to 7.7 percent and would continue its upward trend until it topped 10 percent in October 2009.

Rising unemployment and dire warning about the consequences of inaction led Congress to finally pass a modified version of Bush's rescue package a month after its defeat. But, the crisis had a momentum of its own. All the government could hope for was to help stem the bleeding, not cure the patient, in the short term. Obama would end up bailing out much of the auto industry, passing his own massive stimulus package, and trying to smooth things over with scores of countries dragged down by the flagging U.S. economy and by their own investments in American housing and financial firms that had gone sour.

SHAPING THE U.S. SUPREME COURT

On July 1, 2005, Justice Sandra Day O'Connor announced her retirement from the U.S. Supreme Court. President Reagan had originally appointed O'Connor, who was the first woman to serve on the High Court. Bush nominated Judge John G. Roberts to take her place. However, before the confirmation was complete, Chief Justice William Rehnquist died from complications with thyroid cancer. Bush withdrew his nomination of Roberts to replace O'Connor and pushed him for the chief justice position. Roberts was quickly confirmed, replacing a conservative with another conservative and maintaining a close ideological balance between conservatives and liberals on the court.

Following Roberts's confirmation, Bush chose a loyal confidante to replace O'Connor, nominating his White House counsel Harriet Miers. Miers was a fellow Texan who had worked for a law firm in Dallas most of her professional life before Bush recruited her to work in the White House. Bush touted her accomplishments in urging her confirmation, calling her "a pioneer for women lawyers" because she was "the first woman to be hired at her law firm, the first woman to become president of that firm, the first woman to lead a large law firm in the State of

Texas, the first woman head of the Dallas Bar Association, and the first woman elected as president of the State Bar of Texas."[7]

Bush's fellow Republicans were not so enamored of this Texas trailblazer. Despite her legal career, her work focused largely on managing her law firm rather than litigating. And, unlike most nominees to the High Court, she had never been a judge. The narrowness of her experience with the law showed when the Senate Judiciary Committee began meeting with her and asking questions. Although Bush assured his Republican colleagues that she would be "a good conservative judge," they expressed concerns about her position on core issues like abortion, where what record there was seemed to lean toward supporting abortion rights. Miers's legal career apparently did not prepare her to answer questions about the nuances of constitutional law.

Bush defended his choice in an October 11, 2005, interview on the *Today Show* with NBC's Matt Lauer, insisting that he had taken some senators up on their suggestion to look for candidates outside the "judicial monastery."[8] Lauer noted that leading conservatives, including Senator Trent Lott, Pat Buchanan, George Will, and Bill Kristol had raised concerns about Miers. Bush insisted that the country simply needed to get to know her as he had. He predicted that she would be confirmed. Whether that prediction was a vote of confidence for one who had been loyal to him or the statement of a president out of touch with the politics of the situation, his prediction was way off the mark. Facing an uphill battle, three weeks into the process the White House announced that Miers had withdrawn her nomination.

A week after Miers's withdrawal, Bush nominated Samuel Alito, a Court of Appeals judge with a solidly conservative record, for O'Connor's seat. Alito had a long track record, serving 15 years as a federal judge. He was reliably conservative, defending the display of religious symbols on government property, giving more leeway to police in conducting searches, challenging Congress's authority to ban machine guns, and even insisting that a state could require a pregnant woman to notify her husband before getting an abortion. These positions and others made Alito "a darling of the conservative movement."[9]

Of course, this record also made Alito a villain to many Democrats. Although Democrats threatened to filibuster his nomination, Alito was confirmed on January 31, 2006, in a 58–42 vote largely along party lines. Alito has proved to be more conservative than O'Connor, if only because the first woman on the High Court had been a legislator who preferred to decide issues on narrow grounds and leave greater authority to democratically elected lawmakers.

Bush's nominations to the Supreme Court did not really change the balance between five mostly conservative members and four mostly liberal members, but it maintained the conservative dominance and placed his stamp on the slowest-changing branch of government.

THE U.S. ATTORNEYS SCANDAL

The next year, Bush would find himself embroiled in another controversy with another Texan who had served as his White House counsel: Alberto Gonzales. Gonzales was confirmed as attorney general, replacing the outgoing John Ashcroft, on a mostly party-line vote. Some Democrats were troubled by his defense of presidential powers in warrantless wiretapping and the use of enhanced interrogation techniques that some thought amounted to torture.

But the issue that would hound Gonzales out of office concerned the firing of seven U.S. attorneys. Although these attorneys serve at the pleasure of the president, these firings were unusual because the attorneys in question had been given positive reviews for their work. An e-mail surfaced showing that Gonzales's chief of staff, D. Kyle Sampson, sought to retain U.S. attorneys who were, in his words, "loyal Bushies." This apparent politicization of the Justice Department brought investigations by Congress. Yet when Gonzales appeared before the Senate Judiciary Committee, he repeatedly said he didn't recall how the decisions had been made. Even conservative Republican senator Jeff Sessions of Alabama complained: "Well, I guess I'm concerned about your recollection, really, because it's not that long ago. It was an important issue. And that's troubling to me, I've got to tell you."[10] Congress asked Bush's White House counsel, Harriet Miers, and his domestic adviser, Karl Rove, to testify about the firings, since the White House appeared to be involved. Bush invoked executive privilege and barred the testimony. Only after he left office did a court rule in favor of Congress and the two were forced to testify.

A Justice Department inquiry in 2009 found that political considerations seemed to play a role in at least four of the firings. Most troubling was the firing of David Iglesias, whom Karl Rove accused of not working hard enough to bring voter fraud charges against the Democratic opponent of a Republican candidate running for Congress in Arizona.[11] Gonzales resigned in September 2007, two months after the Senate attempted (and failed) in a vote of no confidence against the attorney general. Bush didn't acknowledge any basis for the controversy. He complained that a good man's name had been dragged through the mud but accepted the resignation. His loyalty did not permit him to acknowledge problems that his own officials had made for themselves.

CHALLENGING DEMOCRATS AND REPUBLICANS ALIKE

Although Bush's second term would be remembered for his failures on Hurricane Katrina, his bold decision to surge the number of troops in Iraq, and his grappling with the worst economy since the Great Depression, he was involved on several other notable fronts. These often put him at odds with his own party or with the Democrats. But he was feistier during his second term—perhaps spurred on by his lame-duck status—and seemed more willing to defy others where he believed in a cause.

In July 2006, he finally decided to veto his first bill—taking longer than any president since John Quincy Adams to do so. But his choice on where to take a stand was a controversial one—his own party was in charge when Congress authorized an extension of funding to support embryonic stem cell research. Although a majority of Americans supported embryonic stem cell research, with its potential to cure cancer, spinal cord injuries, and countless other maladies, Bush rejected the extension of funding, claiming: "This bill would support the taking of innocent human life in the hope of finding medical benefits for others. It crosses a moral boundary that our decent society needs to respect, so I vetoed it."[12]

Bush had demonstrated that same unbending support for innocent life a year and a half earlier when a comatose woman named Terri Schiavo was scheduled to have her feeding tube removed. The case involved a dispute over whether her feeding tube could be removed, with her husband arguing that is what she would have wanted and her parents opposing the move. Bush's brother Jeb, as Florida governor, had fought to prevent the removal of the feeding tube. With all legal obstacles overcome and the removal of the tube imminent, Congress intervened, passing the "Palm Sunday Compromise" on March 20, 2005, with only three senators in session. Bush flew to the White House from his Crawford ranch to sign the bill at 1 A.M. on Palm Sunday. The unprecedented interference of the federal government in this family decision was quickly overturned by the courts, and Schiavo was allowed to die. The American public strongly opposed this federal intrusion into personal medical decisions.

On another medical front, Bush stood against an expansion of the State Children's Health Insurance Program (SCHIP), which would have extended health insurance coverage to 6–10 million children. The Democrats were in charge when this 2007 bill came before Bush, who rejected it as "an incremental step toward the goal of Government-run health care for every American."[13] He argued that it would move millions of poor children from private insurance coverage to government-run insurance coverage, increasing costs and eventually moving the government into the health care business.

Bush was more generous in funding efforts to combat HIV and AIDS in Africa. He first proposed a massive $15 billion plan to fight the African epidemic in his first term. By the end of his second term, in summer 2008, he worked with a Democratic Congress to increase that amount to $48 billion, which also helped with malaria and tuberculosis on that continent. Bush is credited with helping to save tens of millions of Africans suffering from HIV/AIDS. Bush seemed to want to help those unable to help themselves, but to require more from Americans who are poor but able to pay their own way, especially if that risks interfering with the work of the free market. These two decisions on funding medical care reflect a moral stance that supports charity, while defending free markets and encouraging self-reliance.

Bush faced vehement opponents of his own party in trying to develop an immigration policy to deal with the more than 12 million illegal immigrants living in our country. In the interest of national security, Bush had gotten agreement to begin construction of a fence spanning much of the U.S.-Mexican border. Now he wanted to deal with those already inside the country. He proposed allowing those inside to come out of the shadows, register for a two-year guest worker card, and then return briefly to their home country before paying a fee and applying for citizenship.

In one sense, Bush was appealing to his traditional business base. As a former businessman in Texas, he was very familiar with the problems of illegal immigrants crossing over to Texas for better jobs. He also knew that many businesses, especially in agriculture, relied heavily on undocumented workers. His proposal called for a temporary worker program that would meet the needs of business, while alleviating the pressure on the borders from those seeking to enter the country illegally and improving national security. As he urged in his April 8, 2006, weekly radio address:

> A temporary-worker program would create a legal way to match willing foreign workers with willing American employers to fill jobs that no American is available to do. By creating a legal channel for those seeking temporary work in America, we would reduce the number of people trying to sneak across the border. This would free up law enforcement officers to focus on criminals, drug dealers, terrorists, and others who mean us harm. A temporary-worker program would also improve security by creating tamper-proof identification cards, so we can keep track of every temporary worker who is here on a legal basis and identify those who are not.[14]

But the Republican Party was pulled in two directions on this issue: The business interests that aligned with them might support a worker program to avoid penalties for hiring undocumented workers and to ensure the flow of cheap labor. But social conservatives in the party complained that illegal immigrants were breaking the law, changing American society, and taking American jobs. They referred to Bush's plan as "amnesty" for those who broke the law by entering the United States illegally. Although the Senate passed a bipartisan version of the measure, Republican House members facing tight races in the midterm elections stood against the measure. Conservative talk show hosts

lambasted the proposal. Protesters clogged town hall meetings and engaged in letter-writing campaigns to oppose what they saw as reward-
ing illegal behavior through the plan pushed by Bush and the Senate.
Facing concerns from House members about to face voters at the polls,
the measure died in the House.

But avoiding this hot potato issue didn't save many Republicans. The
party was reeling from the indictment of House Majority Leader Tom
DeLay over alleged money laundering in a campaign finance scheme;
a sex scandal involving Republican congressman Mark Foley, who was
discovered to have repeatedly sent suggestive text messages to male
congressional pages while Republican House leaders allegedly turned
a blind eye; and the failure of Congress to even pass a budget, leading
to charges that the 109th was a "do-nothing" Congress. After the midterm elections ended, Democrats controlled of both houses of Congress
for the first time since 1994. Bush commented on the election in his
usual down-home style, admitting: "It was a thumping."[15]

Bush would suffer his own rebuke at the end of his second term.
During his final visit to Iraq in December 2008, he hoped to tout the
achievements of five-and-a-half years of life without Saddam Hussein.
While noting successes in calming the violence and building up Iraq at
a news conference in Baghdad, Iraqi reporter Muntadar al-Zaidi yelled
at the president in Arabic and threw one of his shoes at Bush's head,
then the second one. Bush reacted quickly, dodging both missiles, and
the man was quickly taken into custody. Bush immediately made light
of the attack, noting: "All I can report is that it was a size 10," drawing
laughter from the nervous audience.[16] Other journalists in the room
apologized for the incident, insisting it did not represent Iraqi feelings.
But Iraqi demonstrators hailed the man as a hero before news cameras,
reflecting their frustration with the ongoing occupation and the slow
progress in rebuilding their country.

One of Bush's last acts as president came two weeks before he left
office. The pro-business conservative who had eased many regulations
on industries, rejected concerns over global warming and sought to
work with trade groups to develop what he called "commonsense legislation," decided to leave a physical legacy of his time in the White
House.[17] On January 6, 2009, Bush used his presidential authority
to proclaim three protected environmental areas in the Pacific: the

Marianas Trench, the Pacific Remote Islands, and the Rose Atoll Marine National Monuments. These three areas would now be protected environmental ecosystems spanning 200,000 square miles of ocean. The most remarkable among them is the Marianas Trench, located off the Mariana Islands, a U.S. territory in the Pacific. The underwater trench features the lowest point on earth, stretching almost 7 miles deep, where active thermal vents and unimaginable water pressure has given rise to some of the strangest creatures ever discovered. Bush's executive action ensured that these unique habitats and the wildlife, coral reefs, and geologic features would be protected from destructive activities. Bush quoted and endorsed a sentiment of Theodore Roosevelt, the first great conservationist president, who stated: "Of all the questions which can come before the Nation, short of the actual preservation of its existence in a great war, there is none which compares in importance with leaving this land even a better land for our descendants than it is for us."[18]

THE END OF A TURBULENT PRESIDENCY

On January 15, 2009, Bush gave his final televised address to the nation. Speaking from the East Room of the White House, he noted that he had asked the networks "for a final opportunity to share some thoughts on the journey that we have traveled together and the future of our nation." He congratulated Obama on his election, wishing him well; thanked his supporters; and gave his own account of his job as president. He noted the horror of 9/11 and his response to it. He touted the necessary retooling of our intelligence and security apparatus in light of the new threat, the fight against the terrorists, and the transformation of Afghanistan from a haven for terrorists to a fledgling democracy. He tied the Iraq War to the larger effort to fight terrorism and to promote democracy around the world. He admitted there had been controversy over his decisions in these matters but noted that no other terrorist attacks had been made against the homeland.

On the domestic front he touted higher student test scores, the new Medicare drug benefit, tax cuts, protection for "[v]ulnerable human life," better support for veterans, a cleaner environment, two Supreme Court appointments, and his work on faith-based initiatives. He noted that his administration took "decisive measures to safeguard our economy" in the face of the financial crisis.

He came close to admitting he had made mistakes but urged respect for his convictions, stating:

> Like all who have held this office before me, I have experienced setbacks. And there are things I would do differently if given the chance. Yet I've always acted with the best interests of our country in mind. I have followed my conscience and done what I thought was right. You may not agree with some of the tough decisions I have made. But I hope you can agree that I was willing to make the tough decisions.[19]

He urged Americans to stay vigilant in the face of global threats. He noted that some people were uncomfortable with his language of good and evil, but insisted that "good and evil are present in this world, and between the two there can be no compromise." He expressed faith in the American character, ending his speech with stories of brave American soldiers in Iraq and their families. In concluding, he stated:

> It has been the privilege of a lifetime to serve as your President. There have been good days and tough days. But every day I have been inspired by the greatness of our country and uplifted by the goodness of our people. I have been blessed to represent this nation we love. And I will always be honored to carry a title that means more to me than any other: citizen of the United States of America.[20]

After Barack Obama took the oath of office as the first African American president in U.S. history, he began his inaugural address by acknowledging his predecessor, stating: "I thank President Bush for his service to our Nation, as well as the generosity and cooperation he has shown throughout this transition." Obama's next words were at odds this expression of gratitude and with Bush's gloss on his presidency five days earlier. The new president described what Bush had bequeathed him:

That we are in the midst of crisis is now well understood. Our Nation is at war against a far-reaching network of violence and hatred. Our economy is badly weakened, a consequence of greed and irresponsibility on the part of some, but also our collective failure to make hard choices and prepare the Nation for a new age. Homes have been lost, jobs shed, businesses shuttered. Our health care is too costly. Our schools fail too many. And each day brings further evidence that the ways we use energy strengthen our adversaries and threaten our planet.[21]

Despite Bush's work in fighting terrorism; prosecuting two wars; battling the recession, the financial crisis, housing foreclosures, and unemployment; extending prescription drug coverage; and passing No Child Left Behind, the country appeared to be in a mess. He had never succeeded in developing a national energy policy, and he had dismissed concerns over global warming. On this day of transition, his legacy appeared to be tarnished. Yet he remained upbeat and unshakably certain that history would vindicate his policies.

NOTES

1. George W. Bush, "Statement on the Bombing of the Golden Mosque in Samarra, Iraq," *Weekly Compilation of Presidential Documents* 42, no. 8 (27 February 2006): 322.

2. George W. Bush, "Address to the Nation on the War on Terror in Iraq," *Weekly Compilation of Presidential Documents* 43, no. 2 (15 January 2007): 21.

3. Jeff Zeleny, "Leading Democrat in Senate Tells Reporters, 'This War Is Lost,'" *New York Times*, 20 April 2007, http://www.nytimes.com/2007/04/20/washington/20cong.html.

4. Michael Duffy, "The Surge at Year One," *Time*, 31 January 2008.

5. Michael Muskal, "U.S. Troop Reduction In Iraq Remains On Schedule, Gen. Petraeus Says," *Los Angeles Times*, 16 March 2010, http://latimesblogs.latimes.com/dcnow/2010/03/us-military-decrease-from-iraq-remain-on-schedule-top-general-says.html.

6. George W. Bush, "The President's Radio Address," *Weekly Compilation of Presidential Documents* 44, no. 38 (29 September 2008): 1240.

7. George W. Bush, "The President's Radio Address," *Weekly Compilation of Presidential Documents* 41, no. 41 (17 October 2005): 1523–24.

8. "Interview With Matt Lauer of NBC's *Today Show* in Covington, Louisiana," *Weekly Compilation of Presidential Documents* 41, no. 41 (17 October 2005): 1526.

9. "How to Skin a Cat, "*Economist,* 5 November 2005, 38.

10. David Johnston and Eric Lipton, "Rove Is Linked to Early Query over Dismissals," *New York Times*, 16 March 2007, A1; Dan Eggen and Paul Kane, "Senators Chastise Gonzales at Hearing," *Washington Post*, 20 April 2007, A1.

11. Stephen Ohlemacher, "Testimony Puts Rove at Center of Justice Firings, "Associated Press, 12 August 2009.

12. George W. Bush, "Remarks on Signing the Fetus Farming Prohibition Act and Returning Without Approval to the House of Representatives the Stem Cell Research Enhancement Act of 2005," *Weekly Compilation of Presidential Documents* 42, no. 29 (24 July 2006): 1363.

13. George W. Bush, "The President's Radio Address," *Weekly Compilation of Presidential Documents* 44, no. 41 (15 October 2007): 1315.

14. George W. Bush, "The President's Radio Address," *Weekly Compilation of Presidential Documents* 42, no. 15 (17 April 2006): 671

15. George W. Bush, "The President's News Conference," *Weekly Compilation of Presidential Documents* 42, no. 45 (13 November 2006): 2028.

16. George W. Bush, "Remarks at a Signing Ceremony for the Strategic Framework Agreement and the Status of Forces Agreement and an Exchange With Reporters in Baghdad," *Weekly Compilation of Presidential Documents* 44, no. 50 (22 December 2008): 1522.

17. George W. Bush, "Remarks on Homeownership Financing and an Exchange With Reporters," *Weekly Compilation of Presidential Documents* 43, no. 35 (3 September 2007): 1158.

18. George W. Bush, "Remarks on Signing Proclamations To Establish the Marianas Trench Marine National Monument, Pacific Remote Islands Marine National Monument, and the Rose Atoll Marine National Monument." *Weekly Compilation of Presidential Documents* 45, no. 1 (12 January 2009): 6.

19. George W. Bush, "President Bush Delivers Farewell Address to the Nation," Washington, D.C., 15 January 2009, http://georgewbush-whitehouse.archives.gov/news/releases/2009/01/20090115-17.html.

20. George W. Bush, "President Bush Delivers Farewell Address to the Nation," Washington, D.C., 15 January 2009, http://georgewbush-whitehouse.archives.gov/news/releases/2009/01/20090115-17.html.

21. Barack Obama, "Inaugural Address," *Daily Compilation of Presidential Documents* 45, no. 2 (20 January 2009): 1.

Chapter 11

BUSH'S LEGACY

Before Bush left Washington, D.C., he and Laura purchased an 8,500-square-foot home in Preston Hollow, an exclusive Dallas neighborhood where they had lived when Bush comanaged the Texas Rangers. The house is hardly showy for the neighborhood—Tom Hicks, the Dallas billionaire who bought the Texas Rangers from Bush and his partners in 1998, has a 30,000-square-foot home nearby. But the Bush's new home was considerably larger than the 3,600-square-foot house they lived in a decade earlier.[1]

But Dallas County had changed since the Bushes left. A majority of voters pulled the lever for Obama in 2008, giving him the first Democratic presidential win there since Barry Goldwater lost to Lyndon Johnson in 1964, the same year Bush's father lost a Senate bid to Democrat Ralph Yarborough.[2] Indeed, Bush's presidency had turned much of the country—at least temporarily—toward the Democrats.

BUSH'S STANDING AT THE END
OF HIS PRESIDENCY

Obama's campaign strategy in the general election sought to link his Republican opponent, Senator John McCain, to Bush, whose approval ratings had sunk abysmally below 30 percent in 2007 and to an un-imaginable 25 percent after he pushed through a bank bailout to ad-dress the financial crisis.[3] At the Democratic National Convention, Senator Joe Biden, McCain's long-term Senate colleague who was the vice presidential running mate of Obama, charged that "John sided with President Bush 95 percent of the time." He warned voters: "That's not change. That's more of the same."[4] Voters who overwhelmingly disapproved of Bush by late in his presidency obviously did not want another Bush.

The charge against McCain wasn't exactly fair. He often had been a vocal opponent of Bush's policies. As *Time* magazine noted during the 2008 election: "[O]n campaign finance, tax cuts, health care, judicial nominations, the environment, the use of torture, the fate of Guan-tánamo Bay and other issues, McCain stood apart—and sometimes alone—from both his President and his party." Indeed, in 2004 Sena-tor John Kerry considered recruiting McCain to the Democratic ticket to run against Bush's reelection. But McCain ended up campaigning vigorously for Bush. Bush returned the favor by endorsing McCain for president in 2008. But when McCain was asked whether Bush would campaign for him, he said that the president's busy schedule might pre-vent that. Undoubtedly, the McCain camp was nervous about associ-ating Bush's unpopular face with its campaign. In the end, McCain's "maverick" stances weren't able to distance him enough from Bush, and *Time* noted during the campaign, "his ties to the President now act like leg weights in his race against Barack Obama."[5]

Bush's lack of popularity leading up to his exit from the White House must have been hard on the man from Midland, who enjoyed some of the highest approval ratings in history for a president in the wake of the September 11, 2001, attacks. The number of people dis-approving of Bush's job performance in October 2008 hit a historic 71 percent, which is higher than the disapproval ratings of Richard Nixon just before he resigned, Harry Truman in the midst of the Ko-rean War when he seized ownership of American steel mills, or Jimmy Carter in the midst of a recession and an interminable hostage crisis following the Iranian Revolution.[6] The final nationwide television ad-dress Bush gave just before leaving office had attempted to put a posi-tive spin on his presidency, but in the immediate aftermath of his two terms in office, it seemed that no one had anything good to say about his time in the White House. He left office with only 34 percent approving of the job he had done and 61 percent disapproving.[7] President Obama, struggling with a recession, high unemployment rates, a housing crisis, and ballooning federal deficits, continually reminded those who complained that he wasn't addressing these economic problems quickly enough that he inherited the economic downturn from the former president. Republicans and conservative talk show hosts rarely mentioned Bush's name.

In his last press conference, Bush answered questions about his legacy by noting that the perspective of history would be required to judge his performance as president. Similarly, in an interview with Fox News Sunday, he said:

> As far as history goes and all of these quotes about people trying to guess what the history of the Bush administration is going to be, you know, I take great comfort in knowing that they don't know what they are talking about, because history takes a long time for us to reach.[8]

Bush's point has some merit, though his insistence that history would judge him also was a strategy to draw attention away from the harsh judgments he already was receiving in the polls and in media retrospectives on his presidency. Ignoring today in the hopes of a better assessment in the future helped Bush assure himself that the leadership he felt he had demonstrated would eventually be widely recognized. But for now, Bush was through with Washington and its inside-the-Beltway echo chamber of punditry. He was ready to return to his beloved Texas for good.

LIFE AFTER THE WHITE HOUSE

The Bushes flight departing Washington, D.C., headed straight for their hometown of Midland, where they were greeted warmly with a reception featuring Texas governor Rick Perry and a number of Republican officials. Bush took the opportunity once more to burnish his image, announcing, "I'm coming home with my head held high and a sense of accomplishment." He admitted, "Sometimes what I did wasn't always popular. But that's OK. I did what I thought was right."[9]

In the months following his exit from Washington, Bush was rarely seen in public. Laura Bush, appearing on ABC's *Good Morning America* on June 8, 2009, explained her husband's low profile. She said he felt that he "owes President Obama his silence on issues, and that there's no reason to second-guess any decisions that he makes."[10] (Vice President Cheney was not so reticent, immediately taking on the role of a frequent and vocal critic of Obama, particularly on issues of national security, and even acknowledging and defending the waterboarding of three terror suspects.)

Bush did make a few appearances in Texas in 2009, throwing out the first pitch at a game between his beloved Texas Rangers and the Cleveland Indians in the spring and showing up to do the coin toss in the first game the Dallas Cowboys played in their new football stadium in Arlington, Texas, in the fall. He made a few speeches to private groups early in 2009 but officially joined the Washington Speakers Bureau in the fall of that year. One of his most unusual speeches was an address to 15,000 people at a "GET MOTIVATED!" seminar in Fort Worth, Texas, where he discussed his faith in the face of challenges as president. Bush also noted the changes in his life since leaving office, recalling how he would take Barney, his Scottish terrier, on walks with a plastic bag on his hand to pick up after him. Bush was joined by former secretary of state Colin Powell, former New York mayor Rudy Giuliani, football great Terry Bradshaw, and a host of professional motivational speakers.[11]

When Democratic senator Ted Kennedy, the "Lion of the Senate," died on August 25, 2009, Bush praised the liberal senator who worked across party lines with him on education reform and immigration, noting: "In a life filled with trials, Ted Kennedy never gave in to self-pity or despair."[12] A few days later, Bush joined Bill Clinton, Jimmy Carter, and throngs of people from across the political spectrum at his funeral at the Basilica of Our Lady of Perpetual Help in Boston. President Obama delivered the eulogy. Colleagues from Democratic senators Christopher Dodd and John Kerry to Republican senators John McCain and Orin Hatch praised Kennedy, who was a victim of brain cancer.

On November 5, 2009, an army psychiatrist at Fort Hood, Texas, reportedly opened fire on his colleagues, killing 13 soldiers and wounding 38 others. The Bushes, whose Crawford ranch is an hour's drive from the base, quietly visited the survivors the next day, offering their prayers and condolences.

Outside of such brief appearances, Bush spent his early postpresidency days at home working on his autobiography, tentatively titled *Decision Points*. He signed a multimillion-dollar deal with Crown Publishing, a division of Random House, to recount a dozen challenging decisions he has made in his life, including quitting drinking, deciding to run for the presidency, and sending troops to Afghanistan and Iraq. He reportedly was working two to three hours a day on the manuscript, which is due out in 2010.[13]

The new decade that began in January 2010 was initiated with a massive natural disaster. A 7.0 magnitude earthquake struck the poorest country in the Western Hemisphere, Haiti. The poorly constructed homes and buildings, especially in the crowded capital of Port-au-Prince, collapsed like a house of cards. More than 200,000 people were killed in the late-night disaster, which left an estimated 1 million people homeless. The United States and much of the rest of the world responded quickly with aid. President Obama asked former presidents Bill Clinton and George W. Bush to coordinate efforts to raise funds to support Haiti's recovery. The two former presidents appeared together in nationally broadcast commercials calling for donations to the Clinton Bush Haiti Fund. The fund raised tens of millions of dollars in its first few months of operation, including $200,000 donated from President Obama's Nobel Peace Prize award.

Another project that will take a great deal of Bush's time is his presidential library, which recent presidents have begun constructing shortly after leaving the White House. Bush's will be called the George W. Bush Presidential Center, to be housed on the campus of Southern Methodist University in Dallas, Texas. It will include archives from the Bush presidency, a museum, and a research policy institute. A design of the center already has been developed by architect Robert A. M. Stern, dean of Yale University's School of Architecture. Groundbreaking is scheduled for 2011, and the center should open in 2014. The $400 million center will be funded largely by individual donations. Through February 2010, $230 million had been raised.[14] Until the center is completed, Bush's papers are temporarily housed in Lewisville, Texas.

BUSH THE MAN AND BUSH THE PRESIDENT

The biography of George W. Bush and his tumultuous two terms as president provide materials for an unusually wide range of interpretations of who the man from Midland is.[15] Unlike recent presidents, who are generally acknowledged as smart (Clinton), a great communicator (Reagan), secretive (Nixon), or visionary (Kennedy), Bush is hard to pigeonhole. Despite frequent parodies of the 43rd president as dumb (on *Saturday Night Live*, for example), simple labels don't work well. He is a complex figure who inspires many divergent and competing characterizations. Because of this complexity, I have dubbed him "the Chameleon President."

On the issue of intelligence, for example, Bush has provided a lot of fodder to those who would dismiss him as simply lacking in understanding. Journalist Bob Woodward acknowledged early assumptions about Bush's intelligence in his first of four books on Bush and war, noting: "The widely held view [was] that he was a lightweight, unconcerned with details, removed, aloof and possibly even ignorant."[16] Partly that view came straight from Bush's academic record, where he struggled. As I noted in chapter 2, Bush made fun of his own academic record when he gave a commencement address to Yale's 2001 graduating class, admitting that he was a C student who didn't remember much of his education and slept on couches in the university's library.

More regularly, Bush's intelligence has been tied to his frequent verbal gaffes—his inability to use the English language taken as a sign of ignorance. There are Web sites and books filled with *Bushisms* that provided material for late-night comedians over the eight years of Bush's presidency. Bush acknowledged this problem as well, telling a commencement audience at St. Vincent College in Latrobe, Pennsylvania, in 2007 that he was glad his invitation to speak did not include the introduction: "I'm proud to welcome to the podium a man, the first President for whom English was a second language."[17]

Indeed, Bush's statements often made it sound like he was speaking a foreign language. A few examples illustrate the problem. In developing his education policy, he spoke to a group in Townsend, Tennessee, on February 21, 2001, stating: "You teach a child to read, and he or her will be able to pass a literacy test." Later that year, he was speaking about the problem of crime in Philadelphia, when he cited a troubling statistic: "For every fatal shooting, there were roughly three nonfatal shootings. And, folks, this is unacceptable in America. It's just unacceptable. And we're going to do something about it." He bungled an old saying in Nashville on September 17, 2002, when he insisted: "There's an old saying in Tennessee—I know it's in Texas, probably in Tennessee—that says, fool me once, shame on—shame on you. Fool me—you can't get fooled again." (The correct conclusion, of course, is: "Fool me twice, shame on me.") Six days later in Trenton, New Jersey, he spoke about the need for energy legislation, insisting: "We need an energy bill that encourages consumption." After Saddam Hussein was toppled, he met with a former dissident from Iraq, stating: "I'm honored to shake the hand of a brave Iraqi citizen who had his hand cut off by Saddam Hussein." On August 5, 2004, he sought to ensure Americans that his administration was hard at work trying to prevent terrorist attacks, insisting: "Our enemies are innovative and resourceful, and so are we. They never stop thinking about new ways to harm our country and our people, and neither do we."[18]

Inarticulateness is not an infallible sign of a weak mind, of course. Bush's strong SAT scores suggest that he has raw intelligence. Furthermore, despite such gaffes, he has been an incredibly successful politician, winning elections that seemed out of his reach (particularly in Texas against the verbally gifted Ann Richards). His verbal fumbling and his ability to laugh about it publicly endeared him to many voters and made him appear more human and affable.

On the other hand, if Bush had the brainpower to do well in school, his poor academic performance suggests that he was an underachiever. His problem with alcohol and his interest in partying seems to have taken away from his education. He does not appear to have made up for that deficiency by becoming an avid reader. So, he undeniably was handicapped when he found himself faced with international problems whose complexity challenged some of the best minds. Iraq, in particular, was probably not a place Bush understood well, with its ancient history, religiously and ethnically diverse population, and foreign customs and beliefs. Bush's press secretary, Scott McClellan, admitted Bush's lack of knowledge in this area as plans were made to invade the cradle of the oldest known civilization, but blamed Bush's advisers for failing him, noting:

> [I]t's not asking too much that a well-considered understanding of the circumstances and history of Iraq and the Middle East should have been brought into the decision-making process. The responsibility to provide this understanding belonged to the president's advisers, and they failed to fulfill it.[19]

Without extensive knowledge of the country, its people, and its history, Bush nonetheless concluded that democracy could take root there, providing a foothold to extend it throughout the Middle East. Bush appears to have believed the claims of his own administration officials when they suggested that Americans would be greeted by the people of Iraq as liberators. He appears not to have foreseen the possibility that in allowing the people of Iraq (and also Afghanistan) to determine the direction of their country, they might push it toward a theocratic form of government—a form that could lead to the subjugation of women under Shari'a law and put Iraq's interests at odds with those of the United States.

Given Bush's public references to his poor academic performance, it is reasonable to assume that Bush didn't have full confidence in his understanding of such complex matters. However, he does appear to have had confidence in his world view, his intuition, and those who worked for him, giving him support for the actions he undertook.

Bush's final address to the nation assured Americans that there is good and evil in the world. That view was informed by Bush's religious beliefs as well as his tendency to view the world in black and white. Other presidents have dealt with gray areas and the complexities of presidential decisions much more thoughtfully than Bush. President Clinton was good at this, as it appears President Obama is. Ironically though, the presidents who see and talk about the world in black and white, such as Ronald Reagan, seem to provide greater satisfaction to the American public. Although the world is complex, we *like* to think that we can simplify that complexity and know who the bad guys are and who the good guys are, what is the right path and what is the wrong path. In the midst of a difficult recession and the national malaise following Vietnam, Watergate, and an oil crisis that exposed our vulnerabilities, Reagan told us that "America is a shining city on the hill whose beacon light guides freedom-loving people everywhere."[20] He changed the political landscape for more than a generation in insisting that our domestic problems could be traced to our own big government[21] and our foreign problems were the fault of "an evil empire" (the Soviet Union).[22]

Bush's unshakeable belief in the human desire for freedom, in the righteousness of our democratic cause, and in the unique responsibility of the United States in the world was clear and refreshing to many. That faith seemed to allow him to overlook the means that his administration sometimes used to spread democracy (such as using war to create peace) and to defend our people (such as using enhanced interrogation techniques).

Bush's Texas upbringing undoubtedly reinforced such fundamental beliefs, as well as his suspicion of intellectuals and his reliance on his own intuition. Bush's suspicion of intellectuals went back to his days at Yale. As Bush biographer Ronald Kessler reports:

> "What angered me was the way such people at Yale felt so intellectually superior and so righteous," Bush said years later. "They thought they had all the answers. They thought they could create a government that could solve all our problems for us." . . . There's a "west Texas populist streak in me, and it irritates me when these people come out to Midland and look at my friends with just the utmost disdain," Bush said. He wanted to "get away from the snobs."[23]

In contrast to the intellectual snobs he disdained, Bush relied more on his "gut" in making decisions. As Scott McClellan explained:

> President Bush has always been an instinctive leader more than an intellectual leader. He is not one to delve deeply into all the possible policy options—including sitting around engaging in extended debate about them—before making a choice. Rather, he chooses based on his gut and his most deeply held convictions. Such as the case with Iraq.[24]

Bush confirmed that view with Bob Woodward as well, who quoted the president insisting: "The only thing I can tell you is that I rely on my instincts."[25] Bush believes his instincts are particularly keen when it comes to selecting people to work for him, asserting: "If I have any genius or smarts, it's the ability to recognize talent, ask them to serve and work with them as a team."[26]

Indeed, Bush did choose some very talented people to work in his administration, including Colin Powell, Dick Cheney, and Donald Rumsfeld, who each had decades of experience and were generally regarded an extremely knowledgeable and capable men. However, Bush seems to have relied too heavily upon his selections, standing by them through thick and thin, delegating too much authority to them, and not asking them enough questions.

Bush's loyalty to those in his administration was remarkable. He stuck by George Tenet after the Central Intelligence Agency (CIA) failed to foresee the 9/11 attacks and misjudged the weapons of mass destruction (WMDs) in Iraq. He stuck by Paul Bremer when his de-Baathification efforts contributed to a broad-based insurgency. He stuck by Donald Rumsfeld to the point that he sacrificed Republican mid-term election prospects, only buckling in the face of an overwhelming defeat at the polls. He bucked up Michael Brown, telling him before the cameras that he was doing "a heck of a job," when the FEMA director had obviously bungled the Hurricane Katrina rescue effort. He even stuck by "Scooter" Libby, after the vice president's chief of staff was convicted of lying to the Federal Bureau of Investigation about his knowledge of the outing of CIA agent Valerie Plame (though he drew the line at wiping his criminal record clean).

While loyalty to those who serve you is admirable, Bush appeared to be blinded by that loyalty at times. Giving the Presidential Medal of Freedom to Tenet and Bremer seemed inappropriate. Throwing any relief to "Scooter" Libby was politically damaging and made Bush look like he endorsed the campaign to get critic Ambassador Joe Wilson by any means possible. Supporting Rumsfeld was questionable after his light-footprint approach to invading Iraq was thrown into question in the first few weeks by widespread looting and later by four-and-a-half years of quagmire in Iraq.

But more troubling than blind loyalty was Bush's failure to ask tough questions and demand unvarnished answers from those who served

him. Bush's first treasury secretary, Paul O'Neill, noted this lack of engagement and questioning at his first meeting with Bush. The treasury
secretary, a former CEO of the aluminum giant Alcoa, met with Bush
in the White House in January 2001. He spoke for an hour on the
economy, threats of a recession, steel tariffs, No Child Left Behind, and
global warming and got little more than a nod from Bush, who never
asked questions and never referenced any of the memos O'Neill had
sent to him.[27] As Ron Suskind notes in his book with O'Neill on the
Bush presidency—the first of many kiss-and-tell books from the Bush
administration—the treasury secretary witnessed this lack of engagement again and again. For example, in one cabinet meeting on Vice
President Cheney's Energy Task Force deliberations,

> O'Neill was watching Bush closely. He threw out a few general
> phrases, a few nods, but there was virtually no engagement. These
> cabinet secretaries had worked for over a month on detailed re-
> ports. O'Neill had been made to understand by various colleagues
> in the White House that the President should not be expected to
> read reports. In his personal experience, the President didn't even
> appear to have read the short memos he sent over.
>   That made it especially troubling that Bush did not ask any
> questions. There are so many worth asking about each of these
> areas, O'Neill thought as he sat quietly, dozens of queries running
> through his head.[28]

Those who wish to characterize Bush as lacking intelligence could
point to such meetings to suggest that the president didn't know what
to ask. But, one also might argue that Bush's allegiance led him to
pick good people and delegate responsibility to them. To the extent
that no president can know as much as he or she needs to in order
to make informed decisions concerning the huge range of domestic
and international issues a president confronts, then such dependence
on appointees is understandable. On the other hand, given the consequences of decisions made by the executive, one would hope that the
president would at least scrutinize those decisions carefully, if only to
allow other members of his administration to help him weigh them. For
example, when Jerry Bremer made a decision to fire the Iraq army—a
decision that even Bush admitted flew in the face of what he thought

the administration had decided—Bush let the enormously consequential change in policy stand, even lauding Bremer's work.

Some critics suggest a more cynical view. They believe that Bush had knowledge of the major decisions that were made by his administrators and that he endorsed those decisions. Thus, they contend, he knew the case for WMDs in Iraq was weak, but he didn't scrutinize the intelligence that some of his deputies (especially Paul Wolfowitz) offered because he wanted an excuse to go to war against the dictator who controlled oil reserves important to the United States. They argue that he partially pardoned "Scooter" Libby because Libby was actually carrying out a smear campaign against Wilson on the president's behalf. They argue that the torture at Abu Ghraib happened not because a few bad apples or those who commanded them went too far, but because Bush was pushing those under his command to use any means necessary to get the intelligence he thought he needed to protect the country. So, Bush either is ignorant or blindly loyal, or he's a hard-nosed pragmatist looking out for American interests or perhaps a Machiavellian willing to use any means to get what he wants. The choice of characterizations critics choose to embrace typically depends on their attitude toward Bush and his administration.

THE BUSH LEGACY

Bush is certainly correct that our view of his presidency may change over time. If the instability in Iraq can be arrested to the point that a democratically elected government can take charge, then the view of Bush's seemingly idealistic hopes for Iraq and the Middle East might change. If we discover that Bush's measures to prevent terrorist attacks on the homeland are the only ones that will work, he might be vindicated. If institutions such as his Office of Faith-Based and Community Initiatives (now the Office of Faith-Based and Neighborhood Initiatives) yield good results, then we might credit its founder. If No Child Left Behind survives as a federal program and improves our educational processes, then we can say they began with Bush.

The short-term judgment of commentators and historians does not bode well for Bush's legacy. The History News Channel conducted an informal poll of 109 historians, and more than 98 percent of them said that Bush's presidency was a failure. Sixty-one percent of those surveyed said that he was the worst president in U.S. history. Another third ranked him in the lowest quartile of presidents, while only 4 of 109 ranked him higher than the lowest two-thirds. While such non-scientific polls no doubt drew out those who were adamantly opposed to Bush's presidency, it didn't draw out a corresponding number to his defense.

Whatever his legacy, Bush will be considered a consequential president. He was at the helm when the United States suffered its worst attack in history. He used controversial extensions of executive authority in attempting to thwart additional attacks, potentially creating a precedent for those who follow him. He initiated two major wars, one of which is now the longest U.S. war in history. He also was at the helm when the worst recession in 70 years hit the nation. His way of talking in black-and-white terms about freedom and tyranny, good and evil, God and faith made him unique. His everyman manner made him likeable to millions. Finally, his unshakeable sense that he knew what was right, and that, for good or ill, he would make hard decisions, reflected a personality born of his ideas about leadership, his religious faith, his Texas culture, and his sometimes cocksure personality.

Finally, one must acknowledge that Bush was an unlikely person to become a major influence on U.S. history, given his lackluster beginnings. Nevertheless, like many Bushes before him, he eventually carried on the family tradition.

NOTES

1. Skip Hollandsworth, "Here Comes the Neighborhood [Editorial]," *Texas Monthly*, February 2009, 10–14.

2. Ibid.

3. Jeffrey M. Jones, "Despite Recent Lows, Bush Approval Average Is Midrange," *Gallup.com*, 5 January 2009.

4. Joe Biden, "Democratic Vice Presidential Nomination Acceptance Address," Denver, Colorado, 28 August 2008, http://american rhetoric.com/speeches/convention2008/joebiden2008dnc.htm.

5. "Frenemies," *Time*, 28 July 2008, 24–28.

6. "Presidential Job Approval," *The American Presidency Project*, University of California, Santa Barbara, http://www.presidency.ucsb.edu/data/popularity.

7. "Presidential Job Approval."

8. "Interview with President George W. Bush," *Fox News Sunday*, 10 February 2008, http://www.foxnews.com/story/0,2933,330234,00.html.

9. "Bush Returns 'Home' to Midland," *Texas Politics*, 20 January 2009, http://blogs.chron.com/texaspolitics/archives/2009/01/bush_re turns_ho.html.

10. Lee Ferran, "Laura Bush: George Bush 'Owes' Obama Silence," *ABC News*, 8 June 2009, http://abcnews.go.com/GMA/story?id=7779432.

11. Mary Jordan, "Bush's First Stand on a New Podium," *Washington Post*, 27 October 2009.

12. Kathy Kiely, "Sen. Edward Kennedy, 77, Dies of Cancer," *USA Today*, 27 August 2009, http://www.usatoday.com/news/washing ton/2009-08-26-ted-kennedy-obit_N.htm.

13. Mike Allen, "Tell-All: Bush Inks Deal," *Politico.com*, 18 March 2009; Motoko Rich, "Bush Book on Decisions Is Set for 2010," *New York Times*, 18 March 2009.

14. Paul Bedard, "Washington Whispers: George W. Bush Library Donors Appreciate Him," *U.S. News & World Report Online*, 10 February 2010.

15. My own work supporting this unusual aspect of Bush's public image is *The Chameleon President*, a monograph on George W. Bush that is in draft form.

16. Bob Woodward, *Bush at War* (New York: Simon & Schuster, 2002), 37.

17. George W. Bush, "President Bush Delivers Commencement Address at St. Vincent College," Latrobe, Pennsylvania, 11 May 2007, *White House Documents and Publications*, http://georgewbush-white house.archives.gov/news/releases/2007/05/20070511-8.html.

18. Jacob Weisberg, "The Complete Bushisms," *Slate.com*, http://www.slate.com/id/76886/pagenum/all/#p2.

19. Scott McClellan, *What Happened: Inside the Bush White House and Washington's Culture of Deception* (New York: Public Affairs, 2008), 144.

20. Ronald Reagan, "Remarks Accepting the Presidential Nomination at the Republican National Convention," Dallas, Texas, 23 August 1984, http://www.reagan.utexas.edu/archives/speeches/1984/82384f.htm.

21. Ronald Reagan, "First Inaugural Address," Washington, D.C., 20 January 1981, http://americanrhetoric.com/speeches/ronaldreag andfirstinaugural.html.

22. Ronald Reagan, "The Evil Empire [Remarks at the Annual Convention of the National Association of Evangelicals]," Orlando, Florida, 8 March 1983, http://americanrhetoric.com/speeches/ronald reaganevilempire.htm.

23. Ronald Kessler, *A Matter of Character: Inside the White House of George W. Bush* (New York: Sentinel, 2004), 31.

24. Scott McClellan, *What Happened*, 127.

25. Woodward, *Bush at War*, 168.

26. Ibid., 74.

27. Suskind, *The Price of Loyalty: George W. Bush, the White House, and the Education of Paul O'Neill* (New York: Simon & Schuster, 2004), 56–59.

28. Ibid., 148–49.

SELECTED ANNOTATED BIBLIOGRAPHY

BOOKS ABOUT GEORGE W. BUSH

Scores of books have been written about George W. Bush, his family, his presidency, or parts or combinations thereof. Despite the library of sources on this subject, finding sources that are at once fully informed and also unbiased is a little difficult. This is not a problem peculiar to Bush as a subject, but to many powerful people or people from powerful families. That is because, on the one hand, to get insider information on the life and presidency of George W. Bush requires access to Bush, his family, and/or those in his administration; on the other hand, such access is rarely granted without some understanding or assurance that what is revealed will show the president or family in a good light, which is to say, in a slanted fashion. The only way around this dilemma is for investigative reporters and other authors to dig up sources that Bush or his family do not want talking to the media. When such sources do talk—often anonymously—then their legitimacy can be called into question. "Perhaps they are just aggrieved people who didn't get what they wanted or who had something personally against Bush," one might claim. Perhaps the most credible sources are those that Bush himself brought into his administration who left, disillusioned, and wrote kiss-and-tell books about what they witnessed. This essay discusses some selected sources from among the many available.

Among the most notable sources to write about Bush's presidency is journalist Bob Woodward. Woodward is the Pulitzer Prize–winning author who worked with Carl Bernstein in the 1970s to uncover the Watergate conspiracy and topple President Nixon. He wrote four books about Bush as commander in chief. The first two books were the product of unprecedented access to the president and his cabinet: *Bush at War* (2002) and *Plan of Attack* (2004), which discussed, respectively, Bush's response to the September 11, 2001, attacks and the invasion of Afghanistan, and Bush's decision to invade Iraq. The books include detailed accounts of high-level meetings of Bush's national security team and military advisers. The Bush administration was less supportive of Woodward when he wrote his third book, *State of Denial: Bush at War, Part III* (2006), which criticized the president for mismanaging the war in Iraq and misleading the public about how the war was going. His fourth book in the series, *The War Within* (2008), reflected the dissension over the decision to surge the number of troops in Iraq in 2007, though it presented Bush in a generally favorable light.

Plenty of other journalists have written about Bush, though often they have focused on explaining some controversial policy or action, usually to criticize it, or occasionally to defend the president. Thomas E. Ricks, a Pulitzer Prize–winning Pentagon correspondent for the *Washington Post*, sought to explain the bumbling of the Iraq War in *Fiasco: The American Military Adventure in Iraq* (2006), drawing on military sources. Another Pulitzer Prize winner, *Boston Globe* columnist Thomas Oliphant, took a larger look at the Bush administration, examining problems on both domestic and foreign policy fronts. His 2007 work, *Utter Incompetents: Ego and Ideology in the Age of Bush*, details mismanagement on energy, taxes, Hurricane Katrina, Social Security, and the wars in Afghanistan and Iraq, among other things. Jacob Weisberg, editor of *Slate* magazine, takes a more psychological approach to explaining what he calls *The Bush Tragedy* (2008), looking at the president's family relationships and his reliance on an inner circle that greatly influenced the relatively inexperienced former governor. Barton Gellman took the influence of one of Bush's advisers as his focus, writing extensively about Vice President Cheney's role in the Bush presidency. His book, *Angler: The Cheney Vice Presidency* (2008), builds upon a Pulitzer Prize–winning series he coauthored on the same subject for the *Washington Post*.

One unique book on Bush was by a journalist brought down by the Bush administration. Mary Mapes was a television producer with *60 Minutes II* when Dan Rather reported on a story concluding that George W. Bush had failed to meet his obligations to the Texas Air National Guard. An investigation of the story concluded that Mapes and Rather did not have strong support for the documents they relied upon. Rather ended up stepping down a year early as anchor of *The CBS Evening News*, and Mapes was fired. In *Truth and Duty: The Press, the President, and the Privilege of Power* (2005), Mapes defends the veracity of the story and accuses the parent company of CBS, Viacom, of kowtowing to the White House.

At least three Texans have written books about Bush from the unique standpoint of those who grew up in Bush's home state. The most famous writer is the late, sharp-tongued columnist and humorist Molly Ivins, whose book *Shrub: The Short but Happy Political Life of George W. Bush* (2000; coauthored with Lou Dubose) is a rare look at Bush before he won the presidency. She examines his family, his life and work, and his rise in Texas politics. Bill Minutaglio, a writer for the *Dallas Morning News*, discusses Bush's rise as part of a political dynasty in *First Son: George W. Bush and the Bush Family Dynasty* (1999, with a 2001 update). Michael Lind explains Texas politics and the mind-set of those like Bush who came out of that culture in *Made in Texas: George W. Bush and the Southern Takeover of American Politics* (2003).

One of the most controversial biographies of the Bush family is Kitty Kelley's book, *The Family: The Real Story of the Bush Dynasty* (2004). Kelley previously had written equally controversial biographies of Jacqueline Kennedy Onassis, Elizabeth Taylor, Frank Sinatra, Nancy Reagan, and the British royal family. Kelley released the Bush book just before the 2004 presidential election, painting a critical picture of the family and of Bush 43 in particular. For example, she quoted Neil Bush's ex-wife Sharon (Bush 43's former sister-in-law) in claiming that a younger George W. Bush had sniffed cocaine with his brother Marvin at Camp David when their father was president. While obviously open to criticism for relying on those who might have a grudge against the Bushes and for her use of innuendo, Kelley provides extensive details about the family's history, including dates, family member profiles, photos, quotations from letters, public records, and interviews of scores of people who knew the family.

A string of books by disillusioned former Bush administration officials appeared as early as the 2004 book *The Price of Loyalty: George W. Bush, the White House, and the Education of Paul O'Neill*. The book was written by the Pulitzer Prize–winning journalist Ron Suskind, with help from George W. Bush's first treasury secretary, Paul O'Neill, former CEO of the aluminum giant Alcoa. O'Neill was asked to step down after he argued that Bush's tax cuts would lead to huge federal deficits. The book details meetings that show Bush asked few questions and was strongly influenced by Cheney and other advisers. The same year, former counterterrorism chief Richard A. Clarke published *Against All Enemies: Inside America's War on Terrorism*. Clarke documents how he tried to warn the administration about Osama bin Laden and Al Qaeda, only to be ignored until it was too late. In 2006, the former deputy director of Bush's Office of Faith-Based and Community Initiatives, David Kuo, published *Tempting Faith: An Inside Story of Political Seduction*. Kuo was disappointed with what he saw as inadequate funding for the Bush administration's antipoverty efforts. Worse, he reported that officials like Karl Rove were cynically manipulating people of faith to shore up Bush's political base, rather than seeking to help those in need. Finally, in 2008, former White House press secretary Scott McClellan published the book *What Happened: Inside the Bush White House and Washington's Culture of Deception*. This account, from the perspective of those seeking to spin the image of the president and his administration in an acceptable light, was deeply critical of Bush's advisers and often of the president himself for failing to be honest with the American people in the run-up to war in Iraq, for mismanaging the war, for failing to deal with the Hurricane Katrina disaster, and especially for outing CIA agent Valerie Plame and protecting those who did it.

One of the most unusual books criticizing Bush comes from famed federal prosecutor of Charles Manson, Vince Bugliosi. Bugliosi had written a scathing criticism of the U.S. Supreme Court's decision in

Bush v. Gore for the liberal *Nation* magazine, which he turned into a book, *The Betrayal of America* (2001). (My own book on the court case, *Judging the Supreme Court* [2007], agrees with Bugliosi's assessment regarding the political motives of the conservative justices.) In 2008, Bugliosi published *The Prosecution of George W. Bush for Murder*, arguing that taking the country to war under false pretenses supports a case for murder against the commander in chief.

Although the number of books critical of Bush and his administration are many, there are defenders of the president. Conservative journalists such as Fred Barnes, executive editor of the *Weekly Standard*, have come to the defense of Bush. Barnes's profile of Bush 43, *Rebel-in-Chief: Inside the Bold and Controversial Presidency of George W. Bush* (2006), takes the controversy over Bush as a sign that the president is innovative and shaking up a stodgy bureaucracy in Washington, D.C.; taking bold steps in reshaping American foreign policy; and drawing upon a vision of spreading democracy to the world.

Ronald Kessler, a former reporter for the *Washington Post*, wrote a flattering biography of Bush in 2004, *A Matter of Character: Inside the White House of George W. Bush*. To illustrate how positive his portrait of Bush is, consider his description of Bush's reaction to learning that a second plane had struck the World Trade Towers in New York City. Bush was beginning a reading lesson for children at a Sarasota, Florida, elementary school. Kessler reports: "A few minutes after Bush began to read to the children, Andy Card whispered to him that a second plane had hit the South Tower. 'America is under attack,' Card said. After thinking about what his response would be, Bush cut short his presentation, apologizing to the principal, Gwendolyn Tosé-Rigell" (138). Kessler glosses over the fact that Bush's "thinking about . . . his response" took seven minutes and suggested an indecisive response to a critical situation.

Perhaps the most prolific conservative writer defending George W. Bush has been former *Washington Times* writer and Fox News political analyst Bill Sammon. Publishing in Regnery Press (a conservative publisher that is home to books by Ann Coulter, Newt Gingrich, and William Bennett), Sammon has produced a string of short books on Bush, including *Fighting Back: The War on Terrorism—from Inside the Bush White House* (2002); *Strategery: How George W. Bush Is Defeating*

Terrorists, Outwitting Democrats, and Confounding the Mainstream Media (2006); and *The Evangelical President: George Bush's Struggle to Spread a Moral Democracy throughout the World* (2007). He also published *Misunderestimated: The President Battles Terrorism, John Kerry, and the Bush Haters* (2004) with HarperCollins.

Bush himself has put pen to paper in trying to construct his own image. In 1999, as he was working the campaign trail to win the Republican nomination for president, he published *A Charge to Keep*. In 2010, he will publish *Decision Points*, which will describe several key decisions he made in his life and his presidency, including the decision to go to war in Iraq and the decision to quit drinking.

All told, there is plenty of material on George W. Bush. However, when reading any of these books it is important to keep in mind the authors' reputations, their access to information, and their motives, inasmuch as we can assess them.

BIBLIOGRAPHY

Barnes, Fred. *Rebel-in-Chief: Inside the Bold and Controversial Presidency of George W. Bush*. New York: Crown Forum, 2006.

Bugliosi, Vincent. *The Betrayal of America: How the Supreme Court Undermined the Constitution and Chose Our President*. Forewords by Molly Ivins and Gerry Spence. New York: Thunder's Mouth Press/Nation Books, 2001.

Bugliosi, Vincent. *The Prosecution of George W. Bush for Murder*. Cambridge, MA: Vanguard Press, 2008.

Bush, George W. *A Charge to Keep*. New York: Morrow, 1999.

Bush, George W. *Decision Points*. New York: Crown Publishers, 2010 (forthcoming).

Clarke, Richard A. *Against All Enemies: Inside America's War on Terror*. New York: Free Press, 2004.

Gellman, Barton. *Angler: The Cheney Vice Presidency*. New York: Penguin, 2008.

Ivins, Molly, and Lou Dubose. *Shrub: The Short but Happy Political Life of George W. Bush*. New York: Vintage Books, 2000.

Kelley, Kitty. *The Family: The Real Story of the Bush Dynasty*. New York: Doubleday, 2004.

Kessler, Ronald. *A Matter of Character: Inside the White House of George W. Bush*. New York: Sentinel, 2004.

Kuo, David. *Tempting Faith: An Inside Story of Political Seduction*. New York: Free Press, 2006.

Lind, Michael. *Made in Texas: George W. Bush and the Southern Takeover of American Politics*. New York: Basic Books, 2003.

Mapes, Mary. *Truth and Duty: The Press, the President, and the Privilege of Power*. New York: St. Martin's Press, 2005.

McClellan, Scott. *What Happened: Inside the Bush White House and Washington's Culture of Deception*. New York: Public Affairs, 2008.

Minutaglio, Bill. *First Son: George W. Bush and the Bush Family Dynasty*. New York: Times Books, 1999.

Oliphant, Thomas. *Utter Incompetents: Ego and Ideology in the Age of Bush*. New York: St. Martin's Press, 2007.

Ricks, Thomas E. *Fiasco: The American Military Adventure in Iraq*. New York: Penguin, 2006.

Rountree, Clarke. *Judging the Supreme Court: Constructions of Motives in Bush v. Gore*. Rhetoric and Public Affairs Series. East Lansing: Michigan State University Press, 2007.

Sammon, Bill. *The Evangelical President: George Bush's Struggle to Spread a Moral Democracy throughout the World*. Washington, DC: Regnery Pub., 2007.

Sammon, Bill. *Fighting Back: The War on Terrorism—from Inside the Bush White House*. Washington, DC: Regnery Pub., 2002.

Sammon, Bill. *Misunderestimated: The President Battles Terrorism, John Kerry, and the Bush Haters*. New York: HarperCollins, 2004.

Sammon, Bill. *Strategery: How George W. Bush Is Defeating Terrorists, Outwitting Democrats, and Confounding the Mainstream Media*. Washington, DC: Regnery Pub., 2006.

Suskind, Ron. *The Price of Loyalty: George W. Bush, the White House, and the Education of Paul O'Neill*. New York: Simon & Schuster, 2004.

Weisberg, Jacob. *The Bush Tragedy*. New York: Random House, 2008.

Woodward, Bob. *Bush at War*. New York: Simon & Schuster, 2002.

Woodward, Bob. *Plan of Attack*. New York: Simon & Schuster, 2004.

Woodward, Bob. *State of Denial: Bush at War, Part III*. New York: Simon & Schuster, 2006.

Woodward, Bob. *The War Within: A Secret White House History, 2006–2008*. New York: Simon & Schuster, 2008.

INDEX

Abortion, 80–81

Abu Ghraib scandal, 133–35, 138, 178. *See also* Iraq War

Addington, David, 103, 105

Afghanistan, 106–8

AIG, 152

Alito, Samuel, 155–56

Allbaugh, Joe M., 55, 58, 139

Al Qaeda, 89, 95–96, 107–8. *See also* September 11, 2001 terrorist attacks

Anbar Awakening, 150–51

Andover, 10–11, 24–26

Anthrax attacks, 104

Arbusto Energy, 43

Arlington Stadium, 50

Arsenic, in drinking water, 83

Ashcroft, John, 80, 81–82, 104, 138, 156

Atwater, Lee, 44, 47–48

Baathist Party, 121–23

Baghdad, fall of, 118–23

Bailouts, government, 152–53, 154

Baker, James, 73, 150

Ballots, problems with, 73, 77

Baseball, 3, 20, 48–50

Bear Stearns, 152

Bentsen, Lloyd, 34, 37, 56

Biden, Joe, 168

Bin Laden, Osama, 89, 93, 133. *See also* September 11, 2001 terrorist attacks

Blair, Tony, 110, 123

Blount, Winton "Red," Jr., 38

Bremer, L. Paul "Jerry," III: Bush's loyalty to, 138–39, 176, 177–78; Iraq War, 121–23, 125, 126

Brodhead, Dick, 27

Brooks Brothers riot, 74

Brown, Michael, 139, 140, 141, 176

Buchanan, Pat, 68, 70–71, 77

Bullock, Bob, 57, 58, 60, 62–63

Bumiller, Elisabeth, 133

Bush, Barbara (daughter), 44

Bush, Barbara Pierce (mother): campaigns of sons, 53, 54; children, birth

of, 12, 17, 18, 21; family life, 12, 17;
George W., relationship with, 19;
marriage, 11; Midland, move to,
12, 16

Bush, Dorothy Walker (grandmother),
6–7, 7–8

Bush, Dorothy Walker "Doro" (sister),
21, 41

Bush, George Herbert Walker (father):
alcohol use of George W., 39; campaign for Senate, 37; campaigns for
president, 42–43, 44, 46–48, 53;
campaigns of sons, 54, 56; career, as
ambassador, 37, 40; career, as CIA
director, 40, 42; career, in business,
12, 17, 19–20, 28; career, political,
22–23, 28–29, 43, 44; children,
birth of, 12, 17, 18, 21; education,
10–11, 11–12, 24–25, 27; family life,
10, 12, 17–18; Houston, move to,
21–22; Iran-Contra scandal, 47; Iraq,
113–14; job assistance for George W.,
37–38; marriage, 11; Midland, move
to, 12, 16; military service, 11, 33–34;
presidential library, 60–61; Richards
on, 54; Watergate scandal, 40

Bush, George Walker: abortion policy,
80–81; Abu Ghraib scandal, 133–35,
138, 178; alcohol use and sobriety,
30, 38–39, 41, 45–46, 60; approval
ratings, 131, 168, 169; autobiography,
171; bachelorhood, 36–37; baseball,
20, 48–50; birth, 12; cabinet and
staff, 80, 138, 176–78; campaign for
congressional seat, 41–42; campaigns
for governor, 53, 54–56, 62–63; campaigns for president, 63–64, 67–72,
135–37; campaign work for others,
35–36, 37, 38, 44, 46–47; career, as
Texas governor, 57–64; career, early,
26, 37–38; career, in oil business,
40–41, 43–44; childhood, 16–19,
20, 23; children, 44; China surveillance plane incident, 88; Christian
evangelicals and, 46–47, 63–64; Dallas, move to, 167; decision-making,
174, 175–76; drug culture and, 30,
55; economic crisis, 152, 153, 169;
education, 22, 24–26; education, college, 26–28, 29–30, 39–40, 172, 173,
175; education reform, 59–60, 86–87;
engagement, lack of, 176–77; environmental policy, 83–86, 160–61;
euthanasia, opposition to, 81–82;
executions, in Texas, 61–62; Fort
Hood shooting, 170–71; fraternity
membership, 27–28; gay marriage,
135; global warming policy, 84–85;
Haiti earthquake, 171; HIV/AIDS
funding in Africa, 158; Houston,
move to, 21–22; Hurricane Katrina,
140–43; immigration policy, 158–60;
inaugurations, 57–58, 79–80; intelligence, 172–74, 177; Iraq, 148–49,
160, 173–74; jury duty, 60; Kennedy's
(Ted) death, 170; legacy, 161–63,
167–69, 178–79; loyalty, 138–39,
157, 176, 177–78; marriage, 42;
medical policy, 157–58; Medicare
drug benefit, 87–88; Midland as
childhood home, 12, 16–17; military
service, 33–35, 36, 38, 39; mistakes,
reluctance to admit, 132–33, 157,
162; mother, relationship with, 19;
Plame revealed as CIA operative,
127–28; pranks, 20, 28; presidency,
end of, 161–63, 167–69; presidency,
first year of, 96–97; presidency, life
after, 169–71; presidential library,
171; press, interactions with, 131–33,
161–62, 168–69, 174; religion, 46;
Schiavo case, 157–58; September 11,
2001 terrorist attacks, 88–96; Social
Security reform proposal, 137–38; as
speaker after presidency, 170; State
Children's Health Insurance Program,
158; stem cell research, 81, 157; tax
policy, 60, 82–83; tort reform work,

58–59; U.S. attorneys scandal, 156, 157; U.S. Supreme Court nominees, 154–56; verbal gaffes, 172–73; war on terrorism, 101–10. *See also* Election, presidential (2000); Iraq War

Bush, James Smith, 4

Bush, Jeb (brother): birth, 18; campaigns, 54, 56, 63; childhood, 20; education, 39; George W.'s alcohol use, 39; presidential election (2000), 73, 77; Schiavo case, 158

Bush, Jenna (daughter), 44

Bush, Laura Welch (wife), 42, 44, 46, 170

Bush, Marvin (brother), 20, 39

Bush, Neil (brother), 20, 41

Bush, Prescott (grandfather): career, 7, 8–10, 21; death, 39; early life, 5; education, 27; family life, 7–8; marriage, 6–7; military service, 5–6, 33, 34

Bush, Robin (sister), 17, 18–19

Bush, Samuel Prescott, 4–5

Bush, William "Bucky" (uncle), 20

Bush Doctrine, 108–10

Bush Exploration, 43–44

Bush-Overbey Oil Development Company, 17

Bush v. Gore, 74–77, 78

Carbon emissions, 84

Carter, Jimmy, 113, 168, 170

Central Intelligence Agency (CIA): Bush (George H. W.) as director, 40, 42; interrogation techniques, 108, 134; Iraq War, 115, 116, 126–27; Plame's identity revealed, 127–28, 131

Cheney, Dick: as Bush administration member, 176; Energy Task Force, 84–85; environmental policy, 83–85; Iran-Contra scandal, 103; Iraq War, 116, 127; Plame's identity revealed, 127; presidential election (2002), 69–70, 72; September 11, 2001 ter-

rorist attacks, 90, 91, 92–93, 94; vice presidency, life after, 170; war on terrorism, 103, 105, 107–8, 109

Chertoff, Michael, 140

China, 40, 88

Christian evangelicals, 46–47, 63–64

CIA. *See* Central Intelligence Agency

Clarke, Richard, 89

Clinton, Bill: budget surplus, 72, 82; on Bush (George H. W.), 61; decision-making, 174; financial reforms, 152; Haiti earthquake, 171; impeachment, 67, 71; intelligence, 172; Kennedy's (Ted) funeral, 170; Kyoto Protocol, 84; Mexico City Policy suspension, 80–81; nation building, troop involvement in, 88; presidency, end of, 80; president, election as, 53, 56; regulations, 83

Coalition Provision Authority, 121–22

Collins, LeRoy, 35–36

Columbia space shuttle, 117–18

Cooper, Matt, 128

Credit default swaps, 152

Daley, Bill, 73

Dallas, 167

De-Baathification, 121–23

Delta Kappa Epsilon, 27–28, 29

Derivatives, 152

DeWitt, Bill, Jr., 48–49

Dickerson, John, 132

Diesel emission regulation, 85–86

Dilulio, John, 82

Dole, Bob, 47

Draper, Robert, 123

Dresser Company, 12, 17

Drug benefit, Medicare, 87–88

Dukakis, Michael, 47–48

Economic crisis, 151–54, 169

Education reform, 59–60, 86–87

Election, midterm congressional (2006), 149, 160

Election, presidential (2000): campaign, 63–64, 67–72; general election, 70–72, 137; postelection battle, 72–78; Republican primary, 68–70
Ellington Air Force Base, 35, 36
Energy Task Force, 84–85
Enron, 85
Environmental policy, 83–86, 160–61
Equal Protection Clause of the Fourteenth Amendment, 75–76
Euthanasia, 81–82
Evans, Don, 41, 46, 55, 58
Executions, in Texas, 61–62
Extraordinary rendition, 108

Faith-based initiatives, 82
Federal Bureau of Investigation (FBI), 104, 105
Federal Emergency Management Agency (FEMA), 139, 140, 141
Financial system collapse, 153–54
First United Methodist Church, 44
Fitzgerald, Patrick, 128, 131
Florida electoral votes, 72–78
Florida Supreme Court, 74, 75
Forbes, Steve, 68
Ford, Gerald, 40, 69
Fort Hood shooting, 170–71
Franks, Tommy, 114, 116, 118

Garner, Jay, 119, 121, 122, 123
Gates, Robert, 149
Gay marriage, 135
Gerson, Michael, 94
Gingrich, Newt, 56, 61–62, 71, 122
Global warming policy, 84–85
Goldwater, Barry, 22, 23, 26
Gonzales, Alberto, 58, 138, 156–57
Gore, Al, 64, 70, 71–78, 85, 137
Gow, Robert H., 37
Graham, Billy, 46, 57
Gregory, David, 133
Guantánamo Bay detainees, 107–8

Guest worker program, 159–60
Gurney, Edward, 35, 36

Haiti earthquake, 171
Hance, Kent, 41
Harken Oil and Gas, 43, 49, 55
Harriman, Averell, 3, 7
Harris, Katherine, 73, 74, 77
Harris County Republican Party, 22, 28
Harvard Business School, 39–40
HIV/AIDS funding in Africa, 158
Housing crisis, 151–52, 153–54
Houston, 21–22
Hurricane Katrina, 139–43
Hussein, Saddam, 109–10, 113–14, 115–17, 125–27, 132. See also Iraq

Iglesias, David, 157
Immigration policy, 158–60
Inconvenient Truth, An (Gore), 85
Interrogation techniques, 108, 134
Iran, 113, 148
Iran-Contra scandal, 47, 103
Iran hostage crisis, 113
Iraq: Bush's lack of knowledge on, 173–74; Iran and, 113, 148; Kuwait and, 113–14; preemptive strike on, calls for, 109–10; sectarian violence, 147–49; weapons of mass destruction, 109–10, 114, 115, 125–27, 132–33, 178
Iraq War: Abu Ghraib scandal, 133–35, 138, 178; Baghdad, fall of, 118–23; bipartisan commission on, 150; casualties, American, 150, 151; counterinsurgency, 150–51; insurgency, 123–25, 148; preemptive strike on Iraq, calls for, 109–10; preparing for, 114–17; press questions about, 132–33; sectarian violence, 148–49; troop surge, 149–51; weapons of mass destruction, search for, 125–27
Ivins, Bruce, 104

Johnson, Lyndon, 22, 34, 64

Kay, David, 126, 132
Kennedy, John F., 22, 23, 26, 172
Kennedy, Ted, 86, 170
Kerry, John, 135–37, 168, 170
Kessler, Ronald, 175
King, Martin Luther, Jr., 36
Kinkaid School, 22, 24
Klamath River, endangered salmon in, 83–84
Kuwait, 113–14
Kyoto Protocol, 84

Laney, Pete, 57, 60
Lauer, Matt, 155
Lay, Kenneth, 85
Lehman Brothers, 152
Lewinsky, Monica, 67, 71, 80
Libby, I. Lewis "Scooter," 127, 128, 176, 178
Lieberman, Joe, 70, 71
Liedtke, Hugh, 19–20
Lucas, Henry Lee, 62

Magnet, Myron, 64
Mallon, Neil, 12
Marianas Trench, 160–61
Marks, James "Spider," 125, 126
Mauro, Garry, 62–63
McCain, John, 67–69, 135, 167–68, 170
McClellan, Scott, 127–28, 138, 141, 173–74, 175
Medical policy, 157–58
Medicare drug benefit, 87–88
Mexico City Policy, 80–81
Miami-Dade County, Florida, 74
Midland, Texas, 12, 15–17, 40–41
Miers, Harriet, 154–55, 156
Miller, Zell, 136
Moody Air Force Base, 36
Moran, Terry, 132–33

Nader, Ralph, 70–71, 77
National Guard, 34–36, 38, 39
National Security Letters, 105
New Orleans, 139–43
New York Mets, 3, 20, 49
9/11 Commission, 92–93, 133, 149. See also September 11, 2001 terrorist attacks
Nixon, Richard: approval ratings, 168; Houston support for, 22; press conferences, 131; secretive nature, 172; Watergate scandal, 40, 69
No Child Left Behind legislation, 86–87
Northern Alliance, 94, 107
Novak, Robert, 127

Obama, Barack: abortion policy, 81; Bush and, 170; campaign strategy, 167–68; Cheney as critic of, 170; decision-making, 174; economic crisis, 154, 169; faith-based initiatives, 82; Gates as secretary of defense, 149; Haiti earthquake, 171; inaugural address, 162–63; Iraq War, 151; Kennedy's (Ted) funeral, 170
O'Connor, Sandra Day, 154, 156
Odessa, Texas, 16
Office of Faith-Based and Community Initiatives, 82
Office of Legal Counsel, 108
O'Neill, Joe, 41, 46
O'Neill, Paul, 80, 177
Operation Enduring Freedom, 106–7
Operation Iraqi Freedom. See Iraq War
Overbey, John, 17

Palm Beach County, Florida, 77
Palm Sunday Compromise, 158
Paulson, Henry, 153
Perot, Ross, 53, 56
Petraeus, David, 150–51
Phillips Academy (Andover), 10–11, 24–26

Pierce, Barbara. *See* Bush, Barbara Pierce (mother)

Plame, Valerie, 127–28, 131, 176

Posner, Richard, 76–77

Powell, Colin: as Bush administration member, 80, 138, 176; Iraq War, 110, 115, 119; as motivational speaker, 170; September 11, 2001 terrorist attacks, 89

Presidential libraries, 60–61, 171

Press, interactions with, 131–33, 161–62, 168–69, 174

Project PULL (Professional United Leadership League), 39

Reading instruction, 59–60

Reagan, Ronald: banking industry deregulation, 152; campaign for presidency, 43; *Columbia* space shuttle, 117; communication skills, 172; decision-making, 174–75; Iran-Contra scandal, 47, 103

Reese, Jim, 41

Rice, Condoleezza: Iraq War, 122, 124; as secretary of state, 138; September 11, 2001 terrorist attacks, 89, 90, 91; war on terrorism, 105

Richards, Ann, 54, 55–56, 173

Roberts, John G., 154

Robertson, Pat, 46, 47, 61

Roosevelt, Theodore, 161

Rove, Karl: Bush campaigns, 41, 54–55, 67, 135; Plame's identity revealed, 127–28; as political adviser to Bush as governor, 58; U.S. attorneys scandal, 156, 157

Rumsfeld, Donald: Abu Ghraib scandal, 134, 138; as Bush administration member, 80, 176; Bush's loyalty to, 176; Cheney and, 69; secretary of defense, removal as, 149; September 11, 2001 terrorist attacks, 89; de-Baathification, 122; Iraq War, 114,

116, 118, 119, 121; weapons of mass destruction, 126, 133

Russert, Tim, 132

Ryan, Nolan, 50, 58

Salmon, endangered, 83–84

Sauls, N. Saunders, 74

Sawyer, Diane, 132

Schiavo, Terri, 157–58

September 11, 2001 terrorist attacks, 88–96; attacks, 89–92; press questions about, 133; reaction to, 92–96, 97; warning signs, 89; war on terrorism and, 101–4

Sessions, Jeff, 156

Shiites, 147–48

Shoe throwing, by Iraqi reporter, 160

Skull and Bones society, 5, 29

Social Security reform proposal, 137–38

Spectrum 7 (oil company), 43, 48

State Children's Health Insurance Program, 158

Stem cell research, 81, 157

Stock market collapse, 153

Subprime mortgages, 151–52

Sunnis, 147–48, 150–51

Suskind, Ron, 177

Swift Boat Veterans for Truth, 136

Taliban, 89, 94, 96, 107–8

Tax policy, 60, 82–83

Tenet, George: Bush's loyalty to, 138, 176; Iraq War, 114, 116; September 11, 2001 terrorist attacks, 89, 93, 94

Terrorist Surveillance Program, 105–6. *See also* War on terrorism

Texas: education reform, 59–60; executions, 61–62; tax reform plan, 60; tort reform, 58–59

Texas Rangers baseball team, 48–50

Tort reform, 58–59

Trilateral Commission, 41

Tucker, Karla Faye, 61–62

United Nations Security Council, 110, 115

U.S. attorneys scandal, 156–57

U.S. Department of Education, 86–87

U.S. Department of Homeland Security, 140

U.S. Navy, 88

U.S. Supreme Court, 74–77, 78, 154–56

USA PATRIOT Act, 105

USS *Abraham Lincoln,* 120–21

Vieira de Mello, Sérgio, 124

Vietnam War, 34, 36

W. A. Harriman and Company, 3, 7

Walker, David Davis "D.D.", 2

Walker, George E., 2

Walker, George Herbert, Jr. (great-uncle): as baseball franchise owner, 3, 20, 49; death, 42–43; as investor, 17, 19; support for George H. W. Bush, 3–4, 42–43

Walker, George Herbert "Bert" (great-grandfather), 2–3, 7

War on terrorism, 101–10; Afghanistan, 106–8; anthrax attacks, 104; Bush Doctrine, 108–10; Guantánamo Bay detainees, 107–8; PATRIOT Act, 105; September 11, 2001 terrorist attacks and, 101–4; Terrorist Surveillance Program, 105–6

Waterboarding, 108, 170

Watergate scandal, 40, 69

Wead, Doug, 47

Weapons of mass destruction (WMDs), 109–10, 114, 115, 125–27, 132–33, 178

Welch, Laura. *See* Bush, Laura Welch (wife)

White, John, 39

Whitman, Christine Todd, 80, 83, 84

Wilson, Joseph, 126–27, 176, 178

Wolfman, Cathy Lee, 29

Woodward, Bob, 122, 133, 172, 176

World War I, 5–6

World War II, 11

Yale, 26–28, 29–30, 172, 173, 175

Yarborough, Ralph, 22–23

Zaidi, Mutadar al-, 160

Zapata Off-Shore, 19–20, 23

Zapata Petroleum, 19–20

About the Author

CLARKE ROUNTREE, PhD, has authored dozens of articles and two books that analyze political and judicial discourse. His most recent book, *Judging the Supreme Court: Constructions of Motives in* Bush v. Gore, won the Kohrs-Campbell Prize in Rhetorical Criticism in 2009. He is currently completing a manuscript on George W. Bush entitled *The Chameleon President.* Rountree earned his doctorate in rhetorical studies at the University of Iowa. He is Professor of Communication Arts at the University of Alabama in Huntsville.

2010 14
2014
7 atations